Rus

As Seen and Described

Editor: Esther Singleton

Alpha Editions

This edition published in 2023

ISBN : 9789357931939

Design and Setting By
Alpha Editions
www.alphaedis.com
Email - info@alphaedis.com

Contents

PREFACE

This is intended to be a companion volume to *Japan*, and therefore follows the same general plan and arrangement. It aims to present in small compass a somewhat comprehensive view of the great Muscovite power. After a short description of the country and race, we pass to a brief review of the history and religion including ritual and ceremonial observances of the Greek Church. Next come descriptions of regions, cities and architectural marvels; and then follow articles on the various manners and customs of rural and town life. The arts of the nation are treated comprehensively; and a chapter of the latest statistics concludes the rapid survey. The material is all selected from the writings of those who speak with authority on the subjects with which they deal.

The Russian Empire is so vast that it would be impossible to give detailed descriptions of all its parts in a work of this size: therefore I have been forced to be content with more general descriptions of provinces with an occasional addition of a typical city.

E. S.

New York, April 21, 1904.

THE RUSSIAN EMPIRE

PRINCE KROPOTKINE

The Russian Empire is a very extensive territory in eastern Europe and northern Asia, with an area exceeding 8,500,000 square miles, or one-sixth of the land surface of the globe (one twenty-third of its whole superficies). It is, however, but thinly peopled on the average, including only one-fourteenth of the inhabitants of the earth. It is almost entirely confined to the cold and temperate zones. In Nova Zembla (Novaya Zemlya) and the Taimir peninsula, it projects within the Arctic Circle as far as 77° 2' and 77° 40' N. latitude; while its southern extremities reach 38° 50' in Armenia, about 35° on the Afghan frontier, and 42° 30' on the coasts of the Pacific. To the West it advances as far as 20° 40' E. longitude in Lapland, 18° 32' in Poland, and 29° 42' on the Black Sea; and its eastern limit—East Cape in the Bering Strait—extends to 191° E. longitude.

The Arctic Ocean—comprising the White, Barents, and Kara Seas—and the northern Pacific, that is the Seas of Bering, Okhotsk, and Japan, bound it on the north and east. The Baltic, with its two deep indentations, the Gulfs of Bothnia and Finland, limits it on the north-west; and two sinuous lines of frontier separate it respectively from Sweden and Norway on the north-west, and from Prussia, Austria and Roumania on the west. The southern frontier is still unsettled. In Asia beyond the Caspian, the southern boundary of the empire remains vague; the advance into the Turcoman Steppes and Afghan Turkestan, and on the Pamir plateau is still in progress. Bokhara and Khiva, though represented as vassal khanates, are in reality mere dependencies of Russia. An approximately settled frontier-line begins only farther east, where the Russian and Chinese empires meet on the borders of eastern Turkestan, Mongolia and Manchuria.

Russia has no oceanic possessions, and has abandoned those she owned in the last century; her islands are mere appendages of the mainland to which they belong. Such are the Aland archipelago, Hochland, Tütters, Dagö and Osel in the Baltic Sea; Nova Zembla, with Kolgueff and Vaigatch, in the Barents Sea; the Solovetsky Islands in the White Sea; the New Siberian archipelago and the small group of the Medvyezhii Islands off the Siberian coast; the Commandor Islands off Kamchatka; the Shantar Islands and Saghalin in the Sea of Okhotsk. The Aleutian archipelago was sold to the United States in 1867, together with Alaska, and in 1874 the Kurile Islands were ceded to Japan.

ARCHANGEL.

A vast variety of physical features is obviously to be expected in a territory like this, which comprises on the one side the cotton and silk regions of Turkestan and Trans-caucasia, and on the other the moss and lichen-clothed Arctic *tundras* and the Verkhoyansk Siberian pole of cold—the dry Transcaspian deserts and the regions watered by the monsoons on the coasts of the Sea of Japan. Still, if the border regions, that is, two narrow belts in the north and south, be left out of account, a striking uniformity of physical feature prevails. High plateaus, like those of Pamir (the "Roof of the World") or of Armenia, and high mountain chains like the snow-clad summits of the Caucasus, the Alay, the Thian-Shan, the Sayan, are met with only on the outskirts of the empire.

Viewed broadly by the physical geographer, it appears as occupying the territories to the north-west of that great plateau-belt of the old continent—the backbone of Asia—which spreads with decreasing height and width from the high table-land of Tibet and Pamir to the lower plateaus of Mongolia, and thence north-eastwards through the Vitim region to the furthest extremity of Asia. It may be said to consist of the immense plains and flat-lands which extend between the plateau-belt and the Arctic Ocean, including all the series of parallel chains and hilly spurs which skirt the plateau-belt on the north-west. It extends over the plateau itself, and crosses it beyond Lake Baikal only.

A broad belt of hilly tracts—in every respect Alpine in character, and displaying the same variety of climate and organic life as Alpine tracts usually do—skirts the plateau-belt throughout its length on the north and north-west, forming an intermediate region between the plateaus and the plains.

The Caucasus, the Elburz, the Kopetdagh, and Paropamisus, the intricate and imperfectly known network of mountains west of the Pamir, the Thian-Shan and Ala-tau mountain regions, and farther north-east the Altai, the still unnamed complex of Minusinsk mountains, the intricate mountain-chains of Sayan, with those of the Olekma, Vitim, and Aldan, all of which are ranged *en échelon*,—the former from north-west to south-east, and the others from south-west to north-east—all these belong to one immense Alpine belt bordering that of the plateaus. These have long been known to Russian colonists, who, seeking to escape religious persecutions and exactions by the state, early penetrated into and rapidly pushed their small settlements up the better valleys of these tracts, and continued to spread everywhere as long as they found no obstacles in the shape of a former population or in unfavourable climatic conditions.

As for the flat-lands which extend from the Alpine hill-foots to the shores of the Arctic Ocean, and assume the character either of dry deserts in the Aral-Caspian depression, or of low table-lands in central Russia and eastern Siberia, of lake-regions in north-west Russia and Finland, or of marshy prairies in western Siberia, and of *tundras* in the north,—their monotonous surfaces are diversified by only a few, and these for the most part low, hilly tracts.

As to the picturesque Bureya mountains on the Amur, the forest-clothed Sikhota-alin on the Pacific, and the volcanic chains of Kamchatka, they belong to quite another orographical world; they are the border-ridges of the terraces by which the great plateau-belt descends to the depths of the Pacific Ocean. It is owing to these leading orographical features—divined by Carl Ritter, but only within the present day revealed by geographical research—that so many of the great rivers of the old continent are comprised within the limits of the Russian empire. Taking rise on the plateau-belt, or in its Alpine outskirts, they flow first, like the upper Rhone and Rhine, along high longitudinal valleys formerly filled up with great lakes; next they find their way through the rocky walls; and finally they enter the lowlands, where they become navigable, and, describing great curves to avoid here and there the minor plateaus and hilly tracts, they bring into water-communication with one another places thousands of miles apart. The double river-systems of the Volga and Kama, the Obi and Irtish, the Angara and Yenisei, the Lena and Vitim on the Arctic slope, the Amur and Sungari on the Pacific slope, are instances. They were the true channels of Russian colonization.

A broad depression—the Aral-Caspian desert—has arisen where the plateau-belt has reached its greatest height and suddenly changes its direction from a north-western into a north-eastern one; this desert is now filled only to a small extent by the salt waters of the Caspian, Aral and Balkash inland seas; but it bears unmistakable traces of having been during Post-Pliocene times an immense inland basin. There the Volga, the Ural, the Sir Daria, and the Oxus discharge their waters without reaching the ocean, but continue to bring life to the rapidly drying Transcaspian Steppes, or connect by their river network, as the Volga does, the most remote parts of European Russia.

The above-described features of the physical geography of the empire explain the relative uniformity of this wide territory, in conjunction with the variety of physical features on the outskirts. They explain also the rapidity of the expansion of Sclavonic colonization over these thinly-peopled regions; and they also throw light upon the internal cohesion of the empire, which cannot fail to strike the traveller as he crosses this immense territory, and finds everywhere the same dominating race, the same features of life. In fact, as their advance from the basins of the Volkhoff and Dnieper to the foot of the Altai and Sayan mountains, that is, along nearly a quarter of the earth's circumference, the Russian colonizers could always find the same physical conditions, the same forest and prairies as they had left at home, the same facilities for agriculture, only modified somewhat by minor topographical features. New conditions of climate and soil, and consequently new cultures and civilizations, the Russians met with, in their expansion towards the south and east, only beyond the Caucasus in the Aral-Caspian region, and in the basin of the Usuri on the Pacific coast. Favoured by these conditions, the Russians not only conquered northern Asia—they colonized it.

The Russian Empire falls into two great subdivisions, the European and the Asiatic, the latter of which, representing an aggregate of nearly 6,500,000 square miles, with a population of only sixteen million inhabitants may be considered as held by colonies. The European dominions comprise European Russia, Finland, which is, in fact, a separate nationality treated to some extent as an allied state, and Poland, whose very name has been erased from official documents, but which nevertheless continues to pursue its own development. The Asiatic dominions comprise the following great subdivisions:—Caucasia, under a separate governor-general; the Transcaspian region, which is under the governor-general of Caucasus; the Kirghiz Steppes; Turkestan under separate governors-general, Western Siberia and Eastern Siberia; and the Amur region, which last comprises also the Pacific coast region and Kamchatka.

Climate of Russia in Europe.—Notwithstanding the fact that Russia extends from north to south through twenty-six degrees of latitude, the climate of its different portions, apart from the Crimea and the Caucasus, presents a striking uniformity. The aerial currents—cyclones, anti-cyclones and dry south-east winds—extend over wide surfaces and cross the flat plains freely. Everywhere we find a cold winter and a hot summer, both varying in their duration, but differing little in the extremes of temperature recorded.

Throughout Russia the winter is of long continuance. The last days of frost are experienced for the most part in April, but also in May to the north of fifty-five degrees. The spring is exceptionally beautiful in central Russia; late as it usually is, it sets in with vigour and develops with a rapidity which gives to this season in Russia a special charm, unknown in warmer climates; and the rapid melting of snow at the same time raises the rivers, and renders a great many minor streams navigable for a few weeks. But a return of cold weather, injurious to vegetation, is observed throughout central and eastern Russia between May 18 and 24, so that it is only in June that warm weather sets in definitely, reaching its maximum in the first half of July (or of August on the Black Sea coast). The summer is much warmer than might be supposed; in south-eastern Russia it is much warmer than in the corresponding latitudes of France, and really hot weather is experienced everywhere. It does not, however, prevail for long, and in the first half of September the first frosts begin to be experienced on the middle Urals; they reach western and southern Russia in the first days of October, and are felt on the Caucasus about the middle of November. The temperature descends so rapidly that a month later, about October 10 on the middle Urals and November 15 throughout Russia the thermometer ceases to rise above the freezing-point. The rivers rapidly freeze; towards November 20 all the streams of the White Sea basin are covered with ice, and so remain for an average of 167 days; those of the Baltic, Black Sea, and Caspian basins freeze later, but about December 20 nearly all the rivers of the country are highways for sledges. The Volga remains frozen for a period varying between 150 days in the north and 90 days at Astrakhan, the Don for 100 to 110 days, and the Dneiper for 83 to 122 days. On the Dwina ice prevents navigation for 125 days and even the Vistula at Warsaw remains frozen for 77 days. The lowest temperatures are experienced in January, in which month the average is as low as 20° to 5° Fahr. throughout Russia; in the west only does it rise above 22°.

The flora and fauna of Russia.—The flora of Russia, which represents an intermediate link between those of Germany and Siberia, is strikingly uniform over a very large area. Though not poor at any given place, it appears so if the space occupied by Russia be taken into account, only 3,300 species of phanerogams and ferns being known. Four great regions may be distinguished:—the Arctic, the Forest, the Steppe, and the Circum-Mediterranean.

The *Arctic Region* comprises the *tundras* of the Arctic littoral beyond the northern limit of forests, which last closely follows the coast-line with bends towards the north in the river valleys (70° N. lat. in Finland, on the Arctic Circle about Archangel, 68° N. on the Urals, 71° on West Siberia). The shortness of summer, the deficiency of drainage and the thickness of the layer of soil which is frozen through in winter are the elements which go to the making of the characteristic features of the *tundras*. Their flora is far nearer those of northern Siberia and North America than that of central Europe. Mosses and lichens cover them, as also the birch, the dwarf willow, and a variety of shrubs; but where the soil is drier, and humus has been able to accumulate, a variety of herbaceous flowering plants, some of which are familiar also in western Europe, make their appearance.

The *Forest Region* of the Russian botanists occupies the greater part of the country, from the Arctic *tundras* to the Steppes, and it maintains over this immense surface a remarkable uniformity of character. Viewed as a whole, the flora of the forest region must be regarded as European-Siberian; and though certain species disappear towards the east, while new ones make their appearance, it maintains, on the whole, the same characters throughout from Poland to Kamchatka. Thus the beech, a characteristic tree of western Europe, is unable to face the continental climate of Russia, and does not penetrate beyond Poland and the south-western provinces, reappearing again in the Crimea. The silver fir does not extend over Russia, and the oak does not cross the Urals. On the other hand, several Asiatic species (Siberian pine, larch, cedar) grow freely in the north-east, while several shrubs and herbaceous plants, originally from the Asiatic Steppes, have spread into the south-east. But all these do not greatly alter the general character of the vegetation.

The *Region of the Steppes*, which covers all Southern Russia, may be subdivided into two zones—an intermediate zone and that of the Steppes proper. The Ante-Steppe of the preceding region and the intermediate zone of the Steppes include those tracts where the West-European climate struggles with the Asiatic, and where a struggle is being carried on between the forest and the Steppe.

The Steppes proper are very fertile elevated plains, slightly undulated, and intersected by numerous ravines which are dry in summer. The undulations are scarcely apparent to the eye as it takes in a wide prospect under a blazing sun and with a deep-blue sky overhead. Not a tree is to be seen, the few woods and thickets being hidden in the depressions and deep valleys of the rivers. On the thick sheet of black earth by which the Steppe is covered a luxuriant vegetation develops in spring; after the old grass has been burned a bright green covers immense stretches, but this rapidly disappears under the burning rays of the sun and the hot easterly winds. The colouring of the Steppe changes as if by magic, and only the silvery plumes of the *kovyl* (*Stipa pennata*) wave under the wind, giving the Steppe the aspect of a bright, yellow sea. For days together the traveller sees no other vegetation; even this, however, disappears as he nears the regions recently left dry from the Caspian, where salted clays covered with a few *Salsolaceæ*, or mere sands, take the place of the black earth. Here begins the Aral-Caspian desert. The Steppe, however, is not so devoid of trees as at first sight appears. Innumerable clusters of wild cherries, wild apricots, and other deep-rooted shrubs grow in the depressions of the surface, and on the slopes of the ravines, giving the Steppe that charm which manifests itself in popular poetry. Unfortunately, the spread of cultivation is fatal to these oases (they are often called "islands" by the inhabitants); the axe and the plough ruthlessly destroy them. The vegetation of the *poimy* and *zaimischas* in the marshy bottoms of the ravines, and in the valleys of streams and rivers, is totally different. The moist soil gives free development to thickets of various willows, bordered with dense walls of worm-wood and needle-bearing *Composita*, and interspersed with rich but not extensive prairies harbouring a great variety of herbaceous plants; while in the deltas of the Black Sea rivers impenetrable masses of rush shelter a forest fauna. But cultivation rapidly changes the physiognomy of the Steppe. The prairies are superseded by wheat-fields, and flocks of sheep destroy the true steppe-grass (*Stipa-pennata*), which retires farther east.

The *Circum-Mediterranean Region* is represented by a narrow strip of land on the south coast of the Crimea, where a climate similar to that of the Mediterranean coast has permitted the development of a flora closely resembling that of the valley of the Arno.

REVEL

The fauna of European Russia does not very materially differ from that of western Europe. In the forests not many animals which have disappeared from western Europe have held their ground; while in the Urals only a few— now Siberian, but formerly also European—are met with. On the whole, Russia belongs to the same zoo-geographical region as central Europe and northern Asia, the same fauna extending in Siberia as far as the Yenisei and Lena. In south-eastern Russia, however, towards the Caspian, we find a notable admixture of Asiatic species, the deserts of that part of Russia belonging in reality rather to the Aral-Caspian depression than to Europe.

For the zoo-geographer only three separate sub-regions appear on the East-European plains—the *tundras*, including the Arctic islands, the forest region, especially the coniferous part of it, and the Ante-Steppe and Steppes of the black-earth region. The Ural mountains might be distinguished as a fourth sub-region, while the south-coast of the Crimea and Caucasus, as well as the Caspian deserts, have their own individuality.

As for the adjoining seas, the fauna of the Arctic Ocean off the Norwegian coast corresponds, in its western parts at least, to that of the North Atlantic Gulf Stream. The White Sea and the Arctic Ocean to the east of Svyatoi Nos belong to a separate zoological region connected with, and hardly separable from, that part of the Arctic Ocean which extends along the Siberian coast as far as to about the Lena. The Black Sea, of which the fauna was formerly little known but now appears to be very rich, belongs to the Mediterranean region, slightly modified, while the Caspian partakes of the characteristic fauna inhabiting the lakes and seas of the Aral-Caspian depression.

In the region of the *tundras* life has to contend with such unfavourable conditions that it cannot be abundant. Still the reindeer frequents it for its lichens, and on the drier slopes of the moraine deposits four species of lemming, hunted by the *Canis lagopus*, find quarters. Two species of the white partridge, the lark, one *Plectrophanes*, two or three species of *Sylvia*, one *Phylloscopus*, and the *Motacilla* must be added. Numberless aquatic birds, however, visit it for breeding purposes. Ducks, divers, geese, gulls, all the Russian species of snipes and sandpipers, etc., cover the marshes of the *tundras*, or the crags of the Lapland coast.

The forest region, and especially its coniferous portion, though it has lost some of its representatives within historic times, is still rich. The reindeer, rapidly disappearing, is now met with only in Olonetz and Vologda; the *Cervus pygargus* is found everywhere, and reaches Novgorod. The weasel, the fox and the hare are exceedingly common, as also the wolf and the bear in the north; but the glutton, the lynx, and even the elk are rapidly disappearing. The wild boar is confined to the basin of the Dwina, and the *Bison eropea* to the Bielovyezha forests. The sable has quite disappeared, being found only on the Urals; the beaver is found at a few places in Minsk, and the otter is very rare. On the other hand, the hare and also the grey partridge, the hedgehog, the quail, the lark, the rook, and the stork find their way into the coniferous region as the forests are cleared. The avifauna is very rich; it includes all the forest and garden birds which are known in western Europe, as well as a very great variety of aquatic birds. Hunting and shooting give occupation to a great number of persons. The reptiles are few. As for fishes, all those of western Europe, except the carp, are met with in the lakes and rivers in immense quantities, the characteristic feature of the region being its wealth in *Coregoni* and in *Salmonidæ* generally.

In the Ante-Steppe the forest species proper, such as *Pteromys volans* and *Tamias striatus*, disappear, but the common squirrel, the weasel, and the bear are still met with in the forests. The hare is increasing rapidly, as well as the fox. The avifauna, of course, becomes poorer; nevertheless the woods of the Steppe, and still more the forests of the Ante-Steppe, give refuge to many birds, even to the hazel-hen, the woodcock and the black-grouse. The fauna of the thickets at the bottom of the river-valleys is decidedly, rich and includes aquatic birds. The destruction of the forests and the advance of wheat into the prairies are rapidly impoverishing the Steppe fauna. The various species of rapacious animals are disappearing, together with the colonies of marmots; the insectivores are also becoming scarce in consequence of the destruction of insects, while vermin, such as the suslik (*Spermophilus*), become a real plague, as also the destructive insects which have been a scourge to agriculture during recent years. The absence of *Coregoni* is a characteristic feature of the fish-fauna of the Steppes; the carp, on the contrary, reappears, and the rivers are rich in sturgeons. On the Volga below Nijni Novgorod the sturgeon, and others of the same family, as also a very great variety of ganoids and *Teleostei*, appear in such quantities that they give occupation to nearly 100,000 people. The mouths of the Caspian rivers are especially celebrated for their wealth of fish.

SIBERIA

JEAN JACQUES ÉLISÉE RECLUS

Siberia is emphatically the "Land of the North." Its name has by some etymologists been identified with "Severia," a term formerly applied to various northern regions of European Russia. The city of Sibir, which has given its name to the whole of North Asia, was so called only by the Russians, its native name being Isker. The Cossacks, coming from the south and centre of Russia, may have naturally regarded as pre-eminently the "Northern Land" those cold regions of the Ob basin lying beyond the snowy mountains which form the "girdle of the world."

Long before the conquest of Sibir by the Cossacks, this region was known to the Arab traders and missionaries. The Tatars of Sibir were Mahommedans and this town was the centre of the great fur trade. The Russians themselves had constant relations with the inhabitants of the Asiatic slopes of the Urals, and the Novgorodians were acquainted with the regions stretching "beyond the portages." Early in the Sixteenth Century the Moscow Tsars, heirs of the Novgorod power, called themselves lords of Obdoria and Kondina; that is of all the Lower Ob basin between the Konda and the Irtish confluence, and the station of Obdorsk, under the Arctic Circle. Their possessions—that is, the hunting grounds visited by the Russian agents of the Strogonov family—consequently skirted the great river for a distance of 600 miles. But the Slav power was destined soon to be consolidated by conquest, and such is the respect inspired by force that the successful expedition of a Cossack brigand, on whose head a price had been set, was supposed to have led to the discovery of Siberia, although really preceded by many visits of a peaceful character. Even still the conquering Yermak is often regarded as a sort of explorer of the lands beyond the Urals. But he merely establishes himself as a master where the Strogonov traders had been received as guests. Maps of the Ob and of the Ostiak country had already been published by Sebastian Munster and by Herberstein a generation before the Cossacks entered Sibir. The very name of this town is marked on Munster's map.

In 1579, Yermak began the second plundering expedition, which in two years resulted in the capture of the Tatar kingdom. When the conquerors entered Sibir they had been reduced from over 800 to about 400 men. But this handful represented the power of the Tsars and Yermak could sue for pardon, with the offer of a kingdom as his ransom. Before the close of the Sixteenth Century the land had been finally subdued. Sibir itself, which stood on a high bluff on the right bank of the Irtish, exists no more, having probably been swept away by the erosions of the stream. But ten miles farther down another capital, Tobolsk, arose, also on the right bank, and the whole of the north was gradually added to the Tsar's dominions. The fur trappers, more even than the soldiers, were the real conquerors of Siberia. Nevertheless, many battles had to be fought down to the middle of the Seventeenth Century. The Buriats of the Angora basin, the Koriaks, and other tribes long held out; but most of the land was peacefully acquired, and permanently secured by the forts erected by the Cossacks at the junction of the rivers, at the entrance of the mountain passes, and other strategic points. History records no other instance of such a vast dominion so rapidly acquired, and with such slender means, by a handful of men acting mostly on their own impulse, without chiefs or instructions from the centre of authority.

Even China allowed the Cossacks to settle on the banks of the Amur, though the treaty of Nerchinsk required the Russians to withdraw from that basin in 1689. But during the present century they have been again attracted to this region, and the Government of St. Petersburg is now fully alive to the advantages of a free access by a large navigable stream to the Pacific seaboard. Hence, in 1851, Muraviov established the factory of Nikolaievsk, near the mouth of the Amur, and those of Mariinsk and Alexandrovsk at either end of the portage connecting that river with the Bay of Castries. During the Crimean war its left bank was definitely secured by a line of fortified posts, and in 1859 a ukase confirmed the possession of a territory torn from China in time of peace. Lastly, in 1860, while the Anglo-French forces were entering Pekin, Russia obtained without a blow the cession of the region south of the Amur and east of the Ussuri, stretching along the coast to the Corean frontier.

And thus was completed the reduction of the whole of North Asia, a territory of itself alone far more extensive than the European continent. In other respects there is, of course, no point of comparison between these two regions. This Siberian world, where vast wildernesses still remain to be explored, has a foreign trade surpassed by that of many a third-rate European seaport, such as Dover or Boulogne. Embracing a thirteenth part of the dry land on the surface of the globe, its population falls short of that of London alone; it is even more sparsely peopled than Caucasia and Turkestan, having little over one inhabitant to 1,000 acres.

Accurate surveys of the physical features and frontier-lines are still far from complete. Only quite recently the first circumnavigation of the Old World round the northern shores of Siberia has been accomplished by the Swedish explorer, Nordenskjöld. The early attempts made by Willoughby, Chancellor, and Burrough failed even to reach the Siberian coast. Hoping later on to reach China by ascending the Ob to the imaginary Lake Kitaï—that is, Kathay, or China—the English renewed their efforts to discover the "north-east passage," and in 1580 two vessels, commanded by Arthur Ket and Charles Jackman, sailed for the Arctic Ocean; but they never got beyond the Kara Sea. The Dutch succeeded no better, none of the voyages undertaken by Barents and others between 1594 and 1597 reaching farther than the Spitzbergen and Novaya Zembla waters. Nor were these limits exceeded by Hendrick Hudson in 1608. This was the last attempt made by the navigators of West Europe; but the Russian traders and fishers of the White Sea were familiar with the routes to the Ob and Yenisei Gulfs, as is evident from a map published in 1600 by Boris Godunov. However, sixteen years afterwards the navigation of these waters was interdicted under pain of death, lest foreigners should discover the way to the Siberian coast.

SIBERIAN NATIVES.

The exploration of this seaboard had thus to be prosecuted in Siberia itself by means of vessels built for the river navigation. In 1648, the Cossack Dejnev sailed with a flotilla of small craft from the Kolíma round the north-east extremity of Asia, passing long before the birth of Bering through the strait which now bears the name of that navigator. Stadukhin also explored these eastern seas in search of the islands full of fossil ivory, of which he had heard from the natives. In 1735, Pronchishchev and Lasinius embarked at Yakutsk and sailed down the Lena, exploring its delta and neighbouring coasts. Pronchishchev reached a point east of the Taimir peninsula, but failed to double the headlands between the Lena and the Yenisei estuaries. The expedition begun by Laptiev in 1739, after suffering shipwreck, was continued overland, resulting in the exploration of the Taimir peninsula and the discovery of the North Cape of the Old World, Pliny's Tabin, and the

Cheluskin of modern maps, so named from the pilot who accompanied Pronchishchev and Laptiev. The western seaboard between the Yenisei and Ob estuaries had already been surveyed by Ovtzin and Minin in 1737-9.

But the problem was already being attacked from the side of the Pacific Ocean. In 1728, the Danish navigator, Bering, in the service of Russia, crossed Siberia overland to the Pacific, whence he sailed through the strait now named from him, and by him first revealed to the West, though known to the Siberian Cossacks eighty years previously. Even Bering himself, hugging the Asiatic coast, had not descried the opposite shores of America, and was uncertain as to the exact position of the strait. This point was not cleared up till Cook's voyage of 1778, and even after that the Sakhalin, Yezo and Kurile waters still remained to be explored. The shores of the mainland and islands were first traced by La Pérouse, who determined the insular character of Sakhalin, and ascertained the existence of a strait connecting the Japanese Sea with that of Okhotsk. This completed the general survey of the whole Siberian seaboard.

The scientific exploration of the interior began in the Eighteenth Century with Messerschmidt, followed by Gmelin, Müller, and Delisle de la Croyère, who determined many important physical points between the years 1733 and 1742. The region stretching beyond Lake Baikal was explored by Pallas and his associates in 1770-3. The expeditions, interrupted by the great wars following on the French Revolution, were resumed in 1828 by the Norwegian Hansteen, whose memorable expedition in company with Erman had such important results for the study of terrestrial magnetism. While Hansteen and Erman were still prosecuting their labours in every branch of natural science, Alexander von Humboldt, Ehrenberg, and Gustav Rose made a short visit to Siberia, which, however, remained one of the most important in the history of science. Middendorff's journeys to North and East Siberia had also some very valuable results, and were soon followed, in 1854, by the "expedition to Siberia" undertaken by Schwartz, Schmidt, Glehn, Usoltzev, and associates, extending over the whole region of the Trans-baikal to the Lena and northern tributaries of the Amur. Thus began the uninterrupted series of modern journeys, which are now being systematically continued in every part of Siberia, and which promise soon to leave no blanks on the chart of that region.

The work of geographical discovery, properly so called, may be said to have been brought to a close by Nordenskjöld's recent determination of the north-east passage, vainly attempted by Willoughby, Barents, and so many other illustrious navigators.

Such a vast region as Siberia, affected in the west by Atlantic, in the east by Pacific influences, and stretching north and south across 29° of latitude, must obviously present great diversities of climate. Even this bleak land has its temperate zones, which the Slav colonists are fond of calling their "Italies." Nevertheless as compared with Europe, Siberia may, on the whole, be regarded as a country of extreme temperatures—relatively great heats, and, above all, intense colds. The very term "Siberian" has justly become synonymous with a land of winds, frosts, and snows. The mean annual temperature in this region comprised between the rivers Anabara and Indigirka is 20° Fahr. below freezing point. The pole of cold, oscillating diversely with the force of the lateral pressure from Yakutsk to the Lena estuary, is the meteorological centre round which the atmosphere revolves. Here are to a large extent prepared the elements of the climate of West Europe.

Travellers speak of the Siberian winters with mingled feelings of terror and rapture. An infinite silence broods over the land—all is buried in deep sleep. The animals hibernate in their dens, the streams have ceased to flow, disappearing beneath the ice and snow; the earth, of a dazzling whiteness in the centre of the landscape, but grey in the distance, nowhere offers a single object to arrest the gaze. The monotony of endless space is broken by no abrupt lines or vivid tints. The only contrast with the dull expanse of land is the everlasting azure sky, along which the sun creeps at a few degrees only above the horizon. In these intensely cold latitudes it rises and sets with hard outlines, unsoftened by the ruddy haze elsewhere encircling it on the edge of the horizon. Yet such is the strength of its rays that the snow melts on the housetop exposed to its glare, while in the shade the temperature is 40° to 50° below freezing point. At night, when the firmament is not aglow with the many-tinted lights and silent coruscations of the aurora borealis, the zodiacal light and the stars still shine with intense brightness.

To this severe winter, which fissures the surface and rends the rocks of the rivers into regular basalt-like columns, there succeeds a sudden and delightful spring. So instantaneous is the change that nature seems as if taken by surprise and rudely awakened. The delicate green of the opening leaf, the fragrance of the budding flowers, the intoxicating balm of the atmosphere, the radiant brightness of the heavens, all combine to impart to mere existence a voluptuous gladness. To Siberians visiting the temperate climes of Western Europe, spring seems to be unknown beyond their lands. But these first days of new life are followed by a chill, gusty and changeful interval, arising from the atmospheric disturbances caused by the thawing of the vast snowy wastes. A relapse is then experienced analogous to that too often produced in England by late east winds. The apple blossom is now nipped by the night frosts falling in the latter part of May. Hence no apples can be had in East Siberia, although the summer heats are otherwise amply sufficient for the ripening of fruit. After the fleeting summer, winter weather again sets in. It will often freeze at night in the middle of July; and after the 10th of August the sear leaf begins to fall, and in a few days all are gone, except perhaps the foliage of the larch. The snow will even sometimes settle early in August on the still leafy branches, bending and breaking them with its weight. Below the surface of the ground, winter reigns uninterrupted even by the hottest summers.

With its vast extent and varied climate, Siberia naturally embraces several vegetable zones, differing more from each other even than those of Europe. The southern Steppes have a characteristic and well-marked flora, forming a continuation of that of the Aral, Caspian and Volga plains. The treeless northern *tundras* also constitute a vegetable domain as sharply defined as the desert itself, while between these two zones of Steppe and *tundra* the forest region of Europe stretches, with many subdivisions, west and east right across the continent. Of these subdivisions the chief are those of the Ob, Yenisei, Lena, and Amur basins.

Beyond the northern *tundras* and southern Steppes by far the greatest space is occupied by the forest zone. From the Urals to Kamchatka the dense *taiga*, or woodlands are interrupted only by the streams, a few natural glades and some tracts under cultivation. The term *taiga* is used in a general way for all lands under timber, but east of the Altai it is applied more especially to the moist and spongy region overgrown with tangled roots and thickets, where the *mari*, or peat bogs, and marshes alternate with the *padi*, or narrow ravines. The miners call by this name the wooded mountains where they go in search of auriferous sands. But everywhere the *taiga* is the same dreary forest, without grass, birds, or insects, gloomy and lifeless, and noiseless but for the soughing of the wind and crackling of the branches.

The most common tree in the *taiga* is the larch, which best resists the winter frost and summer chills. But the Siberian woodlands also include most of the trees common to temperate Europe—the linden, alder, juniper, service, willow, aspen, poplar, birch, cherry, apricot—whose areas are regulated according to the nature of the soil, the elevation or aspect of the land. Towards the south-east, on the Chinese frontier, the birch is encroaching on the indigenous species, and the natives regard this as a sure prognostic of the approaching rule of the "White Tsar."

Conflagrations are very frequent in the Siberian forests, caused either by lightning, the woodmen, or hunters, and sometimes spreading over vast spaces till arrested by rivers, lakes or morasses. One of the pleasures of Siberian travelling is the faint odour of the woods burning in the distance.

The native flora is extremely rich in berries of every kind, supplying food for men and animals.

The extreme eastern regions of the Amur basin and Russian Manchuria, being warmer, more humid and fertile, also abound more in animal life than the other parts of Asiatic Russia. On the other hand, the Siberian bear, deer, roebuck, hare, squirrel, marmot and mole are about one-third larger, and often half as heavy again as their European congeners. This is doubtless due partly to the greater abundance of nourishment along the rivers and shores of Siberia, and partly to the fact that for ages the western species have been more preyed upon by man, living in a constant state of fear, and mostly perishing before attaining their full development.

The Arctic Seas abound probably as much as the Pacific Ocean with marine animals. Nordenskjöld found the Siberian waters very rich in molluscs and other lower organisms, implying a corresponding abundance of larger animals. Hence fishing, perhaps more than navigation, will be the future industry of the Siberian coast populations. Cetacea, fishes, molluscs, and other marine organisms are cast up in such quantities along both sides of Bering Strait that the bears and other omnivorous creatures have here become very choice as to their food. But on some parts of the coast in the Chukchi country whales are never stranded, and since the arrival of the Russians certain species threaten to disappear altogether. The *Rhytina stelleri*, a species of walrus formerly frequenting Bering Strait in millions, was completely exterminated between the years 1741-68. Many of the fur-bearing animals, which attracted the Cossacks from the Urals to the Sea of Okhotsk, and which were the true cause of the conquest of Siberia, have become extremely rare. Their skins are distinguished, above all others, for their great softness, warmth, lightness, and bright colours. The more Alpine or continental the climate, the more beautiful and highly prized become the furs, which diminish in gloss towards the coast and in West Siberia, where the south-west winds prevail. The sables of the North Urals are of small value, while those of the Upper Lena, fifteen degrees farther south, are worth a king's ransom. Many species assume a white coat in winter, whereby they are difficult to be distinguished from the surrounding snows. Amongst these are the polar hare and fox, the ermine, the campagnol, often even the wolf and reindeer, besides the owl, yellow-hammer, and some other birds. Those which retain their brown or black colour are mostly such as do not show themselves in winter. The fur of the squirrels also varies with the surrounding foliage, those of the pine forests being ruddy, those of the cedar, *taiga*, and firs inclining to brown, and all varying in intensity of colour with that of the vegetation.

Other species besides the peltry-bearing animals have diminished in numbers since the arrival of the Russian hunters. The reindeer, which frequented the South Siberian highlands, and whose domain encroached on that of the camel, is now found only in the domestic state amongst the Soyotes of the

Upper Yenisei and is met with in the wild state only in the dwarf forests and *tundras* of the far north. The argali has withdrawn to Mongolia from the Siberian mountains and plains, where he was still very common at the end of the last century. On the other hand, cold and want of food yearly drive great numbers of antelopes and wild horses from the Gobi Steppes towards the Siberian lowlands, tigers, wolves and other beasts of prey following in their track, and returning with them in the early spring. Several new species of animals have been introduced by man and modified by crossings in the domestic state. In the north, the Samoyeds, Chukchis, and Kamchadales have the reindeer and dog, while the horse and ox are everywhere the companions of man in the peopled regions of Siberia. The yak has been tamed by the Soyotes of the Upper Yenisei, and the camel, typical of a distinctly Eastern civilization, follows the nomads of the Kirghiz and Mongolian Steppes. All these domesticated animals seem to have acquired special qualities and habits from the various indigenous or Russian peoples of Siberia.

THE RUSSIAN RACES

W. R. MORFILL

The vast Empire of Russia, as may be readily imagined, is peopled by many different races. These may ethnologically be catalogued as follows:

I. Sclavonic races, the most important in numbers and culture. Under this head may be classified:—

(1) The Great Russians, or Russians properly so called, especially occupying the Governments round about Moscow, and from thence scattered in the north to Novgorod and Vologda, on the south to Kiev and to Voronezh, on the east to Penza, Simbirsk, and Viatka, and on the west to the Baltic provinces. Moreover, the Great Russians, as the ruling race, are to be found in small numbers in all quarters of the Empire. They amount to about 40,000,000.

(2) Little Russians (Malorossiani), dwelling south of the Russians, upon the shores of the Black Sea. These, together with the Rusniaks, amount to 16,370,000.

The Cossacks come under these two races.

To the great Russians belong the Don Cossacks, with those sprung from them—the Kouban, Stavropol, Khoperski, Volga, Mosdok, Kizlarski and Grebenski.

SAMOYEDES OF NOVA ZEMBLA.

To the Little Russian: the Malorossiiski, with those sprung from them—the Zaporoghian, Black Sea (Chernomorski), and those of Azov and of the Danube.

(3) The White Russians, inhabiting the Western Governments. Their number amounts to 4,000,000.

(4) Poles, living in the former Kingdom of Poland and the Western Governments of the Empire. Their number amounts to 5,000,000.

(5) Servians, Bulgarians, and other Slavs, inhabiting especially Bessarabia and the country called New Russia. Their number reaches 150,000.

II. The Non-Sclavonic races comprise either original inhabitants of the country who have been subdued by the Russians, or later comers. Among races originally inhabiting the country, and subjugated by the Russians, are included—the Lithuanians and Letts, the Finns, the Samoyeds, the Mongol-Manzhurians, the races of eastern Siberia, the Turko-Tartar, the Caucasian, the German, and the Hebrew.

1. The Lithu-Lettish race inhabits the country between the western Dwina and the Nieman. In numbers they do not amount to more than 3,000,000. The Lithu-Lettish population is divided into the two following branches:—

(a) The Lithuanians properly so called (including the Samogitans or Zhmudes), who inhabit the Governments of Vilno, Kovno, Courland, and the northern parts of those of Augustovo and Grodno (1,900,000).

(b) The Letts, who inhabit the Governments of Courland, Vitebsk, Livonia, Kovno, Pskov, and St. Petersburg (1,100,000).

2. The Finnish race—known in the old Sclavonic chronicles under the name of Chouds—at one time inhabited all the north-eastern part of Russia. The Finns, according to the place of their habitation, are divided into four groups:—the Baltic Finns, the Finns in the Governments of the Volga, the Cis-Oural and the Trans-Oural Finns.

(a) The Baltic Finns: the Chouds (in the Governments of Novgorod and Olonetz); the Livonians (in Courland); the Esthonians (in the Governments of Esthonia, Livonia, Vitebsk, Pskov, and St. Petersburg); the Lopari (in northern Finland and in the Government of Archangel); the Corelians (in the Government of Archangel, Novgorod, Olonetz, St. Petersburg, Tver, and Jaroslav); Evremeiseti (in the Governments of Novgorod and St. Petersburg), Savakoti, Vod, and Izhora.

(b) To the Finns of the Governments of the Volga, who have become almost lost in the Russians, belong the Cheremisians (in the Governments of Kazan, Viatka, Kostroma, Nijni-Novgorod, Orenburg and Perm).

(c) To the Cis-Uralian Finns, who occupy the country from the borders of Finland to the Oural, belong the Permiaks (in the Governments of Viatka and Perm); Zîranians (in the Governments of Archangel and Vologda); Votiaks (in the Governments of Viatka and Kazan); and Vogoulichi (in the Governments of Perm).

(d) Among the Trans-Oural Finns are also to be numbered the Zîranians and Vogoulichi (the first in the Government of Tobolsk, and the second in the Governments of Tobolsk and Tomsk); and the Ostiaks, who, according to the places of their habitation, are called Obski and Berezovski.

The Finns amount altogether to 2,100,000.

3. The Samoyeds, in number 70,000, live in the territory extending from the White Sea to the Yenesei; to these belong the Samoyeds properly so called, the Narîmski and the Yenesei Ostiaks, the Olennie Choukchi, etc.

4. The Mongolo-Manzhourian race amounting to 400,000. Among this race may be remarked the Mongolians properly so called, on the Selenga; the Kalmucks, a nomad people in the Government of Astrakhan, as also in Tomsk, in the country of the Don Cossacks, and partly in the Government of Stavropol. The Kalmucks appeared first on the eastern confines of Russia in the year 1630. About a century later we find them become the regular subjects of the Tsar. They seem, however, to have found the Russian yoke irksome, and resolved to return to their original home on the coasts of Lake Balkach, and at the foot of the Altai Mountains. Nearly the whole nation, amounting to almost 300,000 persons, began their march in the winter of 1770-71. The passage of this vast horde lasted for weeks, but the rear were prevented from escaping by the Kirghiz and Cossacks, who intercepted them. They were compelled to remain in Russia, where their territory was more accurately defined than had been done previously. The Kalmucks are obliged to serve with the Cossack troops, but their duties are mostly confined to looking after the cattle and horses which accompany the army. Their religion is Buddhism, and a conspicuous object in the aouls, or temporary villages which they construct, is the pagoda. Their personal appearance is by no means prepossessing—small eyes and high cheekbones, with scanty hair of a very coarse texture. In every sense of the word they are still strictly nomads; their children and tents are carried by camels, and in a few hours their temporary village, or oulous, is established. To these also belong the Bouriats, by Lake Baikal; the Toungusians from the Yenesei to the Amur; the Lamorets, by the Sea of Okhotsk; and the Olentzi, in the Government of Irkutsk.

5. Races of eastern Siberia: the Koriaks, living in the north-eastern corner of Siberia; the Youkagirs, in the territory of Yakutsk; the Kamchadales, in Kamchatka. Their number amounts to 500,000.

6. The Turko-Tartar race amount in number to 3,000,000. To their branch belong the Chouvashes, in the governments of Orenburg, Simbursk, Saratov and Samaria; the Mordvinians, in the same governments as the Chouvashes,[1] and in those of Tambov, Penza, and Nijni-Novgorod; the Tartars of the Crimea and Kazan; the Nagais, on the Kouban and Don; the Mestcheriaki, in the governments of Orenburg, Perm, Saratov, and Viatka; Koumki, in the Caucasus; Kirghizi, Yakouti, on the Lena; Troukhmentzi and Khivintzi; Karakalpaks (lit. Black Caps), Teleoûti, in the government of Tomsk, Siberia.

[Footnote 1: Some writers consider the Chouvashes to belong to the Finnish race.]

7. The Caucasian races inhabiting Georgia, the valleys and defiles of the Caucasian Mountains have different appellations and different origins. Among them may be noticed the Armenians, Georgians, Circassians, Abkhasians, Lesghians, Osetintzi, Chechentzi, Kistentzi, Toushi, and others. Their number is about 2,000,000.

The languages of the Caucasus must be regarded as a group distinct both from the Aryan and Semitic families. They are agglutinative, and are divided into two branches.

(a) The Northern Division, extending along the northern slopes of the Caucasus, between the Caspian and the northern shores of the Black Sea, as far as the Straits of Yenikale; its subdivisions are Lesghian, Kistian, and Circassian, each with its dialects. Formerly the Circassians numbered about 500,000, but large numbers of them emigrated to European Turkey, where they were dexterously planted by the government to impede the social progress of their Bulgarian and Greek subjects.

(b) The Southern Division, comprising Georgian, Suanian, Mingrelian, and Lazian.

8. The German race, in number about 1,000,000. The Germans are chiefly in the Baltic provinces, in the government of St. Petersburg, in the Grand Duchy of Finland, and the colonies, especially those on the lower Volga, the Don, the Crimea, and New Russia. The Germans have acquired great influence throughout the country; they are represented in the court, in the army, and in the administration. Here also may be mentioned the Swedes, amounting to 286,000.

9. The Jews inhabit especially the former Kingdom of Poland, the Western Governments, and the Crimea. Their number amounts to 3,000,000. Among the Jews the Karaimite are noticeable, living in the governments of Vilno, Volinia, Kovno, Kherson, and the Taurida. Among the Europeans and Asiatics who have come in later times to settle in Russia, are Greeks,

amounting to 75,000, in the governments of New Russia and Chernigov; French, Italians, and Englishmen, in the capitals and chief commercial towns; Wallachians or Moldavians (now generally included under the name of Roumanians), in Bessarabia; Albanians; Gipsies, especially in the territory of Bessarabia, amounting to 50,000; Persians, to 10,000, etc.

THE HISTORY OF RUSSIA

W. R. MORFILL

I shall follow the divisions given in his first volume by Oustrialov. He divides Russian history into two great parts, the ancient and modern.

I. Ancient history from the commencement of Russia to the time of Peter the Great (862-1689).

This first period is subdivided into (*a*) the foundation of Russia and the combination of the Sclavonians into a political unity under the leadership of the Normans and by means of the Christian Faith under Vladimir and the legislation of Yaroslav.

According to the theory commonly received at the present day, the foundation of the Russian Empire was laid by Rurik at Novgorod. The name Russian seems to be best explained as meaning "the seamen" from the Finnish name for the Swedes or Norsemen, Ruotsi, which itself is a corruption of a Scandinavian word. It has been shown by Thomsen, that all the names mentioned in early Russian history admit of a Scandinavian explanation; thus Ingar becomes Igor, and Helga, Oleg. In a few generations the Scandinavian origin of the settlers was forgotten. The grandson of Rurik, Sviatoslav, has a purely Sclavonic name.

Christianity was introduced into the country by Vladimir, and the first code of Russian laws was promulgated by Yaroslav, called Rousskaia Pravda, of which a transcript was found among the chronicles of Novgorod.

(*b*) Breaking up of Russia, under the system of appanages, into some confederate principalities, governed by the descendants of Rurik. This unfortunate disruption of the country paved the way for the invasion of the Mongols, whose domination lasted for nearly two centuries.

During their occupation the Russians were ingrafted with many oriental habits, which were only partially removed by Peter the Great, and in fact many of them have lasted till the present day. The influence of the Mongolians upon the national language has been greatly exaggerated, as the words introduced are confined almost exclusively to articles of dress, money, etc. Had the conquests of the Mongols been permanent, Russia would have become definitely attached to Asia, to which its geographical position seems to assign it.

(*c*) Division of Russia into eastern and western under the Mongolian yoke 1228-1328. This is a very dreary period of the national history.

(*d*) Formation in Eastern Russia of the government of Moscow 1328-1462, which by the energy of its princes became the nucleus of the future empire;

and in Western Russia of the principality of Lithuania, and its union with Poland 1320-1569.

(e) Consolidation of the Muscovite power under Ivan III., who married the daughter of the Greek Emperor, and succeeded in expelling the Tartars, and making himself master of their city Kazan. He was followed by his son Vasilii, who was succeeded by Ivan IV., who has gained a very unenviable reputation on account of his cruelties. Already the yoke of the Tartars had begun to have a very deteriorating effect upon the Russian character, and the more sanguinary code of the Asiatics had effaced the tradition of the laws of Yaroslav. Mutilation, flagellation, and the abundant use of the knout prevailed. The servile custom of chelobitye, or knocking the head on the ground, which was exacted from all subjects on entering the royal presence, was certainly of Tartar origin, as also the punishment inflicted upon refractory debtors, called the pravezh. They were beaten on the shins in a public square every day from eight to eleven o'clock, till the money was paid. The custom is fully described by Giles Fletcher and Olearius.

Another strange habit, savouring too much of the Tartar servitude, was that recorded by Peter Heylin in his *Little Description of the Great World* (Oxford, 1629), who says: "It is the custom over all Muscovie, that a maid in time of wooing sends to that suitor whom she chooseth for her husband such a whip curiously by herself wrought, in token of her subjection unto him." A Russian writer also tells us that it was usual for the husband on the wedding day to give his bride a gentle stroke over the shoulders with his whip, to show his power over her. Herberstein's story of the German Jordan and his Russian wife will perhaps occur to some of my readers. She complained to her husband that he did not love her; but upon his expressing surprise at the doubt, she gave as her reason that he had never beaten her! Indeed the position of a woman in Russia till the time of Peter was a very melancholy one. Her place in society is accurately marked out in the Domostroi, or regulations for governing one's household, written at the time of Ivan the Terrible. As this book presents us with some very curious pictures of Russian family life in the olden time, a few words may be permitted describing its contents. It was written by the monk Sylvester, who was one of the chief counsellors of Ivan, and at one time in great favour with him, but afterwards fell into disgrace and was banished by the capricious tyrant to the Solovetzki monastery, where he died. The work was primarily addressed by the worthy priest to his son Anthemus and his daughter-in-law, Pelagia, but as the bulk of it was of a general character it soon became used in all households. Nothing escapes this father of the church from the duties of religion, down to the minor details of the kitchen and the mysteries of cookery. The wife is constantly recommended to practise humility, in a way which would probably be repulsive to many of our modern ladies. Her industry in weaving and making clothes among her domestics is very carefully dwelt upon. She lived in a kind of Oriental seclusion, and saw no one except her nearest relatives. The bridegroom knew nothing of his bride, she was only allowed to be seen a few times before marriage by his female relatives, and on these occasions all kinds of tricks were played. A stool was placed under her feet that she might seem taller, or a handsome female attendant, or a better-looking sister were substituted. "Nowhere," says Kotoshikhin, "is there such trickery practised with reference to the brides as at Moscow." The innovations of Peter the Great broke through the oriental seclusion of the terem, as the women's apartments were called. During the minority of Ivan IV. the regency was committed to the care of his mother Elena, and was at best but a stormy period. When I van came to the throne the country was not even yet free from the incursions of the Tartars. In Hakluyt's voyages we have a curious account of one of these devastations in a "letter of Richard Vscombe to M. Henrie Lane, touching the burning of the city of Mosco by the Crimme Tartar, written the fifth day of August, 1571." "The Mosco is burnt every sticke by the Crimme, the 24th day of May last, and an innumerable number of people; and in the English house was smothered Thomas Southam, Tosild, Waverley, Green's wife and children, two children of Rafe, and more to the number of twenty-five persons were stifled in oure beere seller, and yet in the same seller was Rafe, his wife, John Browne, and John Clarke preserved, which was wonderful. And there went to that seller Master Glover and Master Rowley also; but because the heat was so great they came foorth againe with much perill, so that a boy at their heeles was taken with the fire, yet they escaped blindfold into another seller, and there as God's will was they were preserved. The emperor fled out of the field, and many of his people were carried away by the Crimme Tartar. And so with exceeding much spoile and infinite prisoners, they returned home againe. What with the Crimme on the one side and his cruelties on the other, he hath but few people left" (Hakluyt, I. 402).

ROOM OF THE TSAR MICHAILOWITCH, MOSCOW.

It is well known that the English first became acquainted with Russia in the time of Ivan the Terrible. In the reign of Edward VI. a voyage was undertaken by Sir Hugh Willoughby and Richard Chancellor, who attempted to reach Russia by way of the North Sea. Willoughby and his crew were unfortunately lost, but Chancellor succeeded in reaching Moscow, and showing his letters to the Tsar, in reply to which an alliance was concluded and an ambassador soon afterwards visited the English court. In spite of his brutal tyrannies, for which no apologies can be offered, although some of the Russian authorities have attempted to gloss them over, the reign of Ivan was distinctly progressive for Russia. The introduction of the printing-press, the conquest of Siberia, the development of commerce, were all in advance of what had been done by his predecessors. He also had the leading idea afterwards fully carried out by Peter the Great of extending the dominions on the north, and ensuring a footing on the Baltic.

The relations of Ivan with England are fully described in the very interesting diary of Sir Jerome Horsey, the ambassador from this country, the manuscript of which is preserved in the British Museum. He was anxious to have an English wife, and Elizabeth selected one for him, Lady Mary Hastings, but when the bride-elect had been made acquainted with the circumstance that Ivan had been married several times before, and was a most truculent and blood-thirsty sovereign, she entreated her father with many tears not to send her to such a man.

The character given of Ivan by Horsey is very graphic, and is valuable as the narration of a person who had frequently been in intimate relations with the Tsar. We give it in the original spelling:—

"Thus much to conclude with this Emperor Ivan Vasiliwich. He was a goodlie man of person and presence, well favoured, high forehead, shrill voice, a right Sithian, full of readie wisdom, cruell, blondye, merciless; his own experience mannaged by direction both his state and commonwealth affairs; was sumptuously intomed in Michell Archangell Church, where he, though guarded daye and night, remaines a fearfull spectacle to the memorie of such as pass by or heer his name spoken of [who] are contented to cross and bless themselves from his resurrection againe."

Passing over his feeble son, we come to the era of Boris Godunov, a man in many respects remarkable, but not the least that he saw the necessity of western culture. His plans for educating Russia were extensive, and several youths were sent abroad for this purpose, including some to England. But his reign ended gloomily, and was followed by the period of the Pretenders (Samozvantzi), during which Russia was rent by opposing factions; and almost ended in receiving a foreign sovereign, in the person of Ladislaus (Wladyslaw), the son of Sigismund III., the King of Poland. The Romanovs finally ascended the throne in the person of Michael in 1613. The son of Michael, Alexis, was a thoroughly reforming sovereign, and took many foreigners into his pay. With the reign of Ivan V., son of Alexis, closes the old period of Russian history.

II. The new history from the days of Peter the Great to the present time.

The reforms introduced into Russia by Peter the Great are too well known to need recapitulation here. There will be always many different opinions about this wonderful man. Some have not hesitated to say that he "knouted" Russia into civilization; others can see traces of the hero mixed with much clay. One of the darkest pages in the annals of his reign, is that upon which is written the fate of his unfortunate son, Alexis. All Russia seems but one vast monument of his genius. He gave her six new provinces, a footing upon two seas, a regular army trained on the European system, a large fleet, an admiralty, and a naval academy; besides these, some educational establishments, a gallery of painting and sculpture, and a public library. Nothing escaped his notice, even to such minutiæ as the alteration of Russian letters to make them more adapted to printing, and changing the dress of his subjects so as to be more in conformity with European costume. All this interference savoured of despotism, no doubt, but it led to the consolidation of a great nationality. The Russians belong to the European family, and must of necessity return to fulfil their destiny, although they had been temporarily diverted from their bondage under the Mongols. Owing to the mistake Peter had committed in allowing the succession to be changed at the will of the ruling sovereign, the country was for some time after his death in the hands of Russian and German adventurers.

On the death of Peter he was succeeded by his wife Catherine, an amiable but illiterate woman, who was wholly under the influence of Menshikov, one of Peter's chief favourites. After a short reign of two years, she was succeeded by Peter II., son of the unfortunate Alexis, in whose time Menshikov and his family were banished to Berezov in Siberia. After his banishment, Peter, who was a weak prince, and showed every inclination to undo his grandfather's work, fell under the influence of the Dolgoroukis.

There is something very touching in the fate of this poor child—he was but fifteen years of age when he died—tossed about amidst the opposing factions of the intriguing courtiers, each of whom cared nothing for the good of the country, but only how to find the readiest means to supplant his rival. The last words of the boy as he lay on his death-bed were, "Get ready the sledge! I want to go to my sister!" alluding to the Princess Natalia, the other child of Alexis who had died three years previously.

On his death Anne, Duchess of Courland, and daughter of Ivan, the elder brother of Peter, was called to the throne. After her death, by a second *révolution de palais*, Elizabeth, the daughter of Peter the Great, was made sovereign. In this reign her alliance was concluded with Maria Theresa of Austria, and during the Seven Years' War, a large Russian force invaded Prussia; another took Berlin in 1760.

During the whole of her reign Elizabeth was under the influence of favourites, or *vremenstchiki*, as the Russians call them. She appears to have been an indolent, good-tempered woman, and exceedingly superstitious. During her reign Russia made considerable progress in literature and culture. A national theatre, of which there had been a few germs even at so early a period as the youth of Peter the Great, was thoroughly developed, and at Yaroslavl, Volkov, the son of a merchant, earned such a reputation as an actor, that he was summoned to St. Petersburg by Elizabeth, who took him under her patronage. Dramatists now sprang up on every side, but at first were merely translators of Corneille, Racine, and Molière. The Russian arms were successful during her reign, and the capture of Berlin in 1760, had a great effect upon European politics. Two years afterwards Elizabeth died, and her nephew Peter III. succeeded, who admired Frederick the Great, and at once made peace with him.

This unfortunate man, however, only reigned six months, having been dethroned and put to death by order of his wife, who became Empress of Russia under the title of Catherine II. However unjustifiable the means may have been by which Catherine became possessed of the throne, and in mere justice to her we must remember that she had been brutally treated by her husband, and was in hourly expectation of being immured for life in a dungeon by his orders, she exercised her power to the advantage of the country.

In 1770, a Russian fleet appeared for the first time in the Mediterranean, and the Turkish navy was destroyed at Chesme. By the treaty of Kutchuk Kainardji (1774), Turkey was obliged to recognize the independence of the Crimea, and cede to Russia a considerable amount of territory. In 1783, Russia gained the Crimea, and in 1793, by the last partition of Poland, a very large portion of that country.

The subsequent events of the history are well known. Paul, who succeeded Catherine, was assassinated in 1801. The reign of this emperor has been made very familiar to Englishmen by the highly coloured portrait given by the traveller Clarke, who laboured under the most aggravated Russophobia. That Paul did many cruel and capricious things does not admit of a doubt, but he was capable of generous feelings, and sometimes surprised people as much by his liberality as by his despotic conduct. Thus he set Kosciusko at liberty as soon as he had ascended the throne; and there was a fine revenge in his compelling Orlov to follow the coffins of Peter and Catherine, when by his order they were buried together in the Petropavlovski church.

Alexander I., his son, added Finland to the Russian empire, and saw his country invaded by Napoleon in 1812. The horrors of this campaign have been well described by Segur, Wilson, and Labaume. At his death in 1825, his brother Nicholas succeeded, not without opposition, which led to bloodshed and the execution of the five Dekabrists (conspirators of December). The schemes of these men were impracticable; so little did the common people understand the very rudiments of liberalism, that when the soldiers were ordered to shout for Konstitoutzia (the constitution, a word the foreign appearance of which shows how alien it was to the national spirit), one of them naively asked, if that was the name of the wife of the Grand Duke Constantine.

The policy of the Emperor Nicholas was one of complete isolation of the country, and the prevention of his subjects as much as possible from holding intercourse with the rest of Europe, hence permission to travel was but sparingly given, nor were foreigners encouraged to visit Russia. In 1826, war broke out with Persia, the result of which was that the latter power was compelled to cede Erivan and the country as far as the Araxes (or Aras). Russia also made further additions to her territory by the treaty of Adrianople in 1829, after Diebich had crossed the Balkans. In 1830, the great Polish rebellion broke out, which was crushed after much bloodshed in Sept. 1831, by the capture of Warsaw. In 1849, the Russians assisted Austria in crushing the revolt of her Hungarian subjects. In 1853 broke out the Crimean War, the details of which are so well known as to require no enumeration. Peace was concluded between Russia and the Allies, after the death of the Emperor Nicholas in 1855, who was succeeded by his son, Alexander II. The two great events of the reign of this monarch have been the emancipation of the serfs in 1861, by which 22,000,000 received their liberty, and the war with Turkey.

CHURCH SERVICE

ALFRED MASKELL

The history of the introduction and early progress of Christianity in Russia is involved in obscurity and overlaid with legendary stories. There is little doubt that it came from Constantinople, and was not only rapidly spread, but firmly established in the country within a short space of time. The date most generally accepted is that of the reign of Vladimir, the great prince of Kief, grandson of Olga. As Dean Stanley remarks in his *Lectures on the Eastern Church*: "It coincides with a great epoch in Europe, the close of the Tenth Century, when throughout the West the end of the world was fearfully expected, when the Latin Church was overclouded with the deepest despondency, when the Papal See had become the prey of ruffians and profligates, then it was that the Eastern Church, silently and almost unconsciously, bore into the world her mightiest offspring."

CHURCH OF THE ASSUMPTION, MOSCOW.

The Eastern Church was then at the zenith of its splendour. The envoys sent by Vladimir to Constantinople to examine and report upon the religion which he had almost decided to adopt were dazzled with the magnificence of the ceremonial. They were wavering in their choice and weighing the merits of the different systems which been brought before them. Rome they had not seen; Mohammedanism was foreign to their tastes; Judaism had been found wanting; but the Eastern Church appealed strongly to their imaginations and barbaric love of splendour. Hers was St. Sophia, magnificent now, but how much more gorgeous then! Every effort was made to win them, and the victory was easy.

The intercourse of the newly formed empire of Russia with Byzantium was at that time great. The change of religion had been very sudden and it was necessary to build at once new edifices for the new order of things. It was naturally to Byzantium that they turned for their form and ornament. Very quickly churches arose. Novgorod, the cradle of the Empire and the capital until the removal to Kief, was the Metropolitan See, and the first cathedral is said to have been built there as early as A. D. 989.

The form of a Russian Church underwent little change up to the Seventeenth Century. In the Thirteenth Century the architects imported from Lombardy brought to bear on the exterior the style of the Lombardic or Romanesque architecture which had so long prevailed in their own country. The gilded dome or cupola, of peculiar onion-shaped form which is so especially Russian, was added soon afterwards. The central cupola, which was adopted from the first, was afterwards surrounded by others; their number reached even to twenty or thirty, and it was not until the Sixteenth Century at the time of the establishment of the patriarchate (1589), that these were authoritatively restricted to five, which is now the orthodox and obligatory number.

The practice of having two, three, five, seven, nine and thirteen cupolas or spires is as early as the Eleventh Century. The numbers were figurative; two signifying the two natures of Jesus Christ, three, a symbol of the Trinity, five, our Lord and the four evangelists or the five wounds, seven, the seven sacraments, the seven gifts of the Holy Spirit, or the seven recumenical councils, nine, the nine celestial hierarchies, and thirteen, our Lord and the twelve apostles.

Within the dimensions are small and the light obscure. Still, the simple, nearly square disposition of the building, the enormous plain-shafted pillars which support the domes, the mass of gilding, the multitude of lamps, produce an undoubtedly grand effect. It is strikingly oriental; and as in Russian churches there are no seats, but the people stand in a mingled throng, now and then prostrating themselves and beating their foreheads on the ground, each as his own devotion may dictate, the resemblance is still more marked. All the interior is covered with fresco pictures; even the pillars have gigantic figures of the saints and doctors of the church painted upon them. From the high roof hang immense brass chandeliers of a peculiar form with many branches, capable of holding hundreds of candles. In the dim distance, seemingly a wall of gold, is the iconostas, the solid screen which in every church divides the sanctuary from the rest of the sacred edifice.

The iconostas is in all cases decorated with a large number of holy pictures or icons, arranged in formal rows one above the other. It is a solid erection from side to side, from floor to roof, and in the centre are the *royal doors*, through which none may pass but the consecrating priest, or the emperor: and the last once only, at the time of his coronation. At no time is any woman permitted to enter the sanctuary.

The iconostas contains sometimes as many as seven rows of images: that of the *Uspenski Sobor*[1] has five. Their arrangement is guided by certain rules and restrictions. Our Lord and the blessed Virgin must be represented on each side of the royal doors, and on the doors themselves the Annunciation and the four evangelists. On the side doors angels must be represented. Above must be the usual symbol of the Trinity figured by Abraham entertaining the three angels.

[Footnote 1: Cathedral of the Assumption, Moscow.]

The whole of the space behind the screen is known as the altar. The altar itself is square, or rather a double cube. Above it four small columns with a canopy form a baldachino; and the cross is laid flat upon it. Here also is placed the tabernacle or *zion* which is often an architectural structure in pure gold with figures. There are five zions of this kind in the cathedrals of St. Sophia at Novgorod and at the Troitsa monastery.

In the apse behind the altar and facing it is the *thronos*, the seat of the archbishop, with seats for priests on either side.

Besides the icons and holy pictures on the screen (and in the Cathedral of the Assumption the latter contains the most highly venerated in Russia) other smaller icons are set apart in various parts of the church. As is now the custom, though it is comparatively a recent one, the greater part of the picture, with the exception of the faces, hands and feet, is covered with an embossed and chased plaque in gold or silver-gilt representing the form and garments. Glories or nimbuses in high relief set thick with gems surround the faces, and sparkle as they reflect the light from the multitude of candles burnt in their honour. Some are covered to overloading with jewels, necklets, and bracelets; pearls, diamonds, and rubies of large size and value adorning them in profusion.

The ceremonial of the Greek church is excessively complex, and the symbolical meanings by which it represents the dogmas of religion are everywhere made the subjects of minute observance. During the greater part of the mass the royal doors are closed: the deacons remain for the most part without, now and again entering for a short time. From time to time a pope or popes pass throughout the church, amongst the crowds, incensing all the holy pictures in turn; the voice of the officiating priest is raised within, and is answered in deep tones by the deacons without. Now from one corner comes a chant of many voices, now for another a single one in tones (it may be), the epistle or gospel of the day. Now the doors fly open and a fleeting glimpse is gained of the celebrant through the thick rolling clouds of incense. Then they are closed again suddenly. To a stranger unable to follow and in ignorance of the meaning, the effect is bewildering.

In writing, even generally, of the arts in Russia some reference to religious music is excusable. That of Russia has a peculiar charm of its own, far above the barbarous discords that are to be heard in Greek and other churches of the East at the present day. There is a sweetness and attractiveness in the unaccompanied chanting of the choir, in the deep bass tones of the men mingling with the plaintive trebles of younger voices, which is indescribable in its harmony. It is unlike any other; yet underneath lies the original tinge of orientalism, the wailing semitones of all barbaric music. No accompaniment, no instrumental music of any kind is permitted. Bass voices of extraordinary depth and power are the most desired. It is said that the tones now used in the Russian church are comparatively modern.

The principal churches and monasteries in Russia possess rich stores of vestments; some of comparatively high antiquity which are preserved with scrupulous care and still used on occasions of great ceremony. In more modern vestments the ancient ornament is to a great extent strictly copied.

The *saccos*, formerly the principal vestment of the patriarchs and an emblem of sovereign power, is now common to all Russian bishops. It is in the shape of a dalmatic, formed of two square pieces of stuff joined together at the neck and open at the sides, having wide short sleeves. Many of the finest of these vestments are elaborately embroidered in gold and silver and ornamented with figures of saints; and in the stuffs themselves sacred subjects are often woven. They are also thickly sown with rows of seed-pearls which follow the lines and edgings of the vestment and border the sacred images. They are besides set with enamelled, nielloed, or jewelled plaques of gold or silver. Texts in Greek or Sclavonic often border the whole of the edges of the garment. These are elaborately worked in gold or silver, or the letters formed completely of seed-pearls. The *saccos* of the Metropolitan Peter (made in 1322), of Alexis (1364), of Photius (1414), and of Dionysius (made in 1583), are remarkable vestments of this character, to be found in the patriarchal sacristy at Moscow. The stoles, which usually correspond, are long, narrow, and nearly straight-sided to the bottom. A peculiar episcopal ornament is the *epigonation*. It is a large lozenge-shaped ornament embroidered and worked in a similar manner to the other vestments, and by bishops is worn hanging from the right side.

The usual form of mitre of a pope of the Russian church is well-known. The earlier kind was a sort of low cap with a border of fur, something like the cap of a royal crown, and probably not different in type from the head-dresses of bishops of the west. Some are sewn thick with pearls bordering and heightening the lines of the figures of saints, and forming the outlines of the Sclavonic inscriptions. Such is that of Joassof, first patriarch of the Russian church (1558). Those of later times are often of metal richly set with precious stones. Sometimes they assume a more conical form, surmounted by a cross, like an imperial crown, as that which is termed the Constantinople mitre, said to have been made in the time of Ivan the Terrible. The mitre of the celebrated Nikon (1655), who aspired to papal prerogatives, is diadem-shaped and remarkable for the richness of the precious stones with which it is set. The most usual shape recalls to some extent the favourite cupola, spreading out from the base to the top.

The form of the chalice used in the Russian church varies considerably, as it does also in that of the Latin church. In general characteristics the two have much in common. In early times the chalice was made of wood or crystal as well as of gold and silver. An ancient chalice of crystal is preserved in the Cathedral of the Assumption at Moscow, and the wooden ones of SS. Sergius and Nikon are in the sacristy at Troitsa. On some old icons our Lord is represented as giving the holy communion to the apostles out of narrow-necked vessels which appear to be made of alabaster.

The Greek rite for the celebration of the holy eucharist requires three things which are not used in the western church. These are the knife or spear, the star or asterisk, and the spoon for the administration of the chalice as the sacrament is received by the laity under both kinds. It may naturally be supposed that such sacred objects would be the subjects of high artistic workmanship. The paten itself is often elaborately enamelled and otherwise decorated, whereas in the western church the rubrics require it to be plain.

The ceremonial of the preparation of the bread (which is leavened and in the form of a small loaf) is exceedingly complex. Portions are cut out for consecration, and for this purpose a knife called a "spear" is used. These portions placed on the paten are covered with a veil, and in order to prevent the latter from touching the elements a piece of metal is placed over them: two strips crossed, and bent so as to have four feet. The tabernacle, or perhaps more properly ciborium, is sometimes in the form of a hill or mount of gold or silver-gilt, or of a temple, and there are many remarkable examples. One at Troitsa is of solid gold with the exception of Judas, which is of brass. Another is in the sacristy of the church of the Assumption at Moscow. From its inscription we learn that it was made for the grand duke Ivan Vassilievitch in 1486, and it is a characteristic specimen of Russian art of the period.

A peculiar ornament or sacred vessel of the Russo-Greek church is known under the name of *panagia*, and of this there are two kinds. One is a jewel or pectoral worn suspended from the neck by bishops, and is an object on which much care and rich decoration are lavished. In a somewhat altered form it is worn by priests in the same way for carrying the holy sacrament on a journey or to the sick.

Pectoral crosses for the dignitaries of the church are of course not uncommon; not only priests, however, but every Russian man, woman or child carries a small cross, more or less ornamental. They are various in form and richness of decoration; from the simple bronze cross, rudely stamped, of the peasant, to the enamelled and jewelled one of the metropolitan or noble. Nearly always the plain three-armed cross is set in the centre of another more elaborate or conventional. Almost invariably also the sacred monograms and invocations in Sclavonic characters are engraved in the field. In some cases it is more a medallion than a cross, the form of the cross being indicated by cutting four segments in the manner of the ancient stone crosses to be seen in many parts of England. Besides the inscriptions, emblems such as the spear and nails and crown of thorns are often to be distinguished though conventionally indicated.

Crosses on church tops are made of silver, wood, lead, and even gold. The open-worked designs of many of them, although intended to be placed at great height, are extremely elegant. They were occasionally ornamented with coins, and those on churches erected by the Tsar are surmounted by an imperial crown.

A crescent as a symbol beneath the cross is very frequent. Various explanations of this symbol have been given. According to some it is in remembrance of the victory of the cross over the crescent on the deliverance from the Mongol yoke. Others think it to have originated simply in the freak of some goldsmith, afterwards copied by others until it came to be accepted as a necessity. It is certain that the use of the crescent is anterior to the Mongol invasion, and was an old symbol in Byzantium, as appears from coins.

The pastoral staff of Russian bishops is tau-shaped; and there are many good old examples, a few in ivory, but for the most part in silver-gilt. Processional crosses are also used.

The censer is a piece of church furniture in constant use in the Russo-Greek church, and we find several examples very characteristic of Russian art. As in the west, the application of architectural forms is very frequent, and it is not surprising that the peculiarities of Russian ecclesiastical ornament should be prominent and especially the dome which naturally suggests itself.

Amongst the objects kept in the sacristy of the patriarchs in the Cathedral of the Assumption, in Moscow, is one which is held in special veneration. This is the vase in which is preserved the deposit of holy chrism used in the annual preparation of holy oils for distribution to the various churches of the empire.

The preparation of this oil is an occasion of great ceremony in Holy Week. From the fourth week in Lent the preliminary mixings of oil, wine, herbs, and a variety of different ingredients begin. In the Holy Week these ingredient are prepared in a public ceremony: two large boilers, several bowls and sixteen vases together with other vessels being used. All of these are of great size of massive silver, and, presented by Catherine II. in 1767, are specimens of silver work of that time.

THE CREEDS OF RUSSIA

ERNEST W. LOWRY

A report was brought to Basil, the Metropolitan of Moscow, in the year 1340, by merchants of Novgorod, who asserted that they had beheld a glimpse of Paradise from the shores of the White Sea. Whether their vision were merely the dazzling reflection of some sunlit iceberg, or only the glow of poetic imagination, it so fired the ardour of the mediæval prelate that he longed to set sail for this golden gleam. Be the old legend true or false, it is certain that to this day the northern Mujik shows an even more marked religious enthusiasm than his brother of the central governments. Fanaticism, mysticism, and fatalism go ever hand in hand in Northern Russia. The Empire of the Tsars being so vast in area and so embracive of races affords space for all forms of belief, or want of belief, within her boundaries. All creeds are represented, from the pagan Samoyede of the *tundras* to the Mohammedan Tartar of the Steppes. Our concern is with but one of these— the Old Believers. But to understand their doctrine, we must glance at the clergy of the State Church from which they dissent.

A RELIGIOUS PROCESSION, LOKA.

The clergy of the Orthodox Russian Church are divided into Black or monks of St. Basil, and the White or parish priests. The latter must be married before they are ordained, and may not marry again (which has led to the saying, "A priest takes good care of his wife, for he cannot get another"), while the monasteries, of course, require celibacy. From the latter the bishops are elected, so that they—in contradistinction to the priests—must be single.

This system is much condemned by the lower clergy, who ask pertinently, "How can the bishop know the hardships of our lives? for he is single and well paid, we poor and married." The rule, observed elsewhere, holds good in Russia, the poorer the priest, the larger the family. Few village priests receive any regular stipend, but are allowed a plot of land in the commune wherein they minister. This allowance is generally from thirty to forty dessiatines (eighty to one hundred and eight acres), and can only be converted into money, or food products, by the labour of the parson and his family upon it—very literally must they put their hand to the plough. Priests are paid for special services, such as christenings or weddings, at no fixed tariff, but at a sliding rate, according to the means of the payer, the price being arrived at by means of prolonged bargaining between the shepherd and his flock. Would-be couples often wait for months until a sum can be fixed upon with his reverence for tying the knot; and sometimes, by means of daily haggling, the amount first asked can be reduced by one-half, for the cost of the ceremony varies—according to the social status of the happy pair—from ten to one hundred roubles. Funerals, too, are at times postponed for most unhealthy periods during this process. Generally, however, the White Clergy[1] are so miserably poor that they cannot be blamed for making the best market they can for their priestly offices. Whether the system or the salary be at fault it is hard to say, but from whatever cause the fact remains that the parish clergy of the villages are not always all they might be; there are many among them who lead upright lives and gain the respect of their parishioners, but it would be idle to deny that there are many whose thoughts turn more to *vodka* than piety, the *kabak* than the Church. Such shepherds have little in common with the best elements of their flocks, and much with the worst, in whose company they are generally seen.

[Footnote 1: The White Clergy wear any colour but that from which they take their name—a deer-skin cap and long felt boots.]

The poor "Pope" spends much of his time going from *izba* to *izba*, giving his blessing and receiving in return drink and a few copecks; from this come, all too easily, the proverbs of his parishioners, "Am I a priest, that I should sup twice?" etc. Count Tolstoi makes his hero remark in the trial scene of the *Resurrection*, when his fellow jurymen are more friendly than he would wish, "The son of a priest will speak to me next." But most of them have a side to their natures which, though not always to be seen, is, nevertheless, latent— the hour of need often lifts them to the lofty plane of their sublime functions; the labouring—often hungry—peasant of the weekdays becomes on Sunday exalted above the petty surroundings of Mujik life, and becomes indeed the "little father" of his people.

From the Established Church of the State, the Church of the few in the North, let us turn to the old faith, the Church of the many. The Old Believers,

Raskolniks, or dissenters, are indeed a numerous, although officially an uncounted, body in the North; half the trade of Moscow, most of that which is Russian at all, in the Port of Archangel, all the Pomor shipping lies in their hands.

The word Raskolnik means, literally, one who splits asunder, and that is just what the Old Believer is—one who has split off from the Orthodox Church.

Two hundred and fifty years ago Nikon, a friar of Solovetsk, an island monastery in the White Sea, having quarrelled alike with equal and superior, was set adrift in an open boat; he reached the mainland at Ki, a small cape in Onega Bay, wandered southward to Olonets, where he got together a band of followers, proceeded to Moscow, obtained the notice of the throne, got preferment, was soon made Patriarch. He ruled with an iron hand, made many enemies, and when at last he obtained from Mount Santo, in Roumelia, authentic Greek Church-service books, and, having had them translated into Sclavonic, forced their use upon the Church, with the aid of the Tsar Alexis, in the place of those previously in use, the revolt began in earnest. In addition to the altered service book, Nikon introduced a cross with but two beams, a new stamp for the holy wafer, a different way of holding the fingers in pronouncing the blessing, and a new way of spelling the name Jesus, to which the Church was unaccustomed. In each of these changes Nikon and his party really wished to go back to older and purer forms of Greek ritual, but many resisted the alterations, believing them to be innovations.

Such was the beginning of Raskol; the end is not yet. Those who could not accept these reforms, or returns to older forms, took up the name of "Staro-obriadtsi," or Old Believers, holding that theirs was indeed the true old faith of their fathers. For them began, in very truth a hard time; a time which has left its mark most clearly upon their descendants to-day. Excommunicated and persecuted under Alexis and Peter I., they were driven in thousands from their village homes to seek refuge where they could, in forest, mountain or island; a party reaching in the year 1767, even to Kolgueff Island, where, as might be expected, they perished during the following year from scurvy. To these brave bands of Old Believers, setting forth under their banner of the "Eight-ended Cross," to find new homes beyond the reach of persecution, is, in large part, due the colonization of the huge province of Archangel and the northern portion of Siberia. That it was not always easy for the Raskolnik to get beyond the range of official persecutions is shown by many an old "*ukas*," and by many an old entry in the books of far-distant communes. Farther north and farther east, from forest to *tundra* and Steppe were they driven, spreading as they went their Russian nationality over regions Asiatic; as exiles they settled among Polish Romanists, Baltic Protestants, and Caucasian Mussulmans, and with the heathen Lapp and Samoyede, and Ostiac, on the Murman coast of Russian Lapland, in the bleak Northern *tundra*, on the Petchora, and away beyond the Ural Spur, they found at last the rest they sought.

Their most dangerous enemy was not, however, the persecution of the dominant Church; they had placed themselves geographically beyond the reach of that: far more dangerous was further Raskol—splitting—among themselves, and it was not long before this overtook them. Cut off by their own faith, as well by excommunication, from the Orthodox Church, the supply of consecrated priests soon gave out; they had lost their apostolic succession and could not renew it, for the one Bishop—Paul of Kalomna— who had joined them, had died in prison, without appointing a successor. Without an episcopate they were soon without a priesthood; and the vital question, "How shall we get priests and through them Sacraments?" was answered in two ways, and according to the answer, so were the Old Believers divided into two main sects. One sect declared that, as there were no longer faithful priests, they were cut off from all the Sacraments except Baptism, which could be administered by laymen. These "Bespopoftsi," or priestless people, were unable to marry; and to this—in a land where the economic unit, is not man, but man and wife, where the ties of family life are so strong—was due their further splitting.

In 1846, however, they persuaded an outcast bishop to join their ranks, and founded a See at Bielokrinitzkaga, in Austrian Bukovina, beyond the Russian Empire; from thence the succession was handed down, and now after long decades of waiting, they have bishops and priests of their own.

The practice of hiring a priest from the Orthodox Church, to conduct a service for the Old Believers, is still very common in the far North, where all villages have not the means to keep a "Pope" of their own; and many an Orthodox clergyman thus adds considerably to his precarious income by officiating for those whom his great-grandfathers excommunicated as heretics; indeed, the Government now encourages this practice, and has made some attempt to heal up the schism by allowing its priests to adopt, to a slight extent, the old customs in villages where all the inhabitants are Raskolniks. This can the more readily be understood when it is remembered that the Old Believers hold in all essential points the same creed as the Orthodox; they are—and their name implies—believers in the old faith of the Russian branch of the Greek Church, as expressed since the day of St. Vladimir until the Seventeenth Century, but not in the so-called innovations of Nikon. The points of difference are so small that it seems impossible a Church should by them have been cleft in twain. The Orthodox sign the Cross with three fingers extended, the dissenters with two, holding that the two raised fingers indicate the dual nature of Christ, while the three bent ones represent the Trinity. It does not seem to have occurred to either party that the reverse holds true as well. The Orthodox Cross has but two beams, while that of the Raskolnik has four, and is made of four woods—cypress, cedar, palm, and olive; the latter, too, repeats his Allelujah thrice, the Orthodox but twice. Such are the points to which in all probability, the peopling of the outlying portions of the Empire of the Tsars is due.

The Raskolniks have set a far higher value upon education than the Orthodox; the instruction given in their settlements often sheds a strong light upon the darkness of Orthodox ignorance around, and with the spread of education so does the sect extend and multiply. Their house can generally be distinguished by cleanliness, the presence of many Eicons, brass and silver crosses, and ancient books; its mistress by her greater thoughtfulness and capability. Old Believers are always glad to seize the opportunity, given so well by the long northern winter, with its almost endless night, of reading, and on their shelves are seen translations of our best authors, from whom, perhaps, it is that they have taken their advanced political views, and the outcome of whose perusal is that the hunter and fisherman will often propound to one questions which show a mind well trained in logical thought. The Raskolnik is generally fairly well to do, for, like the Quaker and the Puritan, he finds a turn for business not incompatible with religious exercise, and to this is in part due the superiority and comfort of their homes. Most of them in the far North are fishers and hunters, sealers and sailors, and in these and kindred trades they make use of better and more modern appliances than their neighbours, and so generally realize more for their commodities.

Far from civilization, in the impenetrable forests of the great lone land of Archangel, the fugitive Raskolniks were able to found retreats for themselves, untroubled and unobserved; these refuges still exist, and are called "Obitel" or cells. In the district of Mezen there are many such establishments, both for men and women; among the former the Anuphief Hermitage, or cells of Koida, stand in a splendid position, on the banks of both lake and river Koida, some 100 versts in summer by river, and 50 in winter, over ice, from the town of that name.

On Nonconformist, as on Orthodox, is laid the burden of severe fasting; as Master Chancellour tells us, in 1553, "This people hath four Lents,"—indeed, the eating working year is reduced to some 130 days. In the North, where vegetables and berries are few and fruit non-existent, the Mujik is left to fast on "*treska*," rotten codfish—and the condition of the man who begins Lent underfed is indeed pitiable when he ends it. The endurance of the Old Believer is marvellous; no offer of food will tempt him from what he considers his duty.

Let us turn our attention from the Raskolniks, or Old Believers of the far North, who, as we have seen, so literally "forsook all" for their ancient Faith, to some few of the many new, or lately developed creeds whose followers are seeking after truth with equal earnestness and vigour, but along very different lines. Sect begets sect in the world of theology, much as cell begets cell in the economy of life. Change seems the active principle of all dissent; new cults are forever springing up in the mystic childlike minds of the Tsar's great peasant family, nor could one expect uniformity of confession, when the size and neighbours of that family are considered, for Mohammedan, Protestant, Catholic, Buddhist, and Shamanist surround it, are made subject to it, and eventually become a part thereof. A Mosque stands opposite the Orthodox church in the great square which forms the centre of Nijni-Novgorod, a Roman Catholic and a German Lutheran church almost face the magnificent Kazan Cathedral, in the Nevski-Prospekt of St. Petersburg. The waiters of nearly all restaurants, from Archangel to Baku, are Mohammedan Tartars, the Jew is in every market-place, the native heathen races, Lapp, Samoyede, Ostiac, Yakout, and a score of others, are closely connected by the bonds of commerce: can it be wondered at if the ideas of the peasant become tinted by his surroundings?

It cannot be gainsaid that the lifelessness and emptiness of the State Church, with its hireling and often ignorant priesthood, fails to satisfy the great mind of Russia—the peasant mind—but now awakening from its long infant slumber, as did the mind of Western Europe three centuries ago. Next perhaps to the extreme literalness with which the Mujik interprets Holy Writ, this dissatisfaction with the official Church is the greatest cause of the grip which the chameleon-like "dissent" has taken hold of the popular mind. With very few exceptions—notably the Skoptsy—the 150 sects which are stated to exist within the pale of Christianity and the borders of the Empire of the Tsar, begin and end with the Mujik; the official world is of necessity Orthodox, the wealthy world careless, and this fact, of the peasant origin and development of the denominations, must be carefully borne in mind when attempting to form any idea of the widely different meanings and shades of meaning which have been put upon the one Bible story.

Of the strictly rational, and more or less Protestant, portion of Russian dissent, the Dukhobortsy, or "Wrestlers with the Holy Spirit," and their descendants in the faith, the Molokans, or "Milk Drinkers," are perhaps the best known to us, from the fact of their having emigrated to English-speaking lands, and from the valiant championing of their cause by Count L. D. Tolstoi. They form the antithesis of the Old Believers, as is well set forth in the conversation between A. Leroy-Beauleau (in the *Empire of the Tsars*) and a fisherman of the persuasion, who said, "The Raskolniks would go to the block for the sign of the Cross with two fingers. As for us, we don't cross ourselves at all, either with two fingers or with three, but we strive to gain a better knowledge of God"; and, indeed, his words may stand for a declaration of the simple faith of his people, for their worship is marked by a deep contempt for tradition, dogma, and ceremony. They have even done away with the church, and, as a rule, use the house of their elders as a meeting-place. Communion has been simplified away, marriage reduced to a simple declaration, and invocation of God's blessing, the priesthood question, the rock which first split the Old Faith, solved by making every man a priest in his own family: surely their motto, "The letter killeth, but the Spirit giveth life," has been well acted up to. Indeed, the whole theology of the Dukhobortsy may be summed up as a bold attempt to depart from the empty Greek formalism and arrive at a spiritual and unconventional worship, an enlargement of the outline given in the shortest and grandest of sermons.

The Molokani are said to have obtained this name from taking milk and butter during fast times when they are forbidden to the Orthodox, but more probably from the fact of their having colonies on either bank of the river Molochnaia, so called from the whiteness of its waters, due to potassium salts. They are very closely akin to the Dukhobortsy, of which sect they are an offshoot. They hope for a millennium, and to this end tend all their communistic experiments; for each of their village settlements is striving to manufacture its own earthly Paradise and run it on its own lines.

SHRINE IN THE CONVENT SOLOVETSKII, KOLA.

The Stunda is perhaps the largest and most rapidly developing faction of nonconformity, for it has ramified from Odessa—its starting point— throughout Tsarland, save in the extreme north and north-east. This faith can be traced directly to the influence of certain Lutherans who emigrated from Würtemberg and settled in the fruitful "*tchenoziom*," or black earth lands, some half-century ago. The Stundist organization is much like that of the "Low Church" division of Protestantism, save that it has no ordained clergy, a body whom it regards as a somewhat expensive luxury, and replaces by elected elders, who lead the very simple services, at which any man or woman who feels called upon to do so may say what he or she will. These gatherings are more prayer-meetings than services, for there is no "Form of Prayer" to be used, but simply informal prayer, praise and song in the best room of a farmhouse, though, now that the Government are not so strict in their search after heretics, regular wooden "meeting-houses" have appeared in some of the Stundist villages.

If few of the rational sects have committed their history and their views, or indeed their creeds, to writing, lest they should fall into the hands of spies and be used in evidence against them, much more is this the case with those whose search after truth has led them to forsake the lines of rationalism and enter the land of mysticism and spiritualism. But two of these mystic schisms need we touch upon in this article, in order to show to what lengths the Mujik will go in his efforts to escape from the trammels of Orthodoxy, and with what logic he will follow up any given line of thought. Most of the irrational sects are older than those already mentioned, and do not seem to have their roots in other lands, but to be the expression of the Mujik's own mind in its waking moments: thus the "Khlystsy"—the name is a nickname taken from the word "Khlyst" (a whip)—date back to the early days of the Seventeenth Century. They hold that Christ has made and still makes repeated appearances on earth and in Russia, and indeed they are seldom without an incarnate God present with them in flesh and blood.

The Khlystsy meet by night, with the utmost secrecy, and are reported to dance, after the manner of the Dervishes, with ever-increasing rapidity, until their feelings are worked up to such a pitch that they are able to receive messages of inspiration, which they shout out to their fellows. If one of their number has a fit—not an uncommon event in some communes where close intermarriage among relations has been the practice for generations—he is safe to be regarded as an inspired messenger and duly honoured as such. Charges of every kind of vice have been laid at the door of the Khlystsy; their secret services have been called cloaks for immorality, and doubtless on occasion have been used as such; but, as the character of their congregation stands for high honesty and industry, it is surely more charitable to assume that their worst feature is their extreme secrecy, and that this, when added to the hatred of orthodox marriage which the sect shows, lies at the base of most of the accusations. Closely connected with these dancing Khlystsy are the jumping Shakuny, whose jumps are said to increase in height as do the circular movements of the former, until the proper state of mind for inspired prophecy is reached.

Among the stockbrokers and money-changers of Russian cities, as well as among peasants, may be seen the pale and almost hairless face, wavering voice, and mild manner of the "Skopets" who has put in practice upon himself the strange doctrine of self-mutilation. These "White Doves" as they call themselves, base their self-sacrifice upon the literal rendering of such texts as, "If thy right eye offend thee, pluck it out," "Except a man become as a little child, he shall not enter into the Kingdom of heaven," and argue that in order to be pleasing to God, man—and in some instances woman—

must become like the angels, whom they assert to be sexless, on the ground that "they neither marry nor are given in marriage."

We notice the hold which religion, in its vast variety of forms, has over the popular mind of Russia. No one who has visited, however casually, a Russian city can doubt this; the icon hangs in the station office, and men bow to it, the cabman crosses himself ere he drives over a bridge; shrines are interposed between shops, many of which latter are devoted to the sale of crucifixes, swinging lamps and sacred pictures; green cupolas and golden crosses gleam against the sky, look which way you will. So it is in the village, the white wooden church stands out in front of the black wooden houses, crosses are placed in the cattle pastures to ward off evil spirits, the folk cross themselves if they yawn, lest "chort," the devil jump in at their mouth, and the drunkard, at the tavern door, kneels and uncovers as the procession passes on its way, may be to bless the waters but now released from the winter grip of ice, or may be to leave some neighbour in the communal graveyard. We notice, too, the stern logic with which the peasant theologian follows up the ideas of his sect, how he works out his own salvation along lines which he himself lays down, and in so doing invents some new creed almost daily; for a Russian newspaper can hardly ever be taken up without seeing the discovery of such in one corner or other of the vast Empire. That he has the full courage of his opinions, that he will suffer for conscience' sake—Russian officials only know how bitterly—that he will lay down his life, or—almost equal sacrifice for him—forsake his land and "*izba*," and face the future among the wild native races which bound European Tsarland on its north and east—not so very long ago—he suffered the knout and the stake rather than recant one iota of what he thinks to be the only true rendering of the Biblical text, all this must in common fairness be allowed to the poor Russian.

ST. PETERSBURG

J. BEAVINGTON ATKINSON

Cronstadt, the strong fortress which stopped the advance of the English squadron in the last Russian war, is as the water-gate of St. Petersburg. A bright July sun made no unpleasing picture of the huge hulks of the men-of-war, and of the many-masted merchant ships which lay within the harbour, or behind the fortifications. Passing Cronstadt the capital soon comes in sight; the water is so smooth and shallow, and the banks are so low, that I was actually reminded of the lagoons of Venice. Far away in the distance glittered in the sunlight cupola beyond cupola, covered with burnished gold or sparkling with bright stars on a blue ground. The river, stretching wide as an estuary, was thronged with merchandise as the Tagus or the Thames: yachts were flying before the wind and steam-tugs laboured slowly against the stream, dragging behind the heavily-laden lighter. Warehouses and wharfs and timber-yards now begin to line either bank; yet the materials for a sketch-book are scanty and uninviting: an artist who, like Mr. Whistler, has etched at Battersea and Blackwell, would find by comparison on the Neva the forms without character, the surface without texture, the masses without light, shade, or colour. As the boat advances the imperial city grows in scale and pomp. The river view becomes imposing, the banks are lined on either side by granite quays, which for solidity, strength, and area, have no parallel in Europe. Beneath the bridges the unruly river rushes, bearing along rafts and merchandise, and in the broad-laid streets people hurry to and fro, as if the day were too short for the press of business: only in great commercial capitals, the centres of large populations, is life thus rapid and overburdened. Throughout Russia generally time hangs heavily, but here at the seat of empire, the focus of commerce, life under high pressure moves at full speed. I know of no European capital, excepting perhaps London and Vienna, which leaves on the mind so strong an impression of power, wealth, and ostentation, as the city of St. Petersburg.

Possibly the first idea which may strike the stranger on driving from the steamer to the hotel, is the large scale on which the city has been planned; the area of squares and streets seems proportioned to the vast dimensions of the Russian empire: indeed the silent solitudes of the city may be said to symbolize the desert tracks of central Russia and Siberia. Only on the continent of America is so much land at command, so large a sweep of territory brought within the circuit of city life. In the old world, Munich offers the closest analogy to St. Petersburg, and that not only by wide and half-occupied areas, but by a certain pretentious and pseudo-classic architecture, common to the two cities alike: the design of the Hermitage in fact came from Munich. St. Petersburg, like Munich too, has been forced into rapid growth; indeed while looking at the works raised by successive Tsars, I was reminded of the boast of Augustus that he found Rome of brick and left her of marble.

St. Petersburg, though sometimes decried as a city of shams, is certainly not surpassed in the way of show by any capital in Europe. As to natural situation she may be said to be at once fortunate and infelicitous: the flatness of the land is not redeemed by fertility, the monotony of the panorama is not broken by mountains; the city rides as a raft upon the waters, so heavily freighted as to run the risk of sinking. And yet I know of no capital more imposing when taken from the strong points of view. Almost beyond parallel is the array of palaces and public buildings which meets the traveller's eye in a walk or sail from the English quay up to the Gardens of the Summer Palace. The structures it is true tend a little too much of what may be termed buckram and fustian styles; indeed there is scarcely a form or a detail which an architect would care to jot down in his note-book. And yet the general effect is grand: a big river rushing with large volume of water through the arches of bridges, along granite quays and before marble palaces, is a noble and living presence in the midst of city life. The waters of "the great Neva" and of "the little Neva" appear as an omnipresence; the rivers are in the streets, and great buildings, such as the Admiralty, the Fortress, and the Cathedral of St. Peter and St. Paul, ride as at anchor on a swelling flood. The views from the three chief bridges—Nicholas Bridge, Palace Bridge, and Troitska Bridge—are eminently palatial and imperial. The Academy of Arts, the Academy of Sciences, St. Isaac's Cathedral, the Admiralty, the Winter Palace, the Hermitage, and the fortress and cathedral of St. Peter and St. Paul, give to the stranger an overpowering impression of the wealth and the strength of the empire. The Englishman, while standing on these bridges, will naturally recall analogous positions on the river Thames; such comparison is not wholly to the disadvantage of the northern capital, yet on the banks of the Neva rise no structures which in architectural design equal St. Paul's Cathedral, Somerset House, Westminster Abbey, and the Houses of Parliament. Indeed, with the exception of the spire of the Admiralty, I did not find in St. Petersburg a single new idea.

ST. PETERSBURG.

Of the famous Nevski-Prospekt, the chief street in St. Petersburg, it may be said as of our London Regent Street, that it can stand neither weather nor criticism. As to style of architecture, strictly speaking the Nevski-Prospekt has none: the buildings, consisting of shops, interspersed with a few churches and public edifices, so much partake of the modern and mongrel Italian manner, that the traveller might easily fancy himself in Paris, Brussels, or Turin. Few cities are so pretentious in outside appearances as St. Petersburg, and yet the show she makes is that of the whited sepulchre: false construction and rottenness of material, façades of empty parade, and plaster which feigns to be stone, constitute an accumulative dishonesty which has few parallels in the history of architecture. Classic pillars and porticos, which have been thrust in everywhere on slightest pretext, are often built up of brick covered with cement and coloured yellow. Columns, here the common and constant expedient, are mostly mismanaged; they are as it were gratuitous intrusions, they seem to be stuck on, they fail to compose with the rest of the building. Neither do the architects of St. Petersburg understand mouldings or the value of shadow, there is scarcely a moulding in the city which casts a deep, broad or delicate shadow: hence the façades look flat and thin as if built of cards. In the same way the details are poor and treated without knowledge; it thus happens that conceptions bold and grand are carried out incompletely. The great mistake is that the architects have made no attempt to gather together the scattered elements of a national style. With the noteworthy exception of the use of fine, fanciful and fantastic domes, often gilt or brightly coloured, the architecture of Russian capitals is either Classic or Renaissance of the most commonplace description.

I shall not think it worth while to dwell on the very many churches which adorn the northern capital, because, with few exceptions, there is nothing in point of art which merits to be recorded. Yet I can scarcely refrain from again referring to the fine fantasy played by many-coloured domes against the blue sky. The forms are beautiful, the colours decorative. The city in its sky outline presents a succession of strange pictures, at one point the eye might seem to range across a garden of gourds, at other positions peer above house-tops groups which might be mistaken for turbaned Turks; and when the sun shines vividly, and throws glittering light on the "patens of bright gold," over these many-domed churches, a stranger might almost fancy that above the city floated fire balloons or bright-coloured lanterns. The large cupola of St. Isaac, covered with copper overlaid with gold, has been said to burn on a bright day like the sun when rising on a mountain top. I can never forget the sight when I returned to St. Petersburg from the most brilliant civic and military spectacle I ever witnessed, the fête of the Empress at Tsarskoé Sélo. It was still dark, but before I reached my hotel for the short repose of a night which already brightened into morning, every cupola on the way was awakening into daylight; the sun, hesitating for a moment on the horizon, announced his coming as by electric light on the golden stars which shone on domes more blue than the grey sky of morning. In Moscow church cupolas playa part in the city panorama still more conspicuous than in St. Petersburg.

The Cathedral of St. Isaac is the most costly and pretentious of Russian churches. The noble edifice has the advantage of a commanding situation; not, it is true, as to elevation—for that is impossible in a city set throughout on a dead level—but the surface area in its wide sweeping circuit at all events contrasts strikingly with that cribbed and cabined church-yard of St. Paul's in London, which the Englishman may have just left behind him. Yet St. Isaac's can scarcely venture on comparison with St. Paul's, though the style of the two buildings is similar. The great Cathedral of St. Petersburg has, however, the advantage of that concentration which belongs to the Greek as distinguished from the Latin Cross, a distinction which has always been to the disadvantage of St. Peter's in Rome. A cross of four equal arms, with columned porticos mounted nobly on steps at the four extremities, the whole composition crowned by central and surrounding cupolas, is assuredly an imposing conception, of which the French artist M. Montferrand has known how to make the most. I may here, by way of parenthesis, remark that the two works which do most honour to St. Petersburg, the Cathedral of St. Isaac and the adjacent equestrian statue of Peter the Great, are severally due not to Russian but to French artists. This is one example among many of the foreign origin of the arts in Russia. But at all events let it be admitted that the materials used, as well as the ideas often brought to bear, are local or national. For example, the grandest of all architectural conceptions, the idea of a dome, is here glorified in true Russian or Oriental manner, not so much by magnitude of proportion as by decorative splendour, heightened to the utmost by a surface of burnished gold. Then the four porticos which terminate each end of the Greek cross with stately columns and entablatures of granite from Finland, albeit in design mere commonplace complications, are wholly national in the material used. I do not now stop to mention the large and bold reliefs in bronze, which though French in design were, I believe, cast in St. Petersburg: indeed here, as in Munich, the government makes that liberal provision which only governments can make, for noble but unremunerative art. The great dome is said to be sustained by iron; indeed the science of construction brought to bear is great, yet again it must be acknowledged that whether the material be iron, bronze, or stone, the art, the skill, and even the commercial capital, are not Russian but foreign, and often English. Russian workmen, however, are employed as mechanics or machines, partly because in copyism and mechanism Russian artisans cannot throughout Europe be surpassed. When I got to St. Petersburg I could scarcely believe the statement to be true that the "English Magazine" and not any Russian factory had executed the eight stupendous malachite pillars within the church, weighing about 34,000 pounds and costing £2,500 sterling. Yet while the organization might be English, the operatives were Russians. The unsurpassed malachite pillars combine in the grand altar-screen with columns of lapis-lazuli: the latter are said to have cost per pair £12,000 sterling. I need scarcely observe that this parade of precious metals partakes more of barbaric magnificence than of artistic taste; indeed these columns of malachite and lapis-lazuli, which to the eye present themselves as solid and honest, have been built up as incrustations on hollow cast-iron tubes. Thus hollow are the most precious arts of Russia. Justice, however, demands that I should speak hereafter in fair appreciation of the interiors of Russian churches, whereof the Cathedral of St. Isaac is among the chief. Nevertheless, material rather than mind, money rather than art, is the governing power; malachite, lapis-lazuli, gold, and other precious substances are heaped together profusely, yet no architect in Europe of the slightest intellectual pretensions, would care to look a second time at the constructive or decorative conceptions which the churches of St. Petersburg display. St. Isaac's in fact is miraculous only in its monoliths. I could scarcely believe my eyes when first I stood beneath the stately porticos and looked from top to bottom of the very many columns, seven feet in diameter and sixty feet high, all polished granite monoliths from Finland. Already I had made the assertion that there was nothing new in St. Petersburg when these granite monoliths at once compelled a recantation.

The monoliths in St. Petersburg are so exceptional in number and often so gigantic in dimension as to call for special mention. The monolith obelisks of ancient Egypt are scarcely more remarkable. In addition to the magnificent columns, each sixty feet high, which sustain the four porticos of the Cathedral of St. Isaac, are fifty-six monoliths, also of granite from Finland, thirty-five feet high in the Kazan Cathedral; likewise the noble entrance-hall of the Hermitage is sustained by sixteen monoliths, and the magnificent room which receives the treasures from the Cimmerian Bosphorus has the support of twenty monoliths. But the greatest single block of modern times stands in front of the Winter Palace, as a monument to Alexander I. The height is eighty-four feet, and the weight nearly four hundred tons. The story goes that the contractor in Finland, finding that he had exceeded the required length, actually cut off ten or fifteen feet. The vast granite quarries of Finland supply the Tsars with these stupendous columns, just as the granite quarries of Syene on the Nile furnished the Pharaohs with obelisks. These enormous masses are too heavy to be conveyed on wheels, the only practicable mode of transit is on rollers. In this way each of the sixty-feet columns for St. Isaac's was transported across country all the way from Finland. Each column represents so incredible an amount of labour as to make it evident that monoliths are luxuries in which only emperors can indulge. And even when these heavy weights have reached their destination the difficulty next occurs how to secure a solid foundation. St. Petersburg was once a swamp, and so rotten is the ground that it would be quite possible for a monolith to sink out of sight and never more be heard of. To provide against such contingencies a forest of piles was driven into the earth at the cost of £200,000 as the foundation of St. Isaac, and yet the cathedral sinks. Like causes render the roads of St. Petersburg the worst in Europe; winter frosts, which penetrate several feet below the surface, seize on the imprisoned waters and tear up the streets. The surface thus broken is so destructive to wheels that I have known an Englishman, who, though he kept four carriages, had not one in a condition to use. The jolting on the roads is so great as to make it wise for a traveller to hold on fast, and when a lady and gentleman ride side by side, it is usual for the gentleman to protect the lady by throwing his arm round his companion's waist. This delicate attention is so much of a utilitarian necessity as in no way to imply further obligations.

St. Petersburg is considerably indebted to the art of sculpture: public monuments adorn her squares and gardens. Indeed the art of sculpture has, like the sister arts of architecture and painting, been forced into preternatural proportions. In the large area within sight of the church of St. Isaac and of the Admiralty, stands conspicuously one of the few successful equestrian statues in modern or ancient times, the colossal bronze to Peter the Great. The huge block of granite, which is said to weigh upwards of 15,000 tons, was conveyed from a marsh, four miles distance from St. Petersburg, by means of ropes, pulleys, and windlasses, worked by men and horses. A drummer stationed on the rock itself gave the signal for onward movement. It would seem that the methods used in Russia to this day for transporting granite monoliths, are curiously similar to the appliances of the ancient Egyptians for moving like masses. In point of art this equestrian statue, though grand in conception, is, after the taste of barbarous nations, colossal in size. Peter the Great is eleven feet in stature, the horse is seventeen feet high. The nobility lies in the action, the horse rears on his hind legs after the favourite manner of Velasquez in well-known equestrian portraits of Ferdinand IV. The attitude assumed by the great Emperor is triumphant, the fiery steed has dashed up the rock and pauses as in mid-air on the brink of the precipice. The idea is that Peter the Great surveys from the height the capital of his creation, as it may be supposed to rise from the waters. His hand is stretched forth for the protection of the city. This work, like many other proud achievements in the empire, unfortunately is not Russian. The design is due to the Frenchman Falconet; Marie Callot is said to have modelled the head, and the casting was done by Martelli, an Italian. Falconet, in order to be true to the life, carefully studied again and again a fine Arab horse, mounted by a Russian general who was famous as a rider; the general day by day made a rush up a mound, artificially constructed for the purpose, and when just short of the precipice the horse was reined in and thrown on its hind legs. The artist watched the action and made his studies; the work accordingly has nature, movement, vigour. I may here mention that I have nowhere found such large masses of stone conveyed from place to place as here in St. Petersburg. It is true I have seen marble fresh from the mountains of Carrara tugged along by teams of bullocks, but I have nowhere witnessed so much power brought to bear as in the transit of the granite used in the immense memorial to the Empress Catherine.

The art collections in St. Petersburg may give the traveller pleasant occupation for several weeks; indeed if the tourist be an art student he will find work for months. The Winter Palace, adjoining the Hermitage, on the Neva, is like the palace at Versailles, conspicuous for rooms or galleries commemorative of military exploits. Here are well-painted battle-pieces by Willewalde and Kotzbue, also naval engagements by Aivasovsky, highly coloured as a matter of course. Likewise are hung the best battle-pieces I have ever seen, by Peter Hess, the renowned Bavarian painter, who appears to less credit in Munich than in the Winter Palace, St. Petersburg. Also may be noted the portrait of Alexander I. by Dawe, the Englishman, who worked much in Russia. Here likewise is the imperial gallery of portraits of all the sovereigns of the reigning Russian house. I pass over these multitudinous works thus briefly, because, though the collection is of importance in the history of the empire, it has little value in art.

"The Crown Jewels" I shall not attempt to describe; no description of jewels can be worth much. I may venture to say, however, that after seeing all the royal jewellery in Europe, I found these Russian crowns, sceptres, etc., richer in diamonds than any other. Also pearls, rubies, Siberian aqua-marines, etc., add colour and splendour to the imperial treasure. The comparison on the spot, which I not unnaturally instituted, was with the imperial treasury at Vienna. Next, a word may be given to the room in which the proud, stern, and unrelenting Nicholas died, where all is kept intact as he left it. I have seldom been more impressed than with this small, simple, and almost penurious apartment, so striking in contrast with the splendour of the rest of the palace. Silence, solitude, and solemnity all the more attach to the spot from the statement to which credence is given that the great emperor, on learning of the reverses in the Crimea, here committed suicide. In other words, it is said that he directed his physician to prepare a medicine which after having taken he died. The sword, helmet, and grey military cloak are where he laid them. Here lies a historic tragedy which remains to be painted; one of the most dramatic pictorial scenes in Europe, the death of Wallenstein in Schiller's drama, painted by Professor Piloty and now in the new Pinakothek, Munich, might in the death of the great Nicholas find a parallel. The emperor lies buried with all the sovereigns of Russia since the foundation of St. Petersburg, in the cathedral fortress of St. Peter and St. Paul. Nothing in Europe is grander in the simplicity and silence which befit a sepulchre—not even the imperial tombs in Vienna—than this stately mausoleum of the Tsars. The Emperor Nicholas lies opposite to Peter the Great. In the Hermitage, or rather in the Winter Palace, is a gallery illustrative of the life and labours of Peter the Great. The collection, besides turning-lathes and other instruments with which the monarch worked, contains curiosities, knickknacks, as well as some works of real art value: the connecting point of the whole collection is in Peter himself. An analogous collection was some years ago opened in the Louvre as the Museum of Napoleon I. Dynasties all the world over thus seek to perpetuate their memories.

THE HERMITAGE, ST. PETERSBURG.

The Academy of Fine Arts is a noble institution, imposing in its architecture, and richly endowed. The Corps des Mines must also be visited, the collection of minerals proves the amazing riches of European and Asiatic Russia. I wish I had knowledge and space to describe this unexampled collection, which though not falling within my art province has direct art relations. Nothing beauteous or wondrous in nature lies beyond the sphere of art; the forms of crystals, the colours of precious stones are specially objects of delight to the artist's eye. The Imperial Public Library is one of the richest libraries in Europe; its literary treasures can hardly be overrated; I regret that I cannot enter into its contents. Private collections, though scarcely numerous, are choice; the celebrated Leuchtenberg Gallery, formerly in Munich, is the richest. The royal residences of Peterhof and Tsarshoé Sélo I also found to contain much in the way of art, and yet scarcely of sufficient importance to need special description.

The Imperial Hermitage alone repays a journey to St. Petersburg; for a whole fortnight I visited almost every day the picture and sculpture galleries of this vast and rich museum, and in the end I left with the feeling that I had done but inadequate justice to these valuable and exhaust-less collections. I am tolerably well acquainted with the great museums in the south and west of Europe, and I was interested to find that the Hermitage does not suffer by comparison with the Vatican, the Museum of Naples, the Galleries of Florence, the Louvre in Paris, or the Great Picture Gallery in Madrid. In some departments, indeed, St. Petersburg has the advantage over other capitals; the collection of gold ornaments from Kertch is not surpassed by the gold work in the Etruscan room of the Vatican; the coins are not inferior to the numismatic collections in Paris, or in the British Museum; the Dutch pictures are not to be equalled save in Holland or in Dresden; the Spanish school has no competitor save in Madrid and Seville; the portraits by Vandyck, and the sketches by Rubens, are only surpassed in England and Bavaria. It is thus obvious that the collective strength of the assembled collections, is very great. The picture galleries contain more than 1,500 works; the number of drawings is upwards of 500, the coins and medals amount to 200,000, the painted vases are above 1,700, the ancient marbles number 361, and the collection of gems is one of the largest in existence. The Hermitage has been enriched partly to the prejudice of other cities or palaces. From the Tauris Palace came classic sculpture. Tsarshoé Sélo also furnished contributions. The policy has been to make one astounding museum, which shall represent not a capital but an empire, and stand before the world as the exponent of the wealth, the resource, and the refined taste of the nation and its rulers.

FINLAND

HARRY DE WINDT

"What sort of a place is Finland?" asked a friend whom I met, on my return from that country, in London. "Very much the same as Lapland, I suppose? Snow, sleighs, and bears, and all that kind of thing?"

My friend was not singular in his idea, for they are probably those of most people in England. At present Finland is a *terra incognita*, though fortunately not likely to remain one. Nevertheless, it will probably take years to eradicate a notion that one of the most attractive and advanced countries in Europe, possessed in summer of the finest climate in the world, is not the eternal abode of poverty, cold, and darkness. It was just the same before the railway opened up Siberia and revealed prosperous cities, fertile plains, and boundless mineral resources to an astonished world. A decade ago my return from this land of civilization, progress, and, above all, humanity was invariably met by the kind of question that heads this chapter, with the addition, as a rule, of facetious allusions to torture and the knout! My ignorance, however, of Finland as she really is was probably unsurpassed before my eyes were opened by a personal inspection, so I cannot afford to criticise.

What is Finland, and what are its geographical and climatic characteristics? I will try to answer these questions briefly and clearly without wearying the reader with statistics. In the first place, Finland (in Finnish, "Suomi") is about the size of Great Britain, Holland, and Belgium combined, with a population of about 2,500,000. Its southern and western shores are washed by the Baltic Sea, while Lake Ladoga and the Russian frontier form the eastern boundary. Finland stretches northward far beyond the head of the Gulf of Bothnia, where it joins Norwegian territory. There are thirty-seven towns, of which only seven have a population exceeding 10,000, viz., Helsingfors, Abo, Tammerfors, Viborg, Uleaborg, Vasa (Nikolaistad), and Bjorneborg.

Finland is essentially a flat country, slightly mountainous towards the north, but even her highest peak (Haldesjock, in Finnish Lapland) is under 4,000 feet in height. South of this a hill of 300 feet is called a mountain; therefore Alpine climbers have no business here. The interior may be described as an undulating plateau largely composed of swamp and forest, broken with granite rocks and gravel ridges and honeycombed with the inland waters known as "The Thousand Lakes" (although ten thousand would be nearer the mark), one of which is three times the size of the Lake of Geneva. The rivers are small and unimportant, the largest being only about the size of the Seine. On the other hand, the numerous falls and rapids on even the smallest streams render their ascent in boats extremely difficult and often impossible.

But lakes and canals are the natural highways of the country; rivers are only utilized as a motive power for electricity, manufactories, and for conveying millions of logs of timber yearly from the inland forests to the sea. A curious fact is that, although many parts of the interior are far below the level of the Baltic, the latter is gradually but surely receding from the coast, and many hitherto submerged islets off the latter have been left high and dry by the waves. You may now in places walk from one island to another on dry land, which, fifty years ago, was many fathoms under water, while signs of primitive navigation are constantly being discovered as far as twenty miles inland! It is therefore probable that the millions of islands which now fringe these shores, formed, at some remote period, one continuous strip of land. How vessels ever find their way, say from Hangö to Nystad, is a mystery to the uninitiated landsman. At a certain place there are no less than 300 islands of various sizes crowded into an area of six square miles! Heaven preserve the man who finds himself there, in thick weather, with a skipper who does not quite know the ropes!

The provinces of which the Grand Duchy is composed are as follows, running from north to south: (1) Finnish Lapland, (2) Ostrobothnia, (3) Satakunta, (4) Tavastland, (5) Savolax, (6) Karelia, (7) Finland proper, (8) Nyland, and (9) the Aland Islands.

Finnish Lapland may be dismissed without comment, for it is a wild, barren region, sparsely populated by nomad tribes, and during the summer is practically impassable on account of its dense forests, pathless swamps, and mosquitoes of unusual size and ferocity. In winter-time journeys can be made quickly and pleasantly in sledges drawn by reindeer, but at other times the country must be crossed in cranky canoes by means of a network of lakes and rivers; and the travelling is about as tough as monotony, short rations, and dirt can make it. I am told that gold has lately been discovered there, but it would need a considerable amount of the precious metal to tempt me into Finnish Lapland in summer-time.

Ostrobothnia, which lies immediately south of this undesirable district, contains the towns of Tornea and Uleaborg. We will pass on to the provinces of Central Finland, viz., Tavastland, Savolax, and Karelia. The Finns say that this is the heart of their country, while Helsingfors and Tammerfors constitute its brains. So crowded and complicated is the lake system in this part of Finland that water almost overwhelms dry land, and the district has been likened to one huge archipelago. Forests abound, especially in Tavastland, whence timber is exported in large quantities, while agriculture flourishes in all these provinces. Crops are generally grown in the valleys, while in other parts the sides and summits of the hills are usually selected for cultivation. Large tracts of country about here once laid out for arable are now converted into grazing grounds, for the number of cattle is yearly on the increase. Dairy-farming is found to be more profitable and less risky than the raising of wheat and barley in a land where one night of frost sometimes destroys the result of a whole year's patient care and labour. The land is cleared for cultivation by felling and burning, and it is then ploughed in primitive fashion and sown, but only one harvest is generally gathered on one spot. The latter is then deserted, and the following year another patch of virgin soil takes its place. There is thus a good deal of waste, not only in land, but also in trees, which are wantonly cut down for any trifling purpose, regardless of their value or the possible scarcity in the future of timber. Accidental forest fires also work sad havoc at times, destroying thousands of pounds' worth of timber in a few hours. Pine resin burns almost as fiercely as petroleum, and it sometimes takes days to extinguish a conflagration.

Many of the poorer people in the central provinces live solely by fishing in the lakes teeming with salmon, which find a ready market both salted and fresh. There is plenty of rough shooting to be had for the asking, but no wild animals of any size. In the far north bears are still numerous, and elk were formerly obtainable. A few of the latter still exist in the wilder parts of the country, but it is now forbidden to kill them. Some years ago the forests of Tavastland were infested with wolves, and during one fatal season a large number of cattle and even some children were devoured, but a *battue* organized by the peasantry cleared the brutes out of the country. You may now shoot hares here, and any number of wild fowl, but that is about all.

The remainder of Finland consists of Finland proper and Nyland on the south and south-western coasts, and as these comprise not only the capital, but also the large towns of Abo and Viborg, they may be regarded as the most important, politically, commercially, and socially, in the country. Here lakes are still numerous, but insignificant in size compared with those of the interior. On the other hand, the vegetation is richer, for the oak, lime, and hazel do well, and the flora, both wild and cultivated, is much more extensive than in the central and northern districts. Several kinds of fruit are grown, and Nyland apples are famous for their flavour, while very fair pears, plums, and cherries can be bought cheaply in the markets. Currants and gooseberries are, however, sour and tasteless. In these southern districts the culture of cereals has reached a perfection unknown further north, for the farms are usually very extensive, the farmers up to date, and steam implements in general use. Dairy-farming is also carried on with excellent results and yearly increasing prosperity. Amongst the towns, Bjorneborg, Nystad, Hangö, and Kotka will in a few years rival the capital in size and commercial importance.

The last on the list is the Aland archipelago, which consists of one island of considerable size surrounded by innumerable smaller ones, and situated about fifty miles off the south-western coast of Finland. Here, oddly enough, Nature has been kinder than almost anywhere on the mainland, for although the greater part of the island is wild and forest-clad, the eternal pines and silver birch-trees are blended with the oak, ash and maple, and bright blossoms such as may and hawthorn relieve to a great extent the monotonous green foliage of Northern Europe.

That the Alander has much of the Swede in his composition is shown by the neatness of his dwellings and cleanly mode of life. He is an amphibious creature, half mariner, half yeoman, a sober, thrifty individual, who spends half of his time at the plough-tail and the other half at the helm. Fishing for a kind of small herring called "strömming" is perhaps the most important industry, and a lucrative one, for this fish (salted) is sent all over the country and even to Russia proper. Farming is a comparatively recent innovation, for the Alanders are born men of the sea, and were once reckoned the finest sailors in Finland. Less than a century ago Aland harboured a fine fleet of sailing-ships owned by syndicates formed amongst the peasantry, and engaged in a profitable trade with Great Britain and Denmark. But steamers have knocked all this upon the head, and the commercial future of the islands would now seem to depend chiefly upon the fishing and agricultural industries.

The population of these Islands is under 25,000, of which the small town of Mariehamm, the so-called capital, contains about 700 souls. Steamers touch here, so that there is no difficulty in reaching the place, which is certainly worth a visit not only for its antiquity (the Alands were inhabited long before the mainland), but on account of the interesting ruins it contains—amongst them the Castle of Castelholm, built by Birger Jarl in the Fourteenth Century, and the time-worn walls of which could tell an interesting history. A part of the famous fortress of Bomarsund, destroyed by an Anglo-French fleet in 1854, may also be seen not far from Mariehamm. Plain but decent fare may be obtained here, but the fastidious will do well to avoid the smaller villages, where the Alander's diet generally consists solely of seal-meat, salt fish, bread and milk. A delicacy eaten with gusto by these people is composed of seal-oil and the entrails of sea-birds, and is almost identical with one I saw amongst the Tchuktchis on Bering Straits. And yet the Alanders are cleanly enough in their habits and the smallest village has its bath-house.

At one time Aland was famous for sport, and in olden days Swedish sovereigns visited the island to hunt the elk, which were then numerous. But these and most other wild animals are now extinct and even wild fowl are scarce. Only one animal appears to thrive,—the hedgehog; but the natives do not appear to have discovered its edible qualities. An English tramp could enlighten them on this point.

HELSINGFORS, FINLAND

The entire population of Finland amounts to rather over 2,500,000, including a considerable number of Swedes, who are found chiefly in the Aland Islands, Nyland, and Finland proper. Helsingfors, the capital, contains over 80,000 souls, and Kemi, the smallest town, near the northern frontier, under 400. Of the other cities, Abo has 30,000, Tammerfors, 25,000, and Viborg, 20,000 inhabitants. I should add that there is probably no country in creation where the population has so steadily increased, notwithstanding adverse conditions, as Finland. After the Russian campaign of 1721 the country contained barely 250,000 souls, and yet, although continually harassed by war and its attendant evils, these had increased thirty years later to 555,000. Fifty years ago the Finns numbered 1,500,000, and the latest census shows nearly double these figures, although in 1868 pestilence and famine swept off over 100,000 victims.

The languages spoken in the Grand Duchy are Finnish and Swedish, the former being used by at least eighty-five per cent. of the population. Russian-speaking inhabitants number about 5,000, while the Lapps amount to 1,000 only, other nationalities to under 3,000. Although Swedish is largely spoken in the towns, Finnish only is heard, as a rule, in the rural districts. There is scarcely any nobility in the country, if we except titled Swedish settlers. Most Finns belong to the middle class of life, with the exception of a few families ennobled in 1809 by the Tsar of Russia on his accession as Grand Duke of Finland. The lower orders are generally quiet and reserved in their demeanour, even on festive public occasions, and make peaceable, law-abiding citizens. "'Arry" is an unknown quantity here, and "'Arriet" does not exist. A stranger will everywhere meet with studied politeness in town and country. Drive along a country road, and every peasant will raise his hat to you, not deferentially, but with the quiet dignity of an equal. The high standard of education, almost legally exacted from the lowest classes in Finland, is unusually high, for the most illiterate plough boy may not marry the girl of his choice until he can read the Bible from end to end to the satisfaction of his pastor, and the same rule applies to the fair sex.

The climate of Finland is by no means so severe as is generally imagined. As a matter of fact, no country of a similar latitude, with the exception of Sweden, enjoys the same immunity from intense cold. This is owing to the Gulf Stream, which also imparts its genial influence to Scandinavia. In summer the heat is never excessive, the rainfall is insignificant, and thunderstorms are rare. July is the warmest, and January the coldest month, but the mean temperature of Helsingfors in mid-winter has never fallen below that of Astrakhan, on the Caspian Sea.

The weather is, however, frequently changeable, and even in summer the thermometer often rises or falls many degrees in the space of a few hours. You may sit down to dinner in the open air in Helsingfors in your shirt-sleeves, and before coffee is served be sending home for a fur coat. But this is an unusual occurrence, for a summer in Finland has been my most agreeable climatic experience in any part of the world.

The winter is unquestionably hard, and lasts about six months, from November till the middle of April. At Christmas time the sun is only visible for six hours a day. The entire surface of the country, land, lake, and river, then forms one vast and frozen surface of snow, which may be traversed by means of sledge, snowshoes, or ski. A good man on the last-named will easily cover his seven miles an hour. Although tourists generally affect this country in the open season, a true Finlander loves the winter months as much as he dislikes the summer. In his eyes boredom, heat, and mosquitoes are a poor exchange for merry picnics on ski, skating contests, and sledge expeditions by starlight with pretty women and gay companions, to say nothing of the nightly balls and theatre and supper parties. Helsingfors is closed to navigation from November until June, for the sea forms an icy barrier around the coast of Finland, now no longer impenetrable, thanks to the ice-breakers at Hangö. In the north the Gulf of Bothnia is frozen for even longer.

Towards April winter shows signs of departure. By the middle of May ice and snow have almost disappeared, except in the north, where Uleaborg is, climatically, quite three weeks behind any of the southern towns. Before the beginning of June verdure and foliage have reappeared in all their luxuriance, and birds and flowers once more gladden field and forest with perfume and song. Even now an occasional shower of sleet besprinkles the land, only to melt in a few minutes, and leave it fresher and greener than before. May and

June are, perhaps, the best months, for July and August are sometimes too warm to be pleasant. October and November are gloomy and depressing. Never visit Finland in the late autumn, for the weather is then generally dull and overcast, while cold, raw winds, mist and sleet, are not the exception. Midwinter and midsummer are the most favourable seasons, which offer widely different but equally favourable conditions for the comfort and amusement of the traveller.

And, if possible, choose the former, if only for one reason. No one who has ever witnessed the unearthly beauty of a summer night in Finland is likely to forget it. The Arctic Circle should, of course, be crossed to witness the midnight sun in all its glory, but I doubt if the quiet *crépuscule* (I can think of no other word) of the twilit hours of darkness is not even more weird and fascinating viewed from amid silent streets and buildings than from the sullen dreariness of an Arctic desert, which is generally (in summer) as drab and as flat as a biscuit. In Arctic Lapland, where for two months the sun never sinks below the horizon, you may read small print without difficulty throughout the night between June and August. This would be impossible in Helsingfors, where nevertheless from sunset till dawn it is never quite dark. In the far north the midnight sun affords a rather garish light; down south it sheds grey but luminous rays, so faint that they cast no shadows, but impart a weird and mysterious grace to the most commonplace surroundings. No artist has yet successfully portrayed the indescribable charm and novelty of a summer night under these conditions, and, in all probability, no artist ever will!

His Majesty the Tsar's manifesto has not as yet (outwardly, at any rate) Russianized the capital of Finland. It will probably take centuries to do that, for Finland, like France, has an individuality which the combined Powers of Europe would be puzzled to suppress. A stranger arriving at the railway station of Helsingfors, for instance, may readily imagine himself in Germany, Austria, or even Switzerland, but certainly not within a thousand miles of Petersburg. Everything is so different, from the dapper stationmaster with gold-laced cap of German build down to the porters in clean white linen blouses, which pleasantly contrast with the malodorous sheepskins of unwashed Russia. At Helsingfors there is nothing, save the soldiery, to remind one of the proximity of Tsarland. And out in the country it is the same. The line from Mikkeli traverses a fair and prosperous district, as unlike the monotonous scenery over the border as the proverbial dock and daisy. Here are no squalid hovels and roofless sheds where half-starved cattle share the misery of their owners; no rotting crops and naked pastures; but snug homestead, flower gardens, and neat wooden fences encircling fields of golden grain and rich green meadow land. To travel in Southern Finland after Northern Russia is like leaving the most hideous parts of the Black Country to suddenly emerge into the brightness and verdure of a sunlit Devonshire.

LAPLAND

ALEXANDER PLATONOVICH ENGELHARDT

The Peninsula of Kola, which forms the District of that name, extends about 650 versts, or 433 miles, from west to east, from the frontiers of Norway and Finland to the White Sea, and about 400 versts, or 266 miles, from north to south, from the Arctic Ocean to the Gulf of Kandalax, covering an area of 131,860 square versts, or 37,022,400 acres. The coast belt from the Norwegian border-line to Holy Cape (or Sweet-nose), is called the Murman Coast, or simply the Murman; the eastern and south-eastern part, from Holy Cape along the White Sea to the mouth of the Varzuga, goes by the name of the Tierski Coast; and the southern part, from the Varzuga to Kandalax, the Kandalax Coast; whilst the whole of the interior bears the name of Russian Lapland. The surface of the Peninsula is either mountainous, or covered with *tundras* (i. e., moss-grown wilds), and swamps. The Scandinavian mountain range, which divides Sweden from Norway, extending to the Kola Peninsula, breaks up into several separate branches. Along the shores of the Murman they form craggy coast cliffs, rising at times to an elevation of 500 feet. Further to the east they become gradually lower, so that near the White Sea they seldom exceed fifty or one hundred feet, with less precipitous descents. The reach their greatest height further inland, to the east of Lake Imandra, where they form the Hibinski and Luiavrout chains, veiled in perpetual snow. Some of the peaks rise to 970 feet above the level of the lake, which, in its turn, is 140 feet higher than the sea-level, so that the mountains surrounding the lake are over 1,000 feet above the level of the sea.

Not far from Lake Imandra is the lofty Mount Bozia, (or Gods' Hill), at the foot of which, according to the traditions of the Lapps, their ancestors offered up sacrifices to their gods. Even at the present time the Lapps of the district speak of this site with peculiar veneration. Between the village of Kashkarantz and the Varzuga rises Mt. Korable, remarkable for its many caverns, studded with crystals of translucent quartz and amethyst, the former, together with fluor and heavy spar, being met with, too, in the eastern parts of the mountain. The Kola Peninsula was carefully explored by Finnish Expeditions in 1887-1892.

The climate of Lapland is not everywhere uniform, but in general it is bleak and raw. Winter begins about the end of September and continues till May. It is colder inland than by the ice-free shores of the Northern Ocean, where the warm currents of the Gulf Stream moderate the cold. And yet the severity of the weather does not injuriously affect the health or longevity of the inhabitants. The winter roads are well set in by the end of October (or early in November), the snow-fall during the winter months amounting to seven quarters, or four feet one inch. The Polar night lasts from the 25th of November to the 15th of January, but the darkness is not by any means so great as one would imagine. The white of the snow gives a certain glimmer of light, and the frequent and prolonged flashes of Aurora Borealis set the heavens in a blaze as with clouds of fire, turning night into twilight, as it were, and by their brilliancy and beauty making some amends to the natives for the absence of the sun's rays. It is easy even to read by their light; while each day, about noon, there is enough daylight for an hour or so to enable one to dispense with candles. So that under the name of Polar Night should be understood not the total absence of light, but rather the season when the sun no longer appears above the horizon. It begins to show itself again about the 17th of January, gradually rising higher and higher as the days advance.

REINDEER TRAVELLING

Snow vanishes from the plains towards the middle (or end) of May, but remains the whole year round in the gorges of the mountains. The rivers are clear of ice about the beginning (or middle) of May, and within a month from that time the first shoots of verdure begin to appear on the meadows and hill-sides. The sun never sets from the 24th of May to the 21st of July. There is neither twilight nor night,—the long Arctic Day has set in. During this period the sun warms the soil only at noon, simply shining for the rest of the day, seemingly a golden orb without heat. Summer, beginning about the middle (i. e., end) of June, barely lasts two months. By July flowers are already shedding their blossoms, their rapid growth being aided by the unbroken daylight.

Any attempts at agriculture in such a climate are, of course, foredoomed to failure, but along the river banks some fairly good meadows enable the settlers of the Murman to rear all the cattle they need. Turnips are the only vegetables that can be raised, with, here and there, a few potatoes.

The southern and western portions of the Peninsula are covered with pretty good timber, mostly pine (*Pinus silvestris*). As you go further north, the timber becomes more and more stunted, consisting chiefly of birchwood, till you reach the open *tundra*, which is clothed in moss and low-growing shrubs.

The Lapps lead a semi-nomadic life. The settlements in which they live are called *pagosts*, each group of Lapps having its particular summer and winter *pagost*. The latter is usually inland near the forests, where they herd their deer in winter. In summer they wander nearer to the coasts and lakes for the sake of the fishing. The winter dwelling of the Lapp is called a *toopa*, a small smoky sod-covered hut, covering some 150 to 200 square feet; whereas in summer he lives in his *vieja*, a large wigwam resembling a Samoyede *choom*, but covered over, not with skins as with the Samoyedes, but with branches, tree-bark and turfs.

The typical Lapp is dwarf-like and thick-set. He usually wears a grey cloth jacket, his head being encircled in a high woollen cap tapering to a tassel at the top, while his feet, wrapped up in rags, are then covered with big shoes. In general, his whole appearance, with his pointed beard, bears a striking resemblance to the familiar representations of "gnomes," as these denizens of the subterranean world are pictured to us in fairy books. Few of the Lapps, however, confine themselves to this characteristic type of Lapp costume, but wear whatever comes to their hands,—hats, caps, clothes "made in Germany" and so on.

Among the women, especially the younger ones, some fairly pretty faces may be met with. Their dress is usually a calico *sarafan*, and generally speaking, there is nothing specially distinguishing about their apparel.

The Lapp race is evidently dying out, or rather, is gradually intermingling with, and being absorbed by, the neighbouring races. With neither written memorials nor a historic past to cling to, nor any particular religious belief, they are all of the Orthodox Faith. In assuming the customs and civilization of the Russians, the Lapps often abandon their own tribe, and assimilate with the stronger race. I have often heard such sayings as the following from Lapps who have more or less settled down: "I'm not a Lapp at all, I'm a Russian now," or "He's a good man" (*i. e.*, active, energetic) "and not a Lapp."

So that they evidently have no particularly high opinion of themselves, and put no great value on their tribal individuality; and yet, as the free-born child of the broad and boundless *tundra*, the Lapp dearly loves his home and open roving life.

The chief occupations of the Lapps are reindeer-rearing and fishing, and in winter, the transport of goods by means of their deer. They are unfortunately bad husbandmen, utterly reckless about the increase of their herds, and never dreaming of looking upon them as sources of gain. Deer-herding is not, in their eyes, a regular business, they merely keep such head as are required for domestic uses, that is, for food, clothing and travelling. Very few Lapps own big herds, while most of them hardly know or care how many in reality they have. In summer, when the deer are not wanted for travelling purposes, they dismiss them to range at large, without any surveillance whatever. To escape the persecutions of gadflies and mosquitoes the deer generally flock to the Hibinski Mountains, or else wander to the sea-shore. When thus at large they multiply freely of themselves, and, by this time half wild, often stray away from the herds altogether.

The rearing of reindeer might easily be made such a profitable business as to be sufficient in itself to insure a comfortable livelihood to the Lapps. The deer itself hardly requires any looking after the whole year round. All through the summer it feeds on various grasses, and in winter on the *yagel*, or reindeer lichen (*Cladonia rangiferina*), which it scratches out from under the snow, with its hoofs. This lichen, or moss, grows in profusion all over the *tundras* and forests of the Kola Peninsula. It is his deer which supply the Lapp with food and clothing, convey his family and goods hundreds of versts in his wanderings, and, finally, give him the opportunity of adding to his income by acting as carrier, and by supplying teams to the government postal-stations, etc. Some years ago some Ziriàns from the Petchora settled in the Kola Peninsula with their herds, numbering some 5,000 head. The Lapps welcomed them into their community, looking upon them, indeed, as benefactors, as the Ziriàns, a smart and enterprising race, get everything needed for household purposes, which they obtain much cheaper than the Lapps themselves could before, at the same time giving good prices for the skins of reindeer and other wild animals killed by the Lapps. So far no want of grazing plots has been felt. The Ziriàns have already over 10,000 head of deer, deriving, comparatively speaking, enormous gains from them. But then, unlike the Lapps, the Ziriàns go about their business in systematic and sensible fashion, safeguarding their stock from the incursions of beasts of prey, tending them carefully winter and summer, driving them from time to time to suitable pastures, etc.

MOSCOW

The Kremlin and its treasuries. The Ancient Regalia. The Romanoff House

ALFRED MASKELL

Moscow is the second capital of the Empire, but by ancient right the first, although now surpassed both in commerce and population by the modern city of Peter the Great. Moscow occupies almost exactly the geographical centre of European Russia. Artistically it is of far greater interest to us than its northern rival. It has preserved the old oriental type: in its palaces has been displayed the barbaric pomp of the Muscovite Tsars of which much yet remains, not only in their renovated halls but also in what is left of the plate, jewels and ornaments with which they once abounded.

The general plan resembles somewhat that of Paris; the different quarters have gradually developed around a centre, and the river Moskva meanders through them as the Seine. The centre is the Kremlin; in shape an irregular triangle surrounded by high walls, outside which is the first walled-in quarter—the Kitai-Gorod, that is the Chinese city, about the meaning of which term there is some dispute. It is not, nor ever has been, in any way Chinese.

The name of Moscow appears first in the chronicles in 1147, when Youri, a son of Vladimir Monomachus, built the first houses of a town on the hill where the Kremlin now stands, but it was not until at least a century later that the city became of any importance. In 1237, it was burned by the Tartars and the real founder was Daniel, a son of Alexander Nevski. He was the first prince buried in the church of St. Michael where, until the time of Peter the Great, all the sovereigns of Russia have been buried; as in the metropolitan Cathedral of the Assumption, but a few steps distant, they have all been crowned up to the present day. From the Fifteenth to the Seventeenth Centuries, at the time when the arts flourished in Russia, in the greatest profusion and magnificence, Moscow was endowed with her richest monuments. It was then the numerous churches arose, the Kremlin, and the palaces of the boyars. At that time the city consisted of the Kremlin and the three walled-in enclosures which encircle it and each other as the several skins and shell inclose the kernel of a walnut. It appears to have been built in a haphazard fashion, though the old plans, with the houses sketched in rows, exhibit an uniformity of streets and buildings. They show us also that the houses were for the most part of wood, having each a covered outside staircase leading to the upper stories. Built so much of wood it was exposed to frequent conflagrations, the last being the great burning at the time of the French invasion in 1812. But so quickly was it always rebuilt and on the same lines that it has ever retained its original and irregular aspect. The Kremlin was at first of wood, but under the two Ivans it was surrounded by the solid stone walls of white stone cut in facets, which have given to the city the name "White Mother," or "Holy Mother Moscow with the white walls."

MOSCOW.

The Kremlin is at the same time a fortress and a city contained within itself, with its streets and palaces, churches, monasteries, and barracks. Eighteen towers and five gateways garnish the long extent of the inclosing wall; two of the gateways are interesting; that of the Saviour built by Pietro Solario in 1491, and that of the Trinity by Christopher Galloway in the Seventeenth Century. Here, among the churches are those of the Assumption and of St. Michael; here are the new palace of the Tsar, the restored Terem (what is left of the old palace), the sacristy and library of the patriarchs, the treasure and regalia, the great tower of Ivan Veliki in which hangs the largest bell in the world that will ring, and beneath it the "Tsar Kolokol," the king of bells, which it is supposed has never been rung and the king of cannons which has never been fired.

The ancient "Kazna," or treasury of the Kremlin, where the riches of the Tsars have been preserved from time immemorial was in the reign of Ivan III. situated within the walls of the Kremlin, between the Cathedrals of St. Michael and of the Annunciation. Here it remained until the great fire of 1737. The treasure had already suffered a heavy loss: in the early part of the Seventeenth Century, at the time of the war with Poland, a large quantity of plate was melted down to provide for the payment of the troops. The fire of

1737 caused a further and greater loss and destroyed also a large part of the armoury. At the time of the French invasion in 1812 the whole of the treasure, together with the regalia, was removed to Novgorod, and thus escaped destruction of seizure. On its return to Moscow in 1814, systematic arrangements were made for its preservation, and for the formation and arrangement of the museum in which it is now exhibited. In the year 1850 the new building of the Orujénaia Palata which forms part of the modern palace of the Kremlin was completed, and to this the entire collection was transferred.

The treasury of Moscow has been almost from the time of the establishment of the Russian Empire the place where the riches of the Tsars have been kept; consisting of the regalia, of the state costumes, of the plate and vases used in the service of their table, of their most magnificent armour and horse-trappings, of their state carriages and sledges and of the presents which from time to time the sovereigns of other countries sent through their ambassadors, of whose embassies so many interesting accounts have come down to us.

The collection of plate is exposed on open stands arranged in tiers round the pillars, or otherwise displayed in a vast hall of the new building of the Orujénaia Palata.

The riches thus brought together have suffered many changes. The court was frequently moved, the state of the empire was continually disturbed, fires were of frequent occurrence, and necessity at times caused much treasure to be melted down. The Tsar's favourites received no doubt from time to time acceptable marks of his approbation in the shape of rich presents, and many specimens of plate found their way probably in a similar manner to the churches and monasteries. But notwithstanding all this, there still remains permanently installed and carefully guarded in the treasury of the Kremlin a collection of plate which, for extent, variety, and interest, may rival that in any other palace in the world.

It appears to have been customary during the last two centuries at least to make a grand display of this treasure on the occasion of the visit of the sovereign, and especially during the ceremonies of the coronation. Then, in the centre of the hall in the ancient *Terem*, known as the gold room, where the Tsar dines in solitary state, a kind of buffet is arranged and other stands disposed, loaded and groaning with this rich accumulation.

Great splendour and richness of material, the lavish use of jewels in the decoration, and the brilliant colour derived from the employment of enamels are characteristics of eastern art in the precious metals. But while we are struck by the delicacy and refinement with which these are employed by many eastern countries, and while we admire the taste and harmony of colour displayed by the workmen of India or of Persia, it must be confessed that the Russian tempted by the glitter and display which are so much in accordance with his own taste, has been unable to use the same judgment as those whom he has taken as his models. Few would deny that there reigns throughout his work that quality which is best expressed by the term—barbaric magnificence. This is not vulgarity: such a term is not applicable; it is the outcome of the desire which is to be found amongst all nations who have attained a certain degree of civilization and riches to impose respect and awe by a lavish display of material wealth or by the use of gorgeous colour, which always calls forth the admiration of the multitude.

In the plate and jewelled ornament which we find in the treasury of the Kremlin, we shall find that Russian taste was fond of solid material and ornament, enriched with many and large precious stones of value. All Oriental nations have ever loved to accumulate riches of this description which, at the same time that they are of use as ornament, are also of intrinsic value. The crowns, and thrones, and sceptres, the ornaments of the imperial costume, the gold and silver plate and vases and other precious objects of the court of the Tsars have, therefore, a character of solid splendour, a want of refinement and delicacy, which is almost uniformly characteristic. Still they are not deficient in a certain grandeur and even elegance, and in details there is much that is admirable, much that is strikingly original.

By far the greater number of pieces that we shall find in the Kremlin and elsewhere belong to the Seventeenth Century. In the treasury of the Kremlin we have but one piece of the Twelfth Century and some few of the Fourteenth and Fifteenth Centuries. All the rest are later.

The entire number of pieces in the Kremlin amounts to sixteen hundred. After the disasters of 1612, all the ancient plate for the service of the Tsar's table was melted down and converted into money; many objects in gold and silver and jewelled work being at the same time given in pledge to the troops of Vladislas IV. There are therefore few examples earlier than the dynasty of the Romanoffs.

The treasure contains also some of the most highly venerated icons, crosses, and reliquaries in Russia. As regards many of these it is difficult to assign a date or a place of production. Many of them have histories more or less legendary, but while some may appear to belong absolutely to the Greek school, we must not forget that Russia sent its workmen to Mount Athos to be instructed and to work there, and on their return the traditions and models of the school were scrupulously observed in the workshops of Moscow.

The regalia of the ancient Tsars scarcely yield in interest to that of any other country. They consist of a large number of crowns or jewelled caps of peculiar form, of orbs and sceptres, of the imperial costume, and especially of that peculiar part of the latter, a kind of collar or shoulder ornament, known as the *barmi*.

Other important pieces of the regalia of Alexis Michailovitch are the orbs and sceptres, the bow and arrow case of the same description of workmanship. These are gorgeous specimens of jewelled and enamelled work attributed to Constantinople. The sceptre of the Tsar Michailovitch is of similar enamelled work, and is probably a good specimen of the effect of western influence on the goldsmiths of Moscow. The figures especially appear to be of the Italian renaissance. Another sceptre is unmistakably Russian work, and if not of pure taste is at least of fine workmanship and imposing magnificence.

The thrones are of high interest from more than one point of view. We must content ourselves with choosing two from amongst them, viz.: the ivory throne of Ivan III. (*Antiquities of the Russian Empire*, ii. 84-100), and the throne known as the Persian throne (*Ibid*, ii. 62-66).

The first was brought from Constantinople in 1472 by the Tsarina Sophia Paleologus, who, by her marriage with Ivan III., united the coats of arms of Byzantium and Russia.

There is a certain resemblance between this throne and that known as the chair of St. Peter at Rome. The general form is the same, as is the manner in which the ivory plaques and their borderings are placed. The second throne is a magnificent work, which, according to a register as the *Book of Embassies*, was sent from Persia in the year 1660 to the Tsar Alexis by a certain Ichto Modevlet, of the Shah's court. M. Weltman, in his enumeration of the treasury of the Kremlin, says: "It was therefore probably made in the workshops of Ispahan about the same time that the globe, sceptre, and *barmi* were ordered from Constantinople."

THE KREMLIN, MOSCOW.

The Kremlin contains a large number of pieces of decorative plate of all kinds made for the service of the table of the Tsars, or displayed on buffets on state occasions. Much of it is the production of other countries, presented by their ambassadors or purchased for the Tsar. The frequent fires and the melting down of treasure during the Polish disturbances have much diminished this collection, and possibly also many of the finest pieces have disappeared. Of the large service of gold plate of the Tsar Alexis, which consisted of 120 covers, two plates are all that remain. These are, however, sufficient evidence of the skill and taste of the Moscow goldsmiths of the period and of their dexterity in the use of enamel.

The Treasury of the Kremlin contains a large number of cups or vases of silver-gilt, for table use, of Russian work. There is no great variety in the cups, but some forms are peculiar to the country. There are especially the cups called *bratini* (loving cups, from *brat*, a brother), the bowls or ladles termed *kovsh*, and the small cups with one flat handle for strong liquors. Tall beakers expanding at the lip and contracted at the middle are also favourite forms, but the bulbous shape is the most frequent. Indeed, that form of bulb or cupola which we see upon the churches is peculiarly characteristic. We find it with more or less resemblance, in the ancient crowns, in the mitres of the popes, in the bowls of chalices and in vases and bowls for drinking. In the *bratini* and *kovsh* the bulging form of ornament, the coving up of the bottoms of the bowls, and the use of twisted lobes are very common.

The Cathedral of the Assumption is one of the many churches situated within the precincts of the Kremlin. It was reconstructed by Fioraventi in 1475 after the model of the Cathedral of Vladimir, and in spite of the frequent calamities and fires which have half ruined Moscow still preserves in a great measure its primitive character. The church of the Assumption has five domes resting in the centre of the building on four massive circular pillars, and the sanctuary is composed of four hemicycles. The Cathedral of the Archangel Michael is close by and was built in 1507 in imitation of it. Near this again is the Cathedral of the Annunciation. This, which was built in 1416, is more original in style and recalls the churches of Mount Athos, or that of Kertch, which dates from the Tenth Century.

Mention must be made of an ancient building, the house known as the Romanoff House in Moscow. It was the birthplace of the Tsar Michael Theodorovitch, founder of the now reigning family, and also of his father Theodore Nikitisch, who became patriarch under the name of Philaret. In its restored state the Romanoff House is still perhaps the most remarkable ancient building existing in Russia as a perfect specimen of the old dwelling-houses of the boyards. It is built of stone, and the solid exterior walls are as they originally stood. The interior restoration, completed by the emperor Alexander in 1859, has been carried out with great care in the exact style of the time, the furniture and ornaments being authentic and placed as they would have been.

VASSILI-BLAGENNOI

(*St. Basil the Blessed*)

THÉOPHILE GAUTIER

We soon reached the Kitai-Gorod, which is the business quarter, upon the Krasnaia, the Red Square, or rather the beautiful square, for in Russia the words red and beautiful are synonymous. Upon one side of this square is the long façade of the Gostinnoi-Dvor, an immense bazaar with streets enclosed by glass-like passages, and which contains no less than 6,000 shops. The outside wall of the Kremlin rears itself on another side, with gates piercing the towers of sharply peaked roofs, permitting you to see above it the turrets, the domes, the belfries and the spires of the churches and convents it encloses. On another side, strange as the architecture of dreamland, stands the chimerical and impossible church of Vassili-Blagennoi, which makes your reason doubt the testimony of your eyes. Although it appears real enough, you ask yourself if it is not a fantastic mirage, a building made of clouds curiously coloured by the sunlight, and which the quivering air will change or cause to dissolve. Without any doubt, it is the most original building in the world; it recalls nothing that you have ever seen and it belongs to no style whatever: you might call it a gigantic madrepore, a colossal formation of crystals, or a grotto of stalactites inverted.

But let us not search for comparisons to give an idea of something that has no prototype. Let us try rather to describe Vassili-Blagennoi, if indeed there exists a vocabulary to speak of what had never been imagined previously.

There is a legend about Vassili-Blagennoi, which is probably not true, but which nevertheless expresses with strength and poetry the sense of wondering stupefaction felt at the semi-barbarous period when that singular edifice, so remote from all architectural traditions, was erected. Ivan the Terrible had this cathedral built as a thank-offering for the conquest of Kasan, and when it was finished, he found it so beautiful, wonderful and astounding, that he ordered the architect's eyes to be put out—they say he was an Italian—so that he could never erect anything similar. According to another version of the same legend, the Tsar asked the originator of this church if he could not erect a still more beautiful one, and upon his reply in the affirmative, he cut off his head, so that Vassili-Blagennoi might remain unrivalled forever. A more flattering exhibition of jealous cruelty cannot be imagined, but this Ivan the Terrible was at bottom a true artist and a passionate dilettante. Such ferocity in matters of art is more pleasing to me than indifference.

Imagine on a kind of platform which lifts the base from the ground, the most peculiar, the most incomprehensible, the most prodigious heaping up of large and little cabins, outside stairways, galleries with arcades and unexpected hiding-places and projections, unsymmetrical porches, chapels in juxtaposition, windows pierced in the walls at haphazard, indescribable forms and a rounding out of the interior arrangement, as if the architect, seated in the centre of his work had produced a building by thrusting it out from him. From the roof of this church which might be taken for a Hindu, Chinese, or Thibetan pagoda, there springs a forest of belfries of the strangest taste, fantastic beyond anything else in the world. The one in the centre, the tallest and most massive, shows three or four stories from base to spire. First come little columns, and toothed string-courses, then come some pilasters framing long mullioned windows, then a series of blank arches like scales, overlapping one another, and on the sides of the spire wart-like ornaments outlining each spire, the whole terminated by a lantern surmounted by an inverted golden bulb bearing on its tip the Russian cross. The others, which are slenderer and shorter, affect the form of the minaret, and their fantastically ornamented towers end in cupolas that swell strangely into the form of onions. Some are tortured into facets, others ribbed, some cut into diamond-shaped points like pineapples, some striped with fillets in spirals, others again decorated with lozenge-shaped and overlapping scales, or honeycombed like a bee-hive, and all adorned at their summit with the golden ball surmounted by the cross.

VASSILI-BLAGENNOI (ST. BASIL THE BLESSED), MOSCOW.

What adds still more to the fantastic effect of Vassili-Blagennoi, is that it is coloured with the most incongruous tones which nevertheless produce a harmonious effect that charms the eye. Red, blue, apple-green and yellow meet here in all portions of the building. Columns, capitals, arches and ornaments are painted with startling shades which give a strong relief. On the plain spaces of rare occurrence, they have simulated divisions or panels framing pots of flowers, rose-windows, wreathing vines, and chimæras. The domes of the bell-towers are decorated with coloured designs that recall the patterns of India shawls; and, displayed thus on the roofs of the church, they recall the kiosks of the Sultans.

The same fantastic genius presided over the plan and ornamentation of the interior. The first chapel, which is very low and in which a few lamps glimmer, resembles a golden cavern; unexpected stars throw their rays across the dusky shadows and make the stiff images of the Greek saints stand out like phantoms. The mosaics of St. Mark's in Venice alone can give an approximate idea of the effect of this astonishing richness. At the back, the iconostas looms up in the twilight shot through with rays like a golden and jewelled wall between the faithful and the priests of the sanctuary.

Vassili-Blagennoi does not present, like other churches, a simple interior composed of several naves communicating and cut at certain points of intersection after the laws of the rites followed in the temple. It is formed of a collection of churches, or chapels, in juxtaposition and independent of each other. Each bell-tower contains a chapel, which arranges itself as it pleases in this mass. The dome is the terminal of the spire or the bulb of the cupola. You might believe yourself under the enormous casque of some Circassian or Tartar giant. These calottes are, moreover, marvellously painted and decorated in the interior. It is the same with the walls covered with those barbaric and hieratic figures, the traditional designs for which the Greek monks of Mount Athos have preserved from century to century, and which, in Russia, often deceive the careless observer regarding the age of a building. It is a peculiar sensation to find yourself in these mysterious sanctuaries, where personages familiar to the Roman Catholic cult, mingle with the saints peculiar to the Greek Calendar, and seem in their archaic Byzantine and constrained appearance to have been translated awkwardly into gold by the childish devotion of a primitive race. These images that you view across the carved and silver-gilt work of the iconostas, where they are ranged symmetrically upon the golden screen opening their large fixed eyes and raising their brown hand with the fingers turned in a symbolic fashion, produce, by means of their somewhat savage, superhuman and immutable traditional aspect, a religious impression not to be found in more advanced works of art. These figures, seen amid the golden reflections and twinkling light of the lamps, easily assume a phantasmagorical life, capable of impressing sensitive imaginations and of creating, especially at the twilight hour, a peculiar kind of sacred awe.

Narrow corridors, low arched passages, so narrow that your elbows brush the walls and so low that you have to bend your head, circle about these chapels and lead from one to the other. Nothing could be more fantastic than these passages; the architect seems to have taken pleasure in tangling up their threading ways. You ascend, you descend, you seem to go out of the building, you seem to return, twisting about a cornice to follow the curves of a bell-tower, and walking through thick walls in tortuous passages that might be compared to the capillary tubes of madrepores, or to the roads made by insects in the barks of trees. After so many turnings and windings, your head swims, a vertigo seizes you, and you wonder if you are not a mollusk in an immense shell. I do not speak of the mysterious corners, of inexplicable cœcums, low doors opening no one knows whither, dark stairways descending into profound depths; for I could never finish talking of this architecture, which you seem to walk through as if in a dream.

POLAND

THOMAS MICHELL

The Tsar still bears the title of King of Poland, but the constitutional kingdom created at the great settlement of political accounts in 1815 has been officially styled "The Cis-Vistula Provinces," ever since the absolute incorporation with the Russian empire in 1868. The provinces in question, ten in number, have an aggregate area of 49,157 English square miles, and a population of eight millions, composed to the extent of sixty-five per cent. of Poles, the remainder being Jews (in the proportion of thirteen per cent., and settled chiefly in towns), Lithuanians, Russians, Germans, and other aliens.

The Poles (the Polacks of Shakespeare), are a branch of the Sclav race, their language differing but little from that of the Russians, Czechs (Bohemians), Servians, Bulgarians, and other kindred remnants. Contact and co-operation with Western civilization, and escape from Tartar subjugation, permitted the Poles to work out their own development on lines so widely apart from those pursued by their Russian brethren, that the complete amalgamation of these two great Sclav branches has long been a matter of practical impossibility.

Polish history begins, like that of Russia, with Scandinavian invasion; Szainocha, a reliable authority of the present century, asserted that the Northmen descended on the Polish coast of the Baltic, and became, as in Russia, ancestors of the noble houses. On the other hand, it is on record that the first Grand Duke of Poland (about A. D. 842), was Piastus, a peasant, who founded a dynasty that was superseded only in 1385 by the Lithuanian Jagellons. Christianity was introduced by the fourth of the Piasts, A. D. 964, and it was a sovereign of the same House, Boleslas I., the Brave, who gave a solid foundation to the Polish State. He conquered Dantzig and Pomerania, Silesia, Moravia, and White Russia, as far as the Dnieper. After being partitioned, in accordance with the principle that long obtained in the neighbouring Russian principalities, the component territories of Poland were reunited by Vladislaf (Ladislaf) the Short, who established his capital, in 1320, at Cracow, where the Polish kings were ever after crowned. Casimir the Great, the Polish Justinian (1334-1370), gained for himself the title of *Rex Rusticorum*, by the bestowal of benefits on the peasantry, who were *adscripti glebæ*, and by the limitation of the power of the nobles, or freeholders. On his death, Louis, King of Hungary, his sister's son, was called to the throne; but in order to insure its continued possession he was compelled to reinstate the nobles in all their privileges, under a *Pacta Conventa*, which, subject to alterations made at Diets, was retained as part of the Coronation Oath so long as there were Polish kings to be consecrated. He was the last sovereign of the Piast period. After compelling his daughter to marry, not William of Austria, whom she loved, but Jagellon, Duke of Lithuania, who offered to unite his extensive and adjacent dominions with those of Poland, and to convert his own pagan subjects to Christianity, the nobles, in virtue of their Magna Charta, elected Jagellon (baptized under the name of Ladislas) to the throne of Poland, which thus became dynastically united (1386), with that of Lithuania.

On the death, in 1572, of Sigismund II., Augustus, the last of the Jagellons, the power of the king, already limited by that of two chambers, was still further diminished, and the crown became elective. While occupied in besieging the Huguenots at Rochelle, and at a time when Poland enjoyed more religious liberty than any other country in Europe, Henry of Valois was elected to the throne, in succession to Sigismund II.; but he quickly absconded from Cracow in order to become Henry III. of France. The Jesuits, introduced in the next reign, that of Stephen Bathori, brought strong intolerance with them, and one of the reasons that led the Cossacks of the Polish Ukraine to solicit Russian protection was the inferior position to which their Greek religion had been reduced in relation to Roman Catholicism. The Russians and Poles had been at war with each other for two centuries. Moscow had been occupied in 1610 by the Poles in the name of Ladislas, son of Sigismund III., of the Swedish Wasa family, elected to the Muscovite throne by the Russian boyars, but soon expelled by the patriots, under Minin and Pojarski. Sobieski, who had saved Vienna for the Austrians, could not keep Kief and Little Russia for the Poles. Such was the outcome of disorders and revolutions in the State, and of wars with Muscovy, Turkey, and Sweden, as well as with Tartars and Cossacks. Frederick Augustus II., Elector of Saxony, succeeded Sobieski, and reigned until 1733, with an interval of five years, during which he was superseded by Stanislas I.

NOWO ZJAZD STREET, WARSAW.

Dissension and anarchy became still more general, in the reign of the next sovereign, Augustus III. Civil war, in which the question of the rights of Lutherans, Calvinists, and other "dissidents" obnoxious to the Roman Catholic Church played a great part, resulted in the intervention of Russia and Prussia, and in 1772 the first partition of Poland was consummated. The second followed in 1793, under an arrangement between the same countries, which had taken alarm at a liberal constitution voted by the Polish Diet in 1791, especially as it had provided for the emancipation of the *adscripti glebæ*. The struggle made by Thaddeus Kosciuszko ended in the entry of Suvoroff into Warsaw over the ashes of the Prague suburb, and in the third dismemberment (1795), of ancient Poland, under which even Warsaw was absorbed by Russia.

Previous to these several partitions, Poland occupied a territory much more extensive than that of France. In addition to the kingdom proper, it included the province of Posen and part of West Prussia, Cracow, and Galicia, Lithuania, the provinces of Volhynia and Podolia, and part of the present province of Kief. In 1772, Dantzig was a seaport of Poland, Kaminets, in Podolia, its border stronghold against Turkey; while to the west and north its frontier extended almost to the walls of Riga, and to within a short distance from Moscow. In still earlier times, Bessarabia, Moldavia, Silesia, and Livonia were embraced within the Polish possessions.

These successive partitions gave the most extensive portion of Polish territory to Russia, the most populous to Austria, and the most commercial to Prussia. Napoleon I. revived a Polish state out of the provinces that had been seized by Prussia and Austria. This was first constituted into a Grand

Duchy under the King of Saxony, and in 1815, when Galicia (with Cracow) was restored to Austria, and Posen to Prussia, Warsaw became again a kingdom under a constitution granted by Alexander I. The old Polish provinces that had fallen to the share of Catherine II. at the partitions remained incorporated with the Russian Empire, but were not fully subjected to a Russian administration until after the great Polish insurrection of 1830, when also the constitution of 1815 was withdrawn, the national army abolished, and the Polish language proscribed in the public offices.

Notwithstanding the wide measures of Home Rule introduced by Alexander II. into the administration of the kingdom, and which, in combination with many liberal and pregnant reforms in Russia Proper appeared to offer to the Poles the prospect of no inconsiderable influence over the destinies of the Russian Empire, the old spirit of national independence began to manifest itself, and in 1862, not without encouragement from Napoleon III., an insurrection broke out at Warsaw.

Outside Warsaw and its immediate vicinity there is little in Russian Poland to interest the tourist. The country is generally level and monotonous, with wide expanses of sand, heath, and forest, and it is only towards the north and east that the ground may be said to be heavily timbered. Dense forests stretch down from the Russian, anciently Polish, province of Grodno, and now form the last retreat in Europe of the *Bison Europeans*, the survivor of the Aurochs (*Bos primigenius*), which is supposed to have been the original stock of our horned cattle. Although much worried by the wolf, the bear, and the lynx, the bison is strictly preserved from the hunter, and are not therefore likely to disappear like the *Bos Americanus*, or buffalo, which has so long been ruthlessly slaughtered in the United States.

Interspersed among these barren or wooded tracts are areas containing some of the finest corn-bearing soil in Europe, supplying from time immemorial vast quantities of superior grain for shipment from ports in the Baltic. It is produced on the larger estates of two hundred to fifteen hundred acres, belonging to more than eight thousand proprietors. The peasantry, who hold more than 240,000 farms—seldom exceeding forty acres—contribute next to nothing towards exportation, their mode of agriculture being almost as rude as that of the Russian peasantry, and their habits of life but little superior, especially in the matter of drink. Towns, large and small, occur more frequently than in Russia, and while some are rich and industrial, others—we may say the great majority—are poor and squalid, affording no accommodation that would render possible the visit of even the least fastidious traveller.

Consequently we confine ourselves to Warsaw, which we take on our way by rail to or from St. Petersburg or Moscow. Founded in the Twelfth Century, and, during the Piast period, the seat of the appanaged Dukes of Masovia, Warszawa, replaced Cracow as the residence of the Polish kings and therefore as the capital of Poland, on the election of Sigismund III. (1586). It has now a population of about 445,000, not including the Russian garrison of 31,500 officers and men. The left bank of the Vistula, on which Warsaw is chiefly built, is high, and the pretty, gay, and animated city, with its stately lines of streets, wide squares, and spacious gardens, is picturesquely disposed along the brow of the cliff and on the plains above. Across the broad sandy bed of the stream, here "shallow, ever-changing, and divided as Poland itself," and which is on its way from the Carpathians to the Baltic, is the Prague suburb, which, formerly fortified, has never recovered from the assault by Suvoroff in 1794, when its sixteen thousand inhabitants were indiscriminately put to the sword. A vast panorama spreads out in every direction from this melancholy and dirty point of vantage. Opposite is the Zamek, or castle, built by the Dukes of Masovia, and enlarged and restored by several of the Polish kings, from Sigismund III. to Stanislas Augustus Poniatovski. Its pictures and objects of art are now at St. Petersburg, and Moscow, and the old royal apartments are occupied by the Governor-General. The square in front of the castle was the scene of the last Polish "demonstrations," in 1861, when it was twice stained with blood.

In the Stare Miasto, or Old Town, strongly old German in aspect, stands the cathedral, built in the Thirteenth Century, and restored on the last occasion by King John Sobieski. A still more ancient sacred edifice is the Church of Our Lady in the Nove Miasto, or New Town; but it certainly retains no traces of deep antiquity. Beyond the great Sapieha and Sierakovski Barracks towers the Alexander Citadel, with its outlying fortifications, built in 1832-35, at the expense of the city, as a penalty for the insurrection in 1830. In the same direction, but a considerable distance from the town, is Mariemont, the country seat of the consort of John Sobieski; also Kaskada, a place of entertainment much frequented by the inhabitants of Warsaw, and Bielany, a pretty spot on the Vistula commanding a fine view. The churches and chapels, mostly Roman Catholic, are numerous (eighty-five), and so are the monasteries and convents (twenty-two).

Near Novi Sviat (New World) Street, we find the Avenues, or *Champs Elysées*, bordered by fine lime-trees, in front of elegant private residences. Crossing a large square, in which the troops are exercised, and the military hospital at Uiazdov, formerly a castle of the kings of Poland, we reach the fine park of Lazienki, a country seat of much elegance built by King Stanislas Augustus, and now the residence of the Emperor when he visits Warsaw. The ceilings of this *château* were painted by Bacciarelli, and its walls are hung with portraits of numerous beautiful women.

Contiguous to the Lazienki Park are the extensive gardens of the Belvedere Palace, in which the Poles attempted in 1830 to get rid of their viceroy, the Grand Duke Constantine. We drive hence in less than an hour to one of the most interesting places near Warsaw. This is the Castle of Villanov, built by John Sobieski, who died in it. To this retreat he brought back the trophies of his mighty deeds in arms, and here sought repose after driving the Turks from the walls of Vienna. The *château*, now the property of Countess Potoçka, is full of historical portraits, objects of art, and other curiosities, of which the most interesting is the magnificent suit of armour presented by the Pope to Sobieski in memory of his great victory. The apartments of his beautiful consort are of great elegance. In the gallery of pictures we notice an admirable Rubens—the *Death of Seneca*; although we are more strongly attracted by an original portrait of Bacon, which is but little known in England.

HOTEL DE VILLE, WARSAW.

For want of space, again we must plead guilty of omitting to describe many palatial residences, and several noticeable monuments, among which is one to Copernicus, the Polish founder of modern astronomy. On the same ground we pass over handsome public buildings, theatres, gardens and cemeteries, in one of which, the Evangelical Cemetery, is buried John Cockerell, to whom Belgium owes so much of her industrial prosperity.

KIEF, THE CITY OF PILGRAMAGE

J. BEAVINGTON ATKINSON

Kief, the Jerusalem of Russia, is by nature marked for distinction; she rises like an Etruscan city from the plain; she is flanked by fortifications; she is pleasantly clothed by trees, and height beyond height is crowned by castle or by church. Fifty thousand pilgrims annually, many of whom are footsore from long and weary journeying, throw themselves on their knees as they see the sacred city from afar: her holy places shine in the sun as a light set upon a hill which cannot be hid. Three holy shrines which I can recall to mind— Kief, Assisi, and Jerusalem—are alike fortunate in command of situation; the approach to each is most impressive. In Kief particularly the natural landscape is heightened in pictorial effect by the picturesque groups of pilgrims, staves in hand and wallets on back, who may be seen at all hours of the day clambering up the hill, resting under the shadow of a tree, or reverently bowing the head at the sound of a convent bell.

Kief is not one city, but three cities, each with its own fortification. The old town, strong in position, and enclosing within its circuit the Cathedral of St. Sophia and the Palace of the Metropolitan, was in remote ages a Sclavonian Pantheon, sacred to the Russian Jupiter and other savage gods. The new town, separated from the old town by a deep ravine, stands on a broad platform which rises precipitously from the banks of the Dnieper. The walls are massive, the fort is strong, and the famous monastery, the first in rank in Russia, with its gilt and coloured domes, shines from out the shade of a deep wood. The third division, "the Town of the Vale," situated between the hills and the river, is chiefly devoted to commerce. Without much stretch of fancy it might be said that Kief, like Rome, Lisbon and some other cities, is built on seven hills. And thus the pictorial aspect changes almost at every step; a winding path will bring to view an unsuspected height, or open up a valley previously hid. The traveller has in the course of his wanderings often to feel thankful that a kind providence has planted sacred places in the midst of lovely scenery. The holy mountain at Varallo, the sacred hill at Orta, are, like the shrines of Kief, made doubly pleasant for pilgrimage through the beauties of nature by which they are surrounded. It is said that at the monastery of the Grande Chartreuse the monks do not permit themselves to look too much at the outward landscape, lest their hearts should by the loveliness of earth be estranged from heaven. I do not think that Russian priests or pilgrims incur any such danger. When they are neither praying nor eating they are sleeping; in short, I did not among the motley multitude see a single eye open to the loveliness of colour in the sky above, or to the beauty of form in the earth beneath. It is singular how obtuse these people are; I have noticed in a crowded railway carriage that not a face would be turned to the glory of the setting sun, but if a church tower came into view on the distant horizon, every hand was raised to make the sign of the cross. While taking my observations among the pilgrims at Kief I was struck with the fact, not only that a superstitious faith, but that a degraded art blinds the eye to the beauty of nature. It is one of the high services of true art to lead the mind to the contemplation, to the love and the better understanding, of the works of creation. But, on the contrary, it is the penalty of this Byzantine art to close the appointed access between nature and nature's God. An art which ignores and violates truth and beauty cannot do otherwise than lead the mind away from nature. This seemed one of the several lessons taught by Kief, the city of pilgrimage.

Sketchers of character and costume will find excellent studies among the pilgrims of Kief. The upper and educated classes, who in Russia are assimilating with their equals in other nations, and are therefore not tempting to the pencil or the brush, do not, as we have already seen, come in any numbers to these sacred shrines. It is the lower orders, who still preserve the manners and customs of their ancestors, that make these church festivals so attractive to the artist. The variety of races brought together from afar—a diversity only possibly within an empire, like Russia, made up of heterogeneous materials—might serve not only to fill a portfolio, but to illustrate a volume; the ethnologist equally with the painter would find at the time of great festivities curious specimens of humanity. I remember some years ago to have met with the French artist, M. Théodore Valerio, when he had brought home the *Album Ethnographique* from Hungary, Croatia, and the more distant borders of the Danube. It was quite refreshing, after the infinite number of costume-studies I had seen from Italian peasantry, to find that art had the possibility of an entirely new sphere among the Sclavonic races. A like field for any painter of enterprise is now open in Russia. The large and famous composition, *The Butter Week (Carnival) in St. Petersburg*, by C. Makowski, may serve to indicate the hitherto undeveloped pictorial resources of the empire. When the conditions are new there is a possibility that the art may be new also. The ethnology, the physical geography, the climate, the religion, the products of the animal and vegetable kingdoms, so far as they are peculiar to Russia, will some day become reflected into the national art. It is true that the painter may occasionally feel a want of colour, the costumes of the peasant are apt to be dull and heavy, yet not unfrequently rags and tatters bring compensation by picturesque outlines and paintable surface-textures. At Kief, however, the traveller is sufficiently south and east to fall in with warm southern hues and Oriental harmonies, broken and enriched, moreover, among the lower orders by that engrained dirt which I have usually noted as the special privilege and prerogative of pilgrims in all parts of the world. The use of soap would seem to be accounted as sacrilege on religious sentiment. What with dust, and what with sun, the wayfarers who toil up the heights leading to the holy hill have gained a colour which a Murillo would delight in. The face and neck bronzed by the hot sun tell out grandly from a flowing mass of hair worthy of a patriarch.

THE DNIEPER AT KIEF.

Beggars, who in Russia are as thick about the churches as the pigeons that pick up crumbs in front of St. Mark's, are almost essential to the histrionic panoramas at these places of pilgrimage. I have never seen so large or so varied a collection of professional and casual mendicants as within and about the sacred enclosures of Kief. Some appeared to enjoy vested rights; these privileged personages would as little endure to be driven from a favoured post as with us a sweeper at a crossing would tolerate a rival broom. Several of these waiters upon charity might be termed literary beggars; their function is to read aloud from a large book in the hearing of the passers-by. They are often infirm, and occasionally blind, but they read just the same. Another class may be called the incurables; in England they would be kept out of sight, but here in Russia, running sores, mutilated hands and legs, are valuable as stock-in-trade. Loathsome diseases are thrust forward as a threat, distorted limbs are extortionate for alms; it is a piteous sight to see; some of these sad objects are in the jaws of death, and come apparently that they may die on holy ground. Another class may be called the pious beggars; they stand at the church doors; they are picturesque and apostolic; long beards and quiet bearing, with a certain professional get-up of misery and desolation, make these sacred mendicants grand after their kind. Such figures are usually ranged on either side of the chief entrance; they are motionless as statues, save when in the immediate act of soliciting alms; indeed I have sometimes noticed how beggars standing before a church façade are suggestive of statuary, the want of which is so much felt in the unsculpturesque architecture of Russia. Pilgrims and beggars—the line of demarcation it is not always easy to define—have an Oriental way of throwing themselves into easy and paintable attitudes; in fact posture plays a conspicuous part in the devotions of such people; they pray bodily almost more than mentally,—the figure and its attendant costume become instruments of worship.

The Cathedral of St. Sophia, which dates back to the Eleventh Century, is of interest from its resemblance to St. Mark's, Venice, in the plan of the Greek cross, in the use of domes and galleries, and in the introduction of mosaics as surface-decorations. I saw the galleries full of fashionable worshippers; the galleries in St. Mark's on the contrary, are always empty and useless, though constructed for use. In the apse are the only old mosaics I have met with in Russia; it is strange that an art which specially pertains to Byzantium was not turned to more account by the Greco-Russian Church. There is in the apse, besides, a subject composition,—a noble female figure, colossal in size, the arms upraised in attitude of prayer, the drapery cast broadly and symmetrically. In the same interior are associated with mosaics, frescoes, or rather wall-paintings in *secco*. On the columns which support the cupola are frescoes which, though of no art value, naturally excited curiosity when they were discovered some few years since, after having been hid for two or more centuries by a covering of whitewash. Some other wall-pictures are essentially modern, and others have been restored, after Russian usage, in so reckless and wholesale a fashion as to be no longer of value as archæologic records. In the staircase leading to the galleries are some further wall-paintings, said to be contemporaneous with the building of the cathedral; the date, however, is wholly uncertain. These anomalous compositions represent a boar-hunt and other sports, with groups of musicians, dancers, and jugglers, intervening. In accord with the secular character of the subjects is the rude naturalism of the style. Positive knowledge as to date being wanting, it is impossible to speak of these works otherwise than to say that they cannot be of Byzantine origin. If of real antiquity they will have to join company with other semi-barbaric products in metal, etc., which prove, as we have seen, that Russia has two historic schools, the Byzantine, on the one hand, debilitated and refined, as of periods of decline, and, on the other, a non-Byzantine and barbarous style, strong and coarse as of races still vital and vigorous. A like conflict is found in the North of Italy between the Byzantine and the Lombard manner; and even in England the west front of Wells Cathedral presents the same unresolved contradictions. It would seem that over the greater part of Europe, Eastern as well as Western, these two hostile arts were practiced contemporaneously; at all events the same buildings are found to display the two opposite styles. It would appear probable, however, that the respective artists or artisans belonged to at least two distinct nationalities.

The Pecherskoi Monastery, or Kievo-Pecherskaya Lavra, at Kief, the Kremlin in Moscow, and the grand monastery of Troitza, have this in common, that the situation is commanding, the site elevated. Also, these three venerable sanctuaries are strongholds, for though the holy places at Kief are not on all sides fortified, yet the approach from the old city, which is the most accessible, lies along bastions and walls. In fact, here we have again a semblance to the ancient idea of a church, a citadel, and a palace united, as in an acropolis—the Church and the State being one; the arm of the flesh sustaining the sword of the spirit,—a condition of things which has always given to the world its noblest art. The walk to this most ancient monastery in Russia passes pleasantly by the side of a wood; then opens a view of the vast plain beneath, intersected by the river Dnieper, over which is flung the great suspension-bridge built by the English engineer, Charles Vignolles, at the cost of £350,000. The immediate approach is lined with open shops or stalls for the sale of sacred pictures, engravings of saints, and other articles which pilgrims love to carry back to their homes. Within the enclosure trees throw a cool shade, under which, as in the courtyards of mosques in Constantinople, the hot and weary may repose.

The cathedral dedicated to the ascension of the Virgin, has not the slightest pretence to external architecture. The walls are mostly whitewashed, and some of the windows have common square heads crowned by mean pediments; the intervening pilasters and floral decorations in relief, and all in the midst of whitewash, are of the poorest character. The seven gilded cupolas or domes may be compared to inverted cups surmounted by crosses. The form resembles the cup commonly combined in the fantastic towers and spires of Protestant churches in Germany, where, however, it has been supposed to signify that the laity partake of the chalice. These domes are made further decorative at the point of the small circular neck which connects the cupola with the upper member or finial; around this surface is painted a continuous series of single saints standing; the effect of these pictures against the sky, if not quite artistic, is striking. Other parts of the exterior may indicate Italian rather than Oriental origin, but the style is far too mongrel to boast of any legitimate parentage. Here, as in the Kremlin, are external wall-paintings of saints, some standing on solid ground, others sitting among clouds; the Madonna is of course of the company, and the First and Second Persons of the Trinity crown the composition. The ideas are trite and the treatment is contemptible—the colours pass from dirty red into brown and black. These certainly are the worst wall-paintings I have ever met with, worse even than the coarsest painted shrines on the waysides of Italy; indeed no Church save the Greek Church would tolerate an art thus debased. A year after my journey to Kief I travelled through the Tyrol on my way from the Ammergau Passion Play. The whole of this district abounds in frescoes, many being on the external walls of private dwellings. This village art of the

Bavarian Highlands, though often the handiwork of simple artisans, puts to shame both the external and the internal wall-paintings at Kief, Troitza, and the Kremlin. Yet this contrast between Russia and Southern nations does not arise so much from the higher ability of the artists, as from the superiority of the one school to the other school. The pictorial arts fostered by the Western Church are fundamentally true, while the arts which the Eastern Church has patronized and petrified are essentially false and effete.

The scene which strikes the eye on entering this parti-coloured Cathedral of the Assumption, though strange, is highly picturesque. To this holy shrine are brought the halt, the lame, and the blind, as to the moving of the waters. Some press forward to kiss the foot of a crucifix, others bow the head and kiss the ground, a servile attitude of worship, which in the Greco-Russian Church has been borrowed from the Mohammedans. The groups which throng the narrow, crowded floor, are wonderfully effective; an artist with sketch-book in hand would have many a good chance of catching graphic heads and costumes, and all the more easily because these pilgrims are not so lively as lethargic. Still, for grand scenic impression, I have never in Russia witnessed any church function so striking as the piazza in front of St. Peter's on Easter Day, when all Rome flocks to receive the Pope's blessing from the balcony. Yet the whole interior of this cathedral is itself a picture, or rather a countless succession of pictures; as to the architecture there is not the minutest space that has not been emblazoned by aid of a paint-pot.

But the greatest marvel in this Cathedral of the Assumption is the iconostas, or screen for the sacred pictures, a structure indispensable to all Russian churches, of which I have withheld the description till now, when I find myself in front of a large and more astounding erection than can be found in St. Petersburg, Moscow, or Troitza. In small churches these sacred placards, bearing the character of drop-scenes, are apt to be paltry, indeed the irreverent stranger may even be reminded of painted caravans at village fairs. But in large cathedrals the screen which stands between the people in the nave and the priests in the holy of holies, presents a vast façade, upon which are ranged, in three, four, or five stories, a multitude of sacred pictures covered with gold and decked with jewels. These elaborate contrivances correspond to the reredos in Western churches, only with this important difference, that they are not behind the holy place but in front of it. They might, perhaps, with more correctness be compared to the rood-screens which in our churches stand between the altar and the people. The sacred screen now before me mounts its head into the dome, and presents an imposing and even an architectonic aspect, but certain details, such as classic mouldings of columns, and a broken entablature, pronounce the edifice to be comparatively modern. The summit is fitly crowned by a crucifix, almost in the flat, in order not to evade the law of the Russian Church, which prohibits statues in the round; the figure of Christ is silver, the cross and the drapery of gold or silver-gilt. On either side of the crucifix stand in their prescriptive stations the Madonna and St. John. On the story beneath comes the entombment, all covered with gold and silver, in a low-relief which indicates the forms of the figures beneath; the heads, which are not in relief but merely pictorial, are the only portions of the picture actually visible.

These altar-screens, which in Russia are counted not by tens but by hundreds and thousands, are highly ornate. Silver and gold and jewellery are conjoined with painting after the nursery and doll-like fashion approved in the South of Spain and at Naples. Only in the most corrupt of Roman Catholic capitals does ecclesiastical art assume the childish forms common in Russia. Resuming the description of the above altar-screen, we find next in range below the entombment a large composition, comprising God the Father surrounded by cherubs, with two full-grown seraphs, encircled by six gold wings, standing on either side. Again, the only parts of the picture permitted to be seen are the heads, crossed hands, black legs and feet. Christ with the open book of judgment is another conspicuous figure; also a companion head, gigantic in size, is the Madonna, directly Byzantine in type, though its smooth and well-kept surface gives little sign of age. The Christ, too, must be accounted but as modernized Byzantine; here is none of the severity or of the tenuity of the early periods. The type is poor though refined, debilitated though ideal. The hair, parted on the forehead, falls thickly on the shoulders. The face is youthful, not more than thirty, and without a wrinkle; the cheeks are a little flushed, the prevailing expression is placidity. The accessories of glory, drapery, and open book are highly decorative; here embossed patterns on the gold coverings enhance the richness of the surface-ornament. Once again the Russians appear supreme in metal-work, especially in the elaboration of decoration in the flat. Most of the pictures above mentioned are evidently supremely holy; they are black and highly gilded; moreover, they move most deeply all sorts and conditions of men, women, and children.

I may here again mention that one purpose of my Russian journey was to discover whether there were heads of Christ in the possession of the Russian Church older or nobler than the ivory carvings, the frescoes, or easel pictures which are found in Italy and other Southern or Western nations. And I was, I confess, disappointed not to meet with any data which could materially enlarge or enrich this most interesting of subjects. As to priority of date, it seems to be entirely on the side of the Roman catacombs and the Latin Church; moreover, in Russia, as I before frequently remarked, chronology is untrustworthy, inasmuch as comparatively modern works assume and parody the style of the most ancient. The heads of Christ in Russia, one of which has been just described, are, as already said, more or less servile reproductions of Byzantine types. Still the typical form is found under varying phases; the general tendency in these replicas of anterior originals would appear to be towards the mitigation of the asperities in the confirmed Byzantine formulas. Thus the more recent heads of the Saviour in the churches of St. Petersburg, Moscow, Troitza and Kief, assume a certain modern manner, and occasionally wear a smooth, pretty and ornamental aspect. In these variations on the prescriptive Eastern type, the hair usually flows down upon the shoulders, as with the Greek and Russian Priests in the present day. As to the beard, it is thick and full, or short and scant, but the cheeks are left uncovered, and show an elongated face and chin.

These Russian heads of the Saviour in softening down the severe and aged type common to Byzantium, assume a physiognomy not sufficiently intellectual for the Greatest of Teachers. These "images" in fact inspire little reverence except with blind worshippers; they are mostly wrought up and renovated, so as to fulfil the preconceived conditions of sanctity: undefined generality, weakness, smoothness, and blackness, are the common characteristics of these supposititious heads of the Saviour. It will thus again be easily understood how opposite has been the practice of the Eastern and Western Churches; it is a striking fact that at the time when, in Italy, under Leonardo da Vinci, Raphael and others, the mystery of a God manifest in the flesh had been as it were solved by a perfected art, this Russian Church was still under bondage to the once accepted but now discarded notion that the Redeemer ought to be represented as one who had no form or comeliness. Art in the Western world gained access to the beautiful, the perfect, and the divine, as soon as it was permitted to the painter or the sculptor to develop to uttermost perfection the idea of the Man-God. All such conceptions of the infinite, whether it be that of Jupiter in pagan periods, or of Christ under our divine dispensation, have always been the life and inspiration of the arts. But in Russia ignoble heads of Christ convinced me that such life and inspiration were denied. And I look upon the head of Christ as the turning point in the Christian art of a nation. If that head be conceived of unworthily there is no possibility that prophets, apostles, martyrs, shall receive their due.

LA LAVRA, KIEF.

NIJNI-NOVGOROD

ANTONIO GALLENGA

Nijni-Novgorod, or Lower New-town, is older than Moscow, and only not so old as Novgorod the Great, which was a contemporary of Venice, and was still new when the semi-fabulaus Ruric and his Varangians are supposed to have given their name to Russia.

Nijni-Novgorod, which everybody here calls simply "Nijni," dates from 1222; and mention of its fair occurs, we are told, in 1366, since which epoch its celebration has suffered very rare and only violent interruption.

To understand why this venerable spot should have been for so many years, and should be still, so extensively favoured by the world's trade, it is hardly necessary to see it. We only need bear in mind that Nijni lies near the confluence of the Oka and the Volga, two of the greatest rivers of this Russia which alone of all countries of Europe may be said to have great rivers; the Volga having a course of 2,320 miles, and the Oka, a mere tributary, of 850 miles.

It is the position which the Saöne and the Rhone have made for Lyons; the position for which St. Louis is indebted to the Mississippi and Missouri; the position which Corientes will soon owe to the Parana and the Paraguay.

Nijni lies at the very centre of that water communication which joins the Caspian and the Black Sea to the White Sea and the Baltic, and which, were it always summer, might almost have enabled Russia to dispense with roads and railroads.

But Nijni is, besides, the terminus of the railway from Moscow. That line places this town and its fair in communication with all the lines of Russia and the Western World, while the Volga, with its tributary, the Kama, leads to Perm, and the Pass of the Ural Mountains, and the vast regions of Siberia and Central Asia.

Nijni-Novgorod is thus one of the most important links between the two great continents, the point of contact between Asiatic wealth and European industry; and its fair the best meeting-place for the interchange of commodities between the nations that still walk, ride, or row at the rate of three to five miles an hour, and those who fly on the wings of steam at the rate of thirty to fifty.

The site of Nijni is somewhat like what I still remember of St. Louis after a seventeen years' interval. We travelled from Moscow over a distance of 273 miles in thirteen hours. For the last hour or two before we reached our journey's end, we had on our right the river Oka and a hilly ridge rising all along it and forming its southern bank.

On alighting at the station we drove through a flat, marshy ground, intersected by broad canals, to a triangular space between the Oka and the Volga at their confluence, where the fair is held.

We went through the maze of bazaars and market buildings, of rows of booths, shops and stalls, eating and drinking sheds, warehouses and counting-houses. We struggled through long lines of heavy-laden country carts, and swarms of clattering *droskies*, all striving to force their way along with that hurry-skurry that adds to confusion and lessens speed; and we came at last to a long pontoon bridge, over which we crossed the Oka, and beyond which rises the hill-range or ravine, on the top and at the foot of which is built the straggling town of Nijni-Novgorod.

Nijni-Novgorod is a town of 45,000 inhabitants, and, like most Russian towns, it occupies a space which could accommodate half a million of people. Like many old Russian towns, also, it is laid out on the pattern of Moscow, as far as its situation allowed; and, to keep up the resemblance, it boasts a Kremlin of its own, a grim, struggling citadel with battlemented walls and mediæval towers over its gates, with its scores of Byzantine churches, most of them with their five cupolas *de rigueur*, clustering together like a bunch of radishes—one big radish between four little radishes—but not as liberally covered with gilding as those which glisten on the top of sacred buildings in St. Petersburg or Moscow; down the slopes and ravines are woods and gardens, with coffee-houses and eating-houses, and other places of popular entertainment.

It is a town to be admired on the outside and at a distance as a picture, but most objectionable as a residence on account of its marvellous distances and murderous pavement, a stroll on which reminds you of the martyrdom of those holy pilgrims who, to give glory to God, walked with dry peas in their shoes.

The pavements are bad in Nijni town, but worse in Nijni fair, for if in the former all is hard, sharp, uneven flint, in the latter, what is not wood is mud, and what is not mud is dust, for heavy showers alternate with stifling heat; and, after a three hours' drought one would say that these good people, who live half in and half out of a swamp, and who drink anything rather than water, can never spare a poor drop to slake the pulverized clay of their much trodden thoroughfares.

With all these drawbacks, however, and even with the addition of its villainous smells, this is an interesting and striking spot. No place can boast of a more sublime view than one can get here from the Imperial Palace and

Terrace, or from the church-domes or spires on the Kremlin; or, even better, from the Esplanade of Mouravief's Folly—a tower erected by the well-known General of that name on the highest and foremost ravine, and on the summit of which he had planned to place a fac-simile of the famous Strassburg clock, but constructed on so gigantic a scale that hours and minutes, the moon's phases, the planets' cycles and all besides, should be distinctly visible from every locality of the town and fair for miles and miles around.

From any of those vantage-grounds on the hill look down. The town is at your feet; the fair—a city, a Babylon of shops—stretches beyond the bridge; the plain, a boundless ocean of green, field and forest, dotted here and there with church-spires and factory-shafts at prodigious distances; and the two broad rivers, bearing the tribute of remote regions from north and south in numberless boats and lighters, and neat gallant steamers; the two streams meeting here at right angles just below the pontoon-bridge where an immense five-domed church of recent construction has been reared to mark and hallow the spot.

Down at the fair, in the centre of its hubbub, rises the governor's summer-place. The governor dwells there with his family during the few weeks of the fair (mid-August to mid-September), coming down hither from the Imperial Palace in the town Kremlin, and occupying the upper floor. The whole basement, the entrance-hall, and all passages—with the exception of a narrow, private, winding staircase—are invaded by the crowd and converted into a bazaar, the noisiest in the fair, where there is incessant life and movement, and music and hurly-burly at every hour between noon and night—a lively scene upon which his Excellency and his guests and friends look down from the balcony after their five o'clock dinner, smoking their cigarettes, and watching the policemen as they pounce like trained hawks on the unwary pick-pockets prowling among the crowd.

Of this immense mass of strangers now in Nijni, the town itself, and especially the upper town, sees and hears but little.

The fair has its own ground, on its own side of the bridge, its own hotels and lodging-houses, its own churches, chapels, theatres, eating, gambling, and other houses, its long straight streets and boulevards, and pleasure as well as business resorts.

It has its fine Chinese Row, though Chinamen have lately discontinued their attendance; it has rich traders' temporary homes, fitted up with comfort, and even taste and luxury; and it has its charity dormitory, a vast wooden shed, built by Court Ignatieff, and bearing his name, intended to accommodate 250 houseless vagrants, but alas! in a place where there must be 20,000, if not 200,000 persons answering that description.

Of women coming to this market the number is comparatively small—one, I should say, for every 100 men; of ladies not one in 10,000, or 100,000.

Of those who muster sufficiently strong at the evening promenade on the Boulevard, indigenous or resident, for the most part, rather the look than the number is formidable; and it is here in Nijni, as it is generally in Russia, that a Mussulman becomes convinced of the wisdom of his Arabian prophet, who invented the yashmak as man's best protection, and hallowed it; for of the charms of most Russian women, blessed are those who believe without seeing!

In working hours only men and beasts are to be seen—a jumble and scramble of men and beasts: car-loads of goods; piles of hogsheads, barrels, bales, boxes, and bundles, merchandise of all kinds, of every shape, colour, or smell, all lying in a mass topsy-turvy, higgledy-piggledy; the thoroughfares blocked up, the foot-paths encumbered; chaos and noise all-pervading; and yet, by degrees, almost imperceptibly, you will see everything going its way, finding its own place; for every branch of trade has, or was at least intended to have, here its appointed abode; and there are Tea Rows; Silversmiths and Calico Streets; Fur Lanes; Soap, Candle, and Caviare Alleys; Photograph, Holy Images, and Priestly Vestments Bazaars; Boot, Slop, Tag and Rag Marts and Depositories—all in their compartments, kin with kin, and like with like; and everything is made to clear out of the way, and all is smoothed down; all subsides into order and rule, and not very late at night—quiet.

The Tartars do the most of the work.

They are the descendants of the old warriors of Genghis Khan and Timour the Lame, of the ruthless savages who for 200 years overran all Russia, spreading death and desolation wherever their coursers' hoofs trod, making slaves of the people, and tributary vassals of their Princes; but, who by their short-sighted policy favoured the rise of that dynasty of Moscow Grand Princes, who presently became strong enough to extend their sway both over Russ and Tartar.

The great merchants of Moscow and St. Petersburg or their representatives and partners come here for a few days, partners and clerks taking up the task by turns, according as business allows them absence from their chief establishments.

They bring here no goods, but merely samples of goods—tea, cotton, woollen and linen tissues, silk, cutlery, jewellery, and generally all articles of European (home Russian) manufacture.

They have most of them good apartments in the upper floors of their warehouses; they see their customers, mostly provincial retail dealers; they show their samples, drive their bargains, receive orders, attend on 'Change (for they have a *Bourse* at the fair, near the bridge), smoke indoors (for in the streets that indulgence is forbidden all over the fair for fear of fire), lunch or dine together often by mutual invitation.

They are gentlemenly men, young men for the most part (for their elders are at home minding the main business), young Russians or Russified Germans, some of whom adopt and even affect and exaggerate Russian feeling and habits; young men to whom it seems to be a principle that easy-made money should be readily spent; leisurely, business young men, who sit up late and get up later, take the world and its work and pleasure at their ease; understand little and care even less about politics; profess to be neither great readers nor great thinkers; but are, as a rule, free-handed, hospitable, sociable, most amiable, and anything rather than unintelligent men.

Of all the articles of trade which come to court public favour in Nijni, the most important and valuable is tea; and although the Moscow merchants, by the excellence of their sea-faring tea, chiefly imported from Odessa or through England, have almost entirely driven from the market the caravan tea, still about one-tenth of the enormous quantity of tea sold here is grown in the north of China, and comes overland from Kiakhta, the city on the border between the Asiatic-Russian and the Celestial Empire.

I was curious to compare the taste of some of the very best qualities of both kinds, and was brought to the conclusion, confirmed by the opinion of gentlemen interested in the sale of sea-faring tea, that, although some of their own is more high-flavoured and stronger, there is in the Kiakhta tea an exquisite delicacy, which will always receive in its favour a higher price. The difference, I am told, mainly arises from the fact that the caravan tea, exposed to the air during its twelve months' journey in loose and clumsy and much-shaken paper and sheep-skin bundles, gets rid of the tannin and other gross substances, a process of purification which cannot be effected in the necessarily sealed and hermetically-closed boxes in which it reaches Europe by the sea-route; so that if sea-faring tea, like port-wine, easily recommends itself to the taste and nerves of a strong, hard-working man, a dainty, refined lady will give preference to a cup of Kiakhta tea, as she would to a glass of Château Yquem.

The interest of a European, however, would be chiefly attracted by what is less familiar in his own part of the world; and, short of an actual journey to the remote regions of Siberia and Central Asia, nothing is calculated to give him a more extensive idea of the produce of those Trans-Uralian Russian possessions than a survey of the goods they send here for sale.

What astonishes a stranger at first sight is the quantity. You may walk for hours along yards and sheds, the repositories of iron from Siberia. You pass hundreds of shops of malachite and lapis-lazuli, and a variety of gold and silver work and precious stones from the Caucasus, cut with all the minute diligence of Asiatic skill. You will see Turkish carpets, Persian silks, and above all things the famous Orenburg shawls, so finely knitted, and with such patience that one can (they say, but I have not made the experiment), be made to pass through a lady's ring, though they be so broad on all sides as to wrap the lady all around from head to foot.

One may, besides, have his choice of hundreds and thousands of those delightful curiosities and knickknacks, recommendable less for their quaintness than for the certainty one feels that there is no possible use in the world they may be put to.

There is no novelty at Nijni; no new shape, pattern, or colour just coming out to catch popular favour; no unknown mechanical contrivance; no discovery likely to affect human progress and brought here for the entertainment of the intelligent, un-commercial visitor. There are only the shop-keeper and his customer, though it is a wholesale shop and on a very large scale.

The fair, moreover, has not the duration that is generally allowed for an Exhibition.

NIJNI-NOVGOROD (BRIDGE OF THE FAIR).

Though officially opened on the 27th of July, the fair does not begin in good earnest till the 18th of August; and it reaches its height on the 27th, when accounts are settled, and payments ensue; after which, goods are removed, and the grounds cleared; only a portion of the business lingering throughout September.

About half a score of days, out of the two months during which the fair is held, are all that may have attraction for the generality of strangers. And although many come from all parts of Russia, and from foreign countries, I do not think they tarry here for pleasure beyond two or three days.

It would be interesting to anticipate what change a few weeks will effect in this scene which is now so full of life, bustle, and gaiety; this stage, where so great a variety of human beings from nearly all regions of the world, with their money or money's worth, with their hopes and fears, their greed and extravagance, all their good and evil instincts and faculties at play.

In a few weeks the flags will be furled, the tents struck; the pontoon-bridge removed; the shops closed; hotels, bazaars, and churches, all private and public edifices, utterly deserted and silent; and every house stripped of the last stick of valuable furniture; every door locked, barred, and sealed; the place left to take care of itself.

For autumn rains and spring thaws must set in, when the seven or eight square miles of the ground of the fair, as well as the country to an immense extent, will be under water.

THE VOLGA BASIN

The Great River—Kasan, Tsaritzin—Astrakhan

ANTONIO GALLENGA

It is hardly possible to travel on the Volga without falling in love with the great river at first sight.

The range of low hills which we had on our right as we descended the Oka continued now on the same side as we came down the Volga. The Volga, however, has nothing of the wild, erratic instincts of its tributary. It is a grand, calm, dignified stream, keeping to its course as a respectable matron, and gliding down in placid loveliness, without weir or leap, fall or rapids, or break of any kind—a fine, broad, almost unrippled sheet of water, with an even, steady, and grandly monotonous flow, like that of the stanzas of Tasso.

Its width, so far as eye can judge, does not greatly exceed that of the Thames at Gravesend, but it is always the same from the bridge at Twer above Moscow to the only other bridge, one mile in length, between Syzran and Samara; everywhere the same "full bumper" for a run of 2,000 English miles.

Though the Volga is numbered among the European rivers, and has its sources on the Valdaï hills between the European cities, St. Petersburg and Moscow, it is a frontier stream, and seemed intended to form the natural line of demarcation between two parts of the world—between two worlds.

Up to the middle of the Sixteenth Century, Kasan was the advanced guard of the Tartar hordes. These wandering tribes, which, profiting by dissensions among the Russian princes, overcame and overran all Russia, weakened in their turn by division, fell back from the main part of the invaded territory, but still held for some time their own on the Volga, from Kasan to Astrakhan, till they were utterly routed and brought under Russian sway by Ivan the Terrible.

Even then, however, though their strength was broken, their spirit was untamed. The men of high warrior caste who survived their defeat sought a refuge among their kindred tribes further east, at Samarkand, Bokhara, and Khiva, where the Russians have now overtaken them; but a large part of the mere multitude laid aside without giving up their arms, passively accepted without formally acknowledging the Tsar's sway, and abided in their tents,— swallowed at once, but very leisurely digested, by the all-absorbing Russian civilization.

Large bodies of the nation, however, migrated *en masse* from time to time, the lands they left vacant being rapidly filled up by bands of Cossacks, and by foreign (chiefly German), colonists.

For more than three centuries, though already mistress of Siberia and victorious in remote Asia, Russia proper might be considered as ending at the Volga; so that most of the older and most important towns south of Kasan and north of Astrakhan, such as Simbirsk, Syzran, Volsk, Saratof, Kamyshin, and Tsaritzin, lie on the right, or Russo-European bank of the stream.

Tsaritzin is at the head of the Delta of the Volga, and it lies 580 versts above Astrakhan, which is said to be at the river's mouth, but which is still 150 versts from the roadstead or anchorage, called the Nine Feet Station; the spot on the Caspian where sea navigation really begins.

At Tsaritzin we might have fancied ourselves in some brand-new town in one of the remote backwoods of America. It was nothing of a place before the railway reached it. No one can foretell what it may become before the locomotive travels past it. For under present circumstances all the postal service, the light goods and time-saving passenger traffic from all parts of Russia to Astrakhan, the Caspian and the Trans-Caspian region, or *vice versâ*, must pass between the Tsaritzin pier on the Volga and the platforms of the Tsaritzin railway station.

We did not see much of the upstart town, for the horrible clouds of thick, dung-impregnated dust would not allow us to keep our eyes open. But we perceived that almost every trace of what was once little better than a second rate fortress and a village was obliterated; the old inhabitants were nowhere, and a bustling set of new settlers were sharing the broad area among themselves, taking as much of it as suited their immediate wants, and extending it to the utmost limits of their sanguine expectations; drawing lines of streets at great distances, tracing the sides of broad squares and crescents, and laying the foundations of what would rise in time into shops and houses, hotels, bazaars, theatres and churches.

Tzaritzin when we saw it was merely the embryo of a city. Those that may visit it a score of years hence will tell us what they find it.

Two more nights and a day down the sluggish waters of the main channel of the Volga landed us on the tenth day after our departure from Nijni-Novgorod, at Astrakhan, where we stayed a whole week.

From Tsaritzin to Astrakhan the Volga flows through the Steppe, the great Asiatic grass desert extending from the Caucasus to the frontier of China. The wild tenants of this wilderness, the various tribes of Tartars, once the terror of East and West, were like a vast ocean of human beings swayed to and fro by nomadic and predatory instincts, which for centuries threatened to overwhelm and efface every vestige of the world's civilization.

The Russians who were first invested and overpowered by the flood, were able by the valour and more by the craft of their princes, first to stem the tide, then to force it back, and in the end to rear such bulwarks as might for ever baffle its fury, and prevent its further onset.

Such bulwarks were once the strong places of Kasan and Astrakhan, the former seats of Tartar hordes, which the Tsars of Moscow made their bases of operations for the indefinite extension of their civilized empire over Tartar barbarism.

For the experience of centuries had proved that the Steppe was not everywhere and altogether an irreclaimable land, nor the Tartars an utterly untameable race.

Astrakhan, like Kasan, is a Russian town, of whose 50,000 inhabitants one-fourth or one-fifth at least are tamed Tartars, and the sands around which can be made to yield grapes and peaches, and a profusion of melons and watermelons. Beyond the immediate neighbourhood, over the whole province or "Government" of Astrakhan, stretches the vast land of the Steppe, the wide and thin pasture-grounds on which the Tartar tribes roam at will with their flocks; a pastoral set of men; without fixed homes, and, in our sense of the word, without laws; and yet perfectly harmless and peaceful—exempt, at least till very lately, from military service, and only paying a tribute of 45,000 roubles, at so much a head for each horse, ox, or camel, ranging over an extent of 7,000,000 dessiatines (20,000,000 acres) of land, an area of 224,514 kilometers, or about half of that of France, with a population, including that of the capital, of 601,514 inhabitants.

Astrakhan is a modern town, with the usual broad, straight streets, most of them boasting no other pavement than sand, with brick side-walks, much worn and dilapidated, and, like those of Buenos Ayres and many other American cities, so raised above the roadway as to require great attention from those who do not wish to run the risk of broken shins.

The town has its own Kremlin, apart from the citadel. The Kremlin is a kind of cathedral-close, with the cathedral and the archbishop's palace, and several monasteries and priests' habitations. The whole town, besides, and the environs, as usual in Russia, muster more churches than they can number priests or worshippers.

In a walk of two or three miles I took outside the town and as far as the cemeteries, I had a scattered group of at least half a score of churches all around me, but there was scarcely a human habitation within sight.

The governor's palace is a low building over a row of shops in the main square of the city. The square itself and the thoroughfares were enveloped in thick clouds of blinding dust, almost as troublesome as that of Tsaritzin; but on the whole, the place is less unclean than one might expect from a population made up of Russians, Tartars, Calmucks, Persians, Armenians and Jews.

The Volga and the hundred channels which constitute its delta, and the northern shores of the Caspian Sea into which they flow, yield more fish than the coasts of Norway and Newfoundland put together. The nets employed in catching them would, if laid side by side on the ground in all their length, extend over a line of 40,000 versts, or twice the distance from St. Petersburg to Tashkend and back. The annual produce of these Astrakhan fisheries—sturgeon, sterlet, salmon, pike, shad, etc.—amounts to 10,000,000 puds of fish (the pud thirty-six English pound weight) of the value of 20,000,000 roubles, the herrings alone yielding a yearly income of 4,000,000 roubles. With the exception of the caviare, which is sold all over the world, the produce of these fisheries, salted or pickled, is destined for home consumption, and travels all over the empire, although as far as I have been, I have found everywhere the waters equally well-stocked by nature with every description of fish; a provident dispensation, since the Russian clergy, like the Roman Catholic, are indefatigable in their promotion of what they call "the Apostles' trade," by their injunction of 226 fast or fish days throughout the year.

The Delta of the Volga and the Caspian Sea lie twenty-five metres below the level of the Black Sea.

The city of Astrakhan, placed on the left bank of the main channel of the Delta, and, as I said, 150 versts above its anchorage, becomes like an island in the midst of a vast sea when the Volga comes down in its might with the thaw of the northern ice in late spring; and most of its lowest wards would be overwhelmed were it not for the dikes that encompass it like a town in Holland.

The eight principal branches and the hundred minor channels and outlets of the Delta, breaking up the land into a labyrinth of hundreds of islets, are then blended together in one watery surface, out of which only the crests of these islets emerge with isolated villages, with log-huts and long whitewashed buildings, and high-domed churches, all dammed and diked up like the town itself—Tartar villages, Calmuck villages, Cossack villages, all or most of them fishers' homes and fishing establishments—a population of 20,000 to 30,000 souls being thus scattered on the bare sand-hills and dunes; men of all race, colour, and faith, all employed in the same fishing pursuit; the Tartars and Calmucks usually as rank and file, the Russians and other Europeans as overseers, foremen, and skilled labourers.

From Astrakhan, the queen of the Steppes, to Tiflis the queen of the Caucasus, we had a choice of routes.

Tourists from England, or from any part of Western Europe, may easily visit the great mountain-chain on which Prometheus was found, by crossing the Black Sea from Constantinople or from Odessa, and landing at Poti, where the Russians have constructed a railway to Tiflis, once the capital of Georgia, now the residence of the Governor-General of the whole Caucasus region.

A traveller from the north, bound to the same goal, can take the train at Moscow, and come down by rail, *via* Rostov-on-the-Don, all the way to Vladikavkas, a distance of 1,803 versts; and about 200 additional versts, by post, over a good military road, and across the main Caucasian chain, will bring him from Vladikavkas to Tiflis.

But we had descended the Volga, and were now near its mouth. We had to go down the Volga to the Nine Feet Station below Astrakhan, embark there on the Caspian Sea, and cross over either to Baku, whence we could go by post round the mountain-chain at its southern extremity as far as Tiflis; or land at Petrofsk, and travel along the chain to Vladikavkas and the good military road across the chain to Tiflis.

We gave our preference to the last-named route.

We left Astrakhan at ten in the evening on board a heavy barge belonging to the Caucasus and Mercury steam-navigation company, towed by a tug down stream at the rate of five or six miles an hour.

We were all that afternoon and night, and part of the following day, descending the main channel of the Volga, and it was past noon before we reached the Nine Feet Station, for so they call the roadstead above which vessels of more than nine feet draught dare not venture.

All sight of land, of the seventy larger islands of the Delta, and even of the minor islets, and of the lowest sand-banks, had been lost for several hours, and we were here in the open sea, though scarcely beyond the boundary that the Creator has elsewhere fixed between land and water. For the Station which, if I can allow myself an apparent Irishism, is a moveable one, has to be pushed forward almost day by day as the sands of the Volga silt up far beyond the choked-up lands of the Delta, encroaching with a steady inroad on the depths of the waves; the Steppe everywhere widening as the sea dwindles, and suggesting the thought that the whole region that is now Steppe must in remote ages have been sea, and that whatever is now sea, must in time become Steppe.

Indeed, it seems not impossible to calculate how many years or centuries it may take for the sands of the Volga, aided by those of the Ural and the Emba on the eastern, and of the Kuma, the Terek, and the Kur or Kura, with its tributary the Aras, on the western shore, to fill up the land-locked Caspian, though its extreme depth, according to the Gazetteers, is 600 feet, and the area covered by it probably exceeds 180,000 square miles, a surface as large as that of Spain.

Kasan, once the residence of a redoubted horde, was probably, under Tartar sway, in a great measure a mere encampment, chiefly a city of tents; for whatever the guide-books may say, there is no positive evidence of its present buildings belonging to a date anterior to the Russian Conquest.

Its situation probably recommended itself to the Tartars chiefly on the score of strength; for although it stands high above the river, its present distance from it is at least three miles, and it is surrounded by a sandy and marshy plain, intersected by the channels of the Kasana river, erratic water-courses which may have proved sufficient obstacles to the onset of an invader, but which raise no less serious hindrances to the conveyance of goods from the landing-place to the town; an inconvenience hitherto not removed by the tramway, as it as yet only carries passengers.

Kasan is on the main line of communication between Central Russia and Siberia.

The travellers bound to that bourne embark here on steamers that go down the Volga as far as its confluence with the Kama, a tributary stream, and thence ascend the Kama, which is navigable all the way to Perm. From Perm a railway runs up to the Pass of the Ural mountains to Ekaterinenburg, probably to be in course of time continued to Tiumen, Tobolsk, Tomsk, Irkutsk, the Baikal Lake, the Chinese frontier at Kiakhta, the banks of the Amoor, and the shores of the Pacific Ocean.

Along this route it is calculated that some £3,000,000 worth of merchandise are brought yearly from Siberia down the Kama and up the Volga to the Nijni-Novgorod fair.

Kasan is a highly flourishing city. It has a population of 90,000 to 100,000 inhabitants, one-fourth of whom are Tartars.

These descendants of the old Nomad race are now here at home, and live in the city perfectly at peace with their Russian fellow-subjects, though being Mahometans, they have distinct, if not separate, quarters, and mosques and a burial-ground of their own. It would seem impossible for two races which have so little reason for mutual good-will, to show so little disposition to quarrel. But it should be remembered that Sclav and Tartar were not in former times so far asunder in manners, in language, in polish, nor so free from admixture in blood as the Russians fondly believe.

The town has its Kremlin, on the site of the old citadel, with its cathedral and other churches, and several "telescope towers," if they may be so called, built on several stories, dwindling in size from floor to floor as they rise one above the other, so that one can conceive how they might easily sink into one another and shut up like a spy-glass. The great brick tower of Pier Crescenzi in Rome is such a tower; and here are many in the same style at Moscow and in most other old Russian cities. Kasan has several public edifices of some pretension: the Admiralty; the University—one of the seven of the Empire, etc. But we had enough of it all after two or three hours, and were glad to shun the heat of the rest of the day in the cool sitting-room of Commonen's Hotel, which alone may be taken as a voucher for the high degree of civilization reached by Kasan.

We gave even less time to the other cities of the Volga, not thinking it always worth while to alight at all the stations, though the steamer stopped at some of these for many a long, weary hour.

With the exception of Kasan, Samara, and Astrakhan, the most important cities are, as I said, on the right or Russian bank of the River; and three of them, Syzran, Saratof, and Tsaritzin, are connected by various railways with Moscow and all the other important centres of life in the Empire.

The Volga, which between Nijni-Novgorod and Kasan flows in an almost straight easterly direction, takes a turn to the southward after leaving Kasan and the confluence of the Kama; but it makes a loop below Simbirsk, turning eastward to Samara, and again west to Syzran, after which it resumes its southerly course to Saratof, Tsaritzin, and Astrakhan.

The railway from Moscow to Syzran, upon reaching Syzran, crosses the Volga on an iron bridge, one verst and a half, or one English mile, in length, and high enough to allow the largest steamer pass without lowering its funnel—a masterpiece of engineering greatly admired by the people here, who describe it as the longest bridge in Russia and in the world.

We went under it at midnight by a dim moonlight which barely allowed us to see it looming in the distance not much bigger than a telegraph-wire drawn all across the valley, the gossamer line of the bridge and all the landscape round striking us as dreamlike and unreal.

After crossing the river the railway proceeds to Samara, and hence 419 versts further to Orenburg, a large and thriving place on the Ural river, the spot from which the straightest and probably the shortest way is, or will be, open to all parts of Siberia or Central Asia; preferable, I should think, to that of Perm and Ekaterinenburg above-mentioned, which is now the most frequented route.

Beyond Syzran and Samara the river scenery, which has hitherto been verdant, assumes a southerly aspect; the hill-sides sloping to the river have a parched and faded brown look; the hill-tops are bared and seamed with chalky ravines; every trace of the forests has disappeared; and it is only at rare intervals that the banks are clad with the verdure of the new growth.

FROM THE RAMPARTS OF THE KREMLIN NIJNI-NOVGOROD.

From Nijni to Tsaritzin we have stopped at more than thirty different stations, and no pen could describe the stir and bustle of goods and passengers that awaited us at every wharf and pier.

Several of these stations are towns of 50,000 to 100,000 inhabitants, and, besides their corn trade and tobacco, they all deal in some articles of necessity or luxury, of which they produce enough for their own, if not always for their neighbours', consumption.

Everywhere one sees huge buildings—steam flour-mills, tobacco-factories, salt-mines, soap and candle factories, tanneries—and last, not least, palaces for the sale of *koumiss* or fermented mare's milk, a sanitary beverage; and extensive establishments, especially near Samara, for the *koumiss* cure,— fashionable resorts as watering-places, frequented by persons affected by consumption, and other real or imaginary ailments.

There is something appalling in the thought that all this busy, and, on the whole, merry life on the banks of the Volga must come to a dead stand-still for six or seven months in the year. I have been vainly taxing my brain to guess what may become of the captains, mates and crews of the 700 steamers, and of the 5,000 heavy barges with which the river is now swarming; of the porters, agents, clerks, and other officials at the various stations; of the thousands of women employed to carry all the firewood from the piers to the steam-boats. What becomes of all these, and of the men and horses toiling at the steam-row and tow-boats on the Oka, the Kama, the Don, the Dnieper, and a hundred other rivers during the long season in which the vast plains of Russia are turned into a howling wilderness of snow and ice from end to end?

Railway communication and sledge-driving may, by doubling their activity, afford employment to some of the men and beasts who would otherwise be doomed to passive and torpid hybernation. But much of the work that is practicable in other countries almost throughout the year—nearly all that is done in the open air—suffers here grievous interruption.

What should we think in England of a six months' winter, in which the land were as hard as a rock, in which all the cattle had to be kept within doors, in which the bricklayer's trowel and the road-mender's roller had to be laid aside?

And, by way of compensation, what mere human bone and muscle can stand the crushing labour by which the summer months, with their long days of twenty hours' sunlight, must make up for the winter's forced idleness; in a climate too, where, as far as my own experience goes, the heat is hardly less oppressive and stifling than in the level lands of Lombardy or the Emilia?

ODESSA

From Yalta to Sebastopol there are two routes. One strikes across the Yaïla hills to Simpheropol, whence we could proceed by rail to Sebastopol; the other runs along the coast, high up on the hills, to the Baidar Gate and through the Baidar Valley leading to Balaclava and the other well-known spots encompassing the ruins of what was once the great naval station of the Russians on the Black Sea.

We chose the coast route, and travelled for five hours in the afternoon over forty-eight versts of the most singular road in the world.

It rambles up and down along the side of the hills—as a road did once on the beautiful Cornice along the Ligurian Riviera—midway between the upper hill crest and the sea, having on the right the mountains, a succession of wall-like, perpendicular, hoary cliffs, between 1,500 feet and 2,000 feet high, a great wall riven into every variety of fantastic shapes of bastions, towers, and pyramids, all bare and rugged, crumbling here and there into huge boulders, strewn along the slopes down to the road, across the road, and further down to the water-edge, a scene which might befit the battle-field of the Titans against the gods; and on the left the wide expanse of the waters, with a coast like a fringe of little glens and creeks and headlines, and the sun's glitter on the waves like Dante's "*tremolar della marina*" on the shore of Purgatory.

Between the road and the sea far below us, in the distance, embosomed in woods still untouched by the autumn frosts, lay the marine villas of Livadia, Orianda, Alupka, etc., very Edens, where on their first annexation of the Crimea the wealthy Russians sought a refuge against the horrors of their wintry climate; more recently, Imperial residences—Livadia, the darling of the late Emperor; Orianda, now a mere wreck from the recent conflagration, the seat of the Grand Duke Constantine; Alupka, the abode of Prince Woronzoff, the son of the benevolent genius of these districts, the road-maker, the patron of Yalta, the second founder of Odessa.

A scene of irresistible enchantment is the whole of what the Russians emphatically call their "southern coast." And, as if to enhance its charm by contrast, everything changes as you pass the Baidar Gate, and when you have crossed the Baidar Valley the balmy air becomes raw and chill, the bald mountains tame and common-place, and the long descent is through an ashy-gray country, swept over by an icy blast, saddened by a lowering sky, unrelieved by a flower, a bush, or a cottage. So marvellous is the power of mere position, so great the difference between the two sides of the same mountain-wall! You pass at once from a garden to a steppe.

Away from these sheltering rocks, away from the southern slopes of the Caucasian ridges, you are in Russia. The only mountains throughout all the rest of the Tsar's European territories are the Urals, which nowhere reach even the heights of the Apennines, which do not form everywhere a continuous chain, and which run in almost a straight line from north to south. From the icy pole the wind sweeping over the frozen ocean and the snowy wastes of the northern provinces finds nowhere a hindrance to its cruel blasts, and spreads its chill over the whole land with such steady keenness as to make the climate of the exposed parts of the Black Sea coast almost as wintry as that of the White Sea. At Odessa in the early days of October both our hotel and the private houses we had occasion to enter had already put up double doors and windows, and people lived in apartments as hermetically closed as if their homes had been in St. Petersburg.

We slept at Baidar, a Tartar village, where a maiden of that Moslem race was the only attendant at the Russian inn, and on the morrow we drove in three hours to Sebastopol, a distance of forty-two versts.

Sebastopol has still not a little of that Pompeian look which it bore on the day after its surrender to the Western Allies in 1856. We drove through miles of ruins, the roofless walls staring at us from the dismantled doors and windows, the dust from the rubbish-heaps of brick and mortar blinding us at every turning of the streets, though, we were told, the city is looking up and thriving, and both house-rent and building-ground are rising in price from day to day.

We had to wait two days for the "Olga," detained by stress of weather, and it was with a hope of enlivening ourselves that, under the escort of the English Consul, a Crimean veteran who takes care of the heroic dead, and actually lives with as well as for them, we drove out to some of the eleven English cemeteries, to the house where Lord Raglan died, and the monument marking the spot where "the six hundred rode into the jaws of death"—those localities made forever memorable by a war than which none was ever undertaken with less distinct aims, none fought with greater valour, none brought to an end with less important results.

We left Sebastopol at three in the afternoon in the "Olga," and landed at Odessa in the morning at ten. Throughout the first week after our arrival, we never caught a single glimpse of the sun. Odessa, like Sebastopol, like Kertch, like Astrakhan, and other places lying on the edge of the Russian Steppe, seems habitually, under the influence of the wind in peculiar quarters, to be haunted by fogs that set in at sunrise and only sometimes clear off after sunset. During this gloomy state of the atmosphere the night is usually warmer than the day.

PLACE TUREMNAJA ODESSA.

Odessa has a magnificent position, for it lies high on ravines, which give it a wide command over its large harbour, lately improved, as well as on the open sea and coast, the striking feature of the place being its *boulevard*, a terrace or platform about 500 yards in length, laid out and planted as a promenade, looking out seawards and accessible by a flight of stairs of 150 steps from the landing-place.

Odessa is not an old town, but it looks brand-new, for there has been of late a great deal of building, and the crumbling nature of the stone keeps the mason and white-washer perpetually at work. It is lively, though monotonous, for its broad, straight streets are astir with business, and the rattle of hackney-carriages, heavy-laden vans, and tramway-cars is incessant. It boasts many private palaces and has few public edifices, and in its municipal institutions it is, or used to be, taxed with consulting rather more the purposes of luxury and ornament than the real wants of the people or the interests of charity.

Odessa is in Russia, but not of Russia, for among its citizens, we are told, possibly with exaggeration, more than one-third (70,000) are Jews, besides 10,000 Greeks and Germans, and Italians in good number. It is unlike any other Russian city, for it is tolerably well paved, has plenty of drinking-water, and rows of trees—however stunted, wind-nipped, and sickly—in every street. It is not Russian, because few Russians succeed here in business; but strenuous efforts are made to Russify it, for the names of the streets, which were once written in Italian as well as in Russian, are now only set up in Russian, unreadable to most foreign visitors; and the so-called "Italian Street"

(Strada Italiana), reminding one of what the town owes to its first settlers, has been rebaptized as "Pushkin Street." Of the three French newspapers which flourished here till very lately, not one any longer exists, for whatever is not Russian is discountenanced and tabooed in a town which, in spite of all, is not and never will be, Russian. French is, nevertheless, more generally understood than in most Russian cities, but Italian is dying off here as in all the Levant and the north coast of Africa, Italy losing as a united nation such hold as she had as a mere nameless cluster of divided states.

It is difficult to foresee what results the great change that is visibly going on in the economical and commercial conditions of the Russian Empire may have on the destinies of Odessa.

Half a century ago, if we may trust the statistics of the *Journal d' Odessa*, this city had only the third rank among the commercial places of Russia. At the head of all then was St. Petersburg, whose harbour was frequented by 1,500 to 2,000 vessels, the exports being 100,000,000 to 120,000,000 roubles, and the imports 140,000,000 to 160,000,000 roubles. Next in importance came Riga, with 1,000 to 1,500 vessels, 35,000,000 to 50,000,000 roubles exports, and 15,000,000 to 20,000,000 roubles imports; and Odessa, as third, received 600 to 800 vessels, her exports amounting from 25,000,000 to 30,000,000 roubles, and her imports from 20,000,000 to 25,000,000 roubles. The relative commercial importance of the three ports was, therefore, as twenty-five to six and five.

Matters have undergone a considerable alteration since then. St. Petersburg, whose imports and exports doubled in amount those of all the other ports of the Empire put together, has been gradually declining, the ports of Esthonia, Livonia, and Courland threatening to deprive her inconvenient harbour of a great part of the Baltic trade, and the centre of general business being rapidly removed from the present seat of Government to the old capital, Moscow. Riga, also, has been and is slowly sinking from its high position in the Baltic, and may, perhaps, eventually succumb to the active rivalry of Revel and Libau. Odessa, on the contrary, has been looking up for these many years, absorbing nearly all the Russian trade in the Black Sea, and rapidly rising from the third to the second rank as a seaport.

The main cause of the rise and progress of Odessa was owing to the development of agricultural enterprise in the provinces of what is called "Little" and "New Russia," or the "Black Earth Country" the granary of the Empire and for a long time of all Europe.

Beyond the steppes which encompass the whole southern seacoast of Russia, from the Sea of Azof to the Danube, there spreads far inland a fertile region, embracing the whole or part of the Governments of Podolia, Poltava, Kharkof, Kief, Voronei, Don Cossacks, etc., including the districts of what was once known as the "Ukraine," which was for many years debatable land between Poland, Turkey, and Russia, and on which roamed the mongrel bands of the Cossacks, an uncouth population recruited among the many tramps and vagabonds from the northern provinces, mixed with all the races of men with whom they came into contact, settling here and there in new, loose, and almost lawless communities, organized as military colonies, and perpetually shifting their allegiance from one to the other of these three Powers, till the policy and good fortune of Peter the Great and Catherine II. extended the sway of Russia over the whole territory.

At the close of the last century, and contemporaneously with the foundation of Odessa (1794), the bountiful nature of the soil of this region became known, and the country was overrun by colonists from "Great" or "Northern Russia," from Germany, and from Bulgaria and Wallachia; and its rich harvests were soon sufficient, not only to satisfy, but to exceed the wants of the whole Empire.

Odessa, endowed by its founder, Catherine II., with the privilege of a free port, which it enjoyed till after the war of the Crimea, monopolized during that time the export of the produce of this southern land, consisting chiefly of grain and wool; and its prosperity went on, always on the increase—affected only temporarily by wars and bad harvests—to such an extent that the total value of the exports, which was, in round numbers, about 52,000,000 roubles in 1871, rose to 86,000,000 roubles in 1878, to 88,000,000 roubles in 1879, and fell, owing to the bad harvest, to 56,000,000 roubles in 1880.

The Odessa trade was for a long time in the hands of Greek and Italian merchants, the original settlers in the town at its foundation, the produce being, before the invention of steamers, conveyed to Italy, France and England in Italian bottoms. But, of late years, preference being given to steamers over sailing vessels, and the Italians, either failing to perceive the value of time and the importance of the revolution that steam had effected, or lacking capital to profit by it, allowed the English to have the lion's share of the Black Sea trade, so that, in 1879, the English vessels entering the port of Odessa were 549 steamers and four sailing vessels, with 500,000 tons, while the Italians had only fifty steamers and 119 sailing vessels, with 85,700 tons. Next to the English were, in the same year, the Austrians (eighty-seven steam and 119 sailing vessels, 119,000 tons). The Russians, at home here, had 150 steam and eight sailing vessels and 180,000 tons.

Odessa, however, though she had so much of the trade to herself, had not of late years the whole of it. As the means of land and water conveyance improved, and especially after the construction of railways, a number of minor rivals arose all along the coast—Rostov, at the mouth of the Don;

Taganrog, Mariupol or Marianopolis, and Berdianski, on the north coast of the Sea of Azof, where Greek colonies are flourishing; Kherson, at the mouth of the Dnieper; Nicolaief, at the mouth of the Bug; and others. Odessa was thus reduced to the trade of the region to the west of the last-named river, having lost that of the provinces of Poltava, Kharkof, Kursk, Orel, Ekaterinoslaf, etc., and only retaining Kherson, Bessarabia, Volhynia, Kief, etc., which would still be sufficient for her commercial well-being.

But Odessa is threatened with a new and far more formidable rival in Sebastopol. Sebastopol, with all its inlets, is by far the most perfect harbour in the Black Sea, and has the inestimable advantage that it never freezes, while in Odessa the ice brings all trade to a standstill for two or three weeks every winter, and all the ports of Azof and the mouths of the rivers are frozen from November to March or even mid-April. Sebastopol has the additional advantage of being in the most direct and nearest communication by rail with Kharkof, the very heart of the Black Earth Country, and with Moscow, the centre of the Russian commercial and industrial business.

The people in Sebastopol have hopes that the Imperial Government, giving up all thought of bringing back their great Black Sea naval station from Nicolaief to its former seat, may not be unwilling that their fine harbour be turned to the purposes of trading enterprise, and even to favour it for a few years with the privileges of a free port.

SEBASTOPOL.

The citizens of Odessa, on the other hand, scout such expectations as over-sanguine, if not quite chimerical, laugh to scorn the idea that the Government may at any time lay aside its intention of going back with its naval establishment to Sebastopol; and, in that case, they contend that the juxtaposition of a commercial with an Imperial naval port would be as monstrous a combination as would be in France that of Marseilles and Toulon, or in England that of Portsmouth and Liverpool, in one and the same place.

They add that the railway between Moscow and Sebastopol is ill-constructed and almost breaking down; that, although it is by some hundred miles shorter than that from Odessa to Moscow, the express and mail trains are so arranged that the most rapid communication between north and south is effected between Odessa and St. Petersburg, which route is travelled over in less than three days.

Whichever of the contending parties may have the best of the argument, there is no doubt that, were even the Government to be favourable to the wishes of the people of Sebastopol, there would be no just reason for jealousy between the two cities, for Odessa has already proved that she can manage to grow richer than ever upon one-half of the trade of Southern Russia, while Sebastopol might safely rely on carrying on the other half— that other half which is now already in the hands of Taganrog, Mariupol, Nicolaief, etc. For all these ports of Azof and the mouths of the rivers, besides being closed by ice for at least four months in the year, are so shallow that no amount of dredging can keep back the silting sands, and vessels must anchor at distances of ten to twenty and even thirty miles outside the harbours.

THE DON COSSACKS

THOMAS MICHELL

Coming from the north, the first town of any importance in Southern Russia is Kursk, three hundred and thirty-five miles from Moscow in an almost direct line, the railway passing through the cities of Tula (the Russian Birmingham), and Orel, the centre of a rich agricultural district connected by rail, on the west, with Riga on the Baltic, and on the south-east with Tsaritzin on the Volga. Authentic records attest the existence of Kursk in 1032, and in 1095 it was held by Isiaslaf, son of Vladimir Monomachus, from whom it passed alternately to the Princes of Chernigof and of Pereyaslasl. In the Thirteenth Century it was razed to the ground by the Tartars. In 1586 the southern frontiers of Moscovy were fortified, and Kursk became one of the principal places on that line of defence against the Crimean Tartars and the Poles. Its disasters and sufferings as a military outpost ceased only towards the end of the Seventeenth Century, after Little Russia (the more southerly districts watered by the Dnieper), submitted to the Tsar Alexis.

We are now almost in the heart of the *Chernozem*, or black soil country, so called from the rich black loam of which its surface is composed to a depth of two and three yards and more. These vast plains were known to Herodotus, Strabo, and other ancient geographers only in their present *Steppe*, or flat and woodless condition. It is a great relief to the eye to see at last a handsomely-built city like Kursk, perched, relatively to the surrounding flatness, on an elevation and almost smothered in the verdure of numerous gardens. There is, however, not much to see within it, for even the churches are mostly not older than the second half of the Eighteenth Century.

The more southerly part of the province of Kursk is in the *Ukraine*, or ancient border country. Its semi-nomadic population obtained in early days the designation of Cossacks. This word is not Sclavonic, but Turkish; and although it long denoted in Russia a free man, or, rather, a man free to do anything he chose, it had been used by the Tartar hordes to designate the lower class of their horsemen. From the princes of the House of Rurik these southerly districts passed into the possession of Lithuania, and, later, into those of Poland. Little Russia was another arbitrary name anciently given to a great part of what has been also known as the Ukraine. No fixed geographical limits can be assigned to either of these designations, and especially to the Ukraine of the Poles or the Muscovites; for as the borders or marshes became safe and populated, they were absorbed by the dominant power, and ultimately incorporated into provinces. Little Russia is, in fact, a term now used only to denote the Southern Russians as distinguished principally from the Great Russians of the more central part of the empire.

There is a strongly-marked difference in the outward appearance, the mode of life, and even the cast of thought of these two branches of the Sclav race. The language of the Little Russian, or *Hohol*, as he is contemptuously called by his more vigorous northern brother, is a cross between the Polish and the Russian, although nearer akin to the Muscovite than to the Polish tongue. Ethnographically, also, the Little Russians become gradually fused with the White Russians of the north-west (Mohilef and Vitebsk) and with the Slovaks of the other side of the Carpathians. The *Malo-Ros* (Little Russian) is physically a better, though a less muscular man than the *Veliko-Ros*, or Great Russian. He is taller, finer-featured, and less rude and primitive in his domestic surroundings. The women have both beauty and grace, and make the most of those qualities by adorning themselves in neat and picturesque costumes, resembling strongly those of the Roumanian and Transylvanian peasantry. Their houses are not like those of other parts of Russia—log huts, full, generally, of vermin and cockroaches; but wattled, thatched, and whitewashed cottages, surrounded by gardens, and kept internally in order and cleanliness.

Their lives are altogether more happy, although their songs, full of deep feeling, and not without a vein of romance are, like those of all Sclavs, plaintive and in the minor key. The men sing of the daring exploits of their Cossack forefathers, who were not free-booters like the old Cossacks of the Volga, but courageous men engaged in a life-and-death struggle with nomadic hordes, and later with internal enemies, Poles and rebels. The greater refinement of the women of Little Russia is attributable to the comparative ease of their lives in a fertile country, with a climate more genial than that of the more northerly parts of the empire. There the Great and the White Russians had to contend with a soil much less productive, with swamps which had to be drained, with thick forests which had to be cleared, with wild beasts which had to be destroyed or guarded against, and with frost and snow that left scarcely four months in the year for labour in the field.

The upper classes of South Russia, enriched by the cultivation of large and fertile estates, and favoured in their social development by long contact with the ancient Western civilization of Poland, exhibit a similar superiority over the bulk of their compeers in Great Russia. Except, however, in the case of the larger landed proprietors, the everyday life of the Southern Russian bears a strong resemblance to that of the Irish squireen. There is a strong tinge of the same *insouciance* as to the material future, and an equal propensity to reckless hospitality, to sport (principally coursing), social jollification, and to a great extent to card-playing. Indeed, there are well-appointed country seats in the South of Russia in which the long summer days are entirely spent in card-playing, with interruptions only for meals. There are horses in plenty in the stable, and vehicles of every description to which they can be harnessed;

but "taking a drive" through endless cornfields along natural roads or tracks, parched, cracked, and dusty one day, and presenting the next a surface of black mud, offers but few attractions to the ladies, and vehicular locomotion is therefore resorted to only as a matter of necessity, on journeys to estates or towns often fifty to one hundred miles distant. Country life, indeed, has no great attractions in any part of Russia Proper, and ever since the Emancipation of the Serfs and the accompanying extinction of the power and authority of the proprietary classes, absenteeism has been largely on the increase, to the advantage solely of the principal provincial towns, and of certain capitals and watering-places in Western Europe. Thus, while Kursk and Kharkof owe much of their riches and progress to the immigration of landed proprietors from the northerly and eastern districts of the "Black Soil Zone," Kief is the resort of more princely landlords of the south-western districts, strongly and favourably affected by Polish culture.

Kharkof, to the east of Kief, is the principal seat of trade in South Russia, being a centre from which the products and manufactures of Northern and Central Russia are spread throughout the provinces to the east and south, down even to the Caucasus.

Sugar, largely produced in this part of Russia from beet-root and "bounty-fed," and corn, brandy, wool and hides from the central provinces, are largely sold at the five fairs held each year at Kharkof, which has also reason to be proud of its university with upwards of six hundred students, and of its connection by rail with the shores of the Baltic and those of the Black and Azof Seas. In 1765, Kharkof became the capital of the Ukraine, after having been a Cossack outpost town since 1647, when Poland finally ceded the province to Muscovy. Anciently, this was the camping-ground of nomadic tribes, particularly of the Khazars, and later the high road of the Tartar invaders of Russia, whether from the Crimea or the shores of the Caspian. In the province of Kharkof are found those remarkable idols of stone which we have seen in the Historical Museum at Moscow, and a vast number of tumuli, which have yielded coins establishing the fact of an early intercourse both with Rome and Arabia.

Poltava, also a place of extensive trade, principally in wool, horses, and cattle, is familiar to us in connection with the defeat of Charles XII. by Peter the Great in 1709. The centre of the field so disastrous to the Swedes is marked by a mound which covers the remains of their slain. Two monuments commemorate the victory.

At Ekaterinoslaf we are again on the great Dnieper. It was only a village when Catherine II., descending the river from Kief in a stately barge accompanied by Joseph II. of Austria, King Stanislaus Augustus of Poland and a brilliant suite, raised it to the dignity of a town bearing her own name. On that occasion she laid the first stone of a cathedral which was not destined to be completed on the imposing scale she had projected, and which has been reduced to one-sixth in the edifice that was consecrated only in 1835. The town consists of only one row of buildings, almost concealed in gardens and running for nearly three miles parallel with the Dnieper. Catherine's Palace, a bronze statue which represents her clad in Roman armour and crowned, and the garden of her magnificent favourite, Prince Potemkin, constitute the "sights" of Ekaterinoslaf, the more striking feature of which, however, is its Jewish population, huddled together in a special quarter between the river and the bazaar. A considerable number of them pursue the favourite Jewish occupation of money-changing, and the Ekaterinoslaf Prospekt is dotted with their stands and their money-chests, painted blue and red.

A drive over forty miles of Steppe, somewhat relieved in its monotony by numerous ancient tumuli, bring those who do not proceed by steamer to the great naval station and commercial port of Nicolaief, at the junction of the Ingul with the Bug. It was the site until 1775 of a Cossack *setch*, or fortified settlement, and in 1789 it received its present appellation in commemoration of the capture of Otchakof from the Turks on the feast-day of St. Nicholas. Destined from the first by Potemkin to be the harbour of a Russian fleet in the Black Sea, temporarily neglected by the naval authorities, Nicolaief reasserted its claim to that proud position after the fall of Sebastopol. It owes much of its present affluence to the sound administration of Admiral Samuel Greig, son of the admiral of Scotch parentage who, with the aid of some equally gallant countrymen, won for the Russians the naval battle of Chesmé in 1769. Next to Odessa, Nicolaief is the handsomest town in New Russia, as this part of the country was called after its conquest from the Turks and Tartars. Its large trade, mostly in grain, has been greatly promoted by the railway, which now connects this important harbour with Kharkof and other rich agricultural centres.

Of the six ports on the neighbouring Sea of Azof, Taganrog, where Alexander I. died in 1825, is the most considerable, although steamers have to anchor at a considerable distance from it, owing to the shallowness of the roadstead. The annual value of its exports of corn, wool, tallow, etc., is about five millions sterling, and, as at Nicolaief, British shipping is chiefly employed in the trade. Much of the produce shipped here comes from Rostov-on-the-Don, the chief centre of inland trade in the south-east provinces of Russia, and one in which many industries (especially the manipulation of tobacco grown in the Caucasus and the Crimea), are pursued. A short distance above this great mart is Novocherkask, the capital of the "Country of the Don Cossacks," anciently the abode of Scythians, Sarmatians, Huns, Bolgars, Khazars and Tartars. The present population dates from the Sixteenth Century, when renegades from Muscovy and vagrants of every description formed themselves into Cossack, or robber communities. They attacked the Tartars and Turks, and in 1637 took the Turkish fortress of Azof. Under the reign of Peter the Great the powerful and independent Cossacks were not much interfered with, but from 1718 they were gradually brought under subjection to the Tsar, whom they powerfully assisted in subsequent wars. The town was founded in 1804, and is adorned with a bronze monument to the famous Hetman (Ataman or chief) Platof, leader of the Cossacks between 1770 and 1816. It is usual to bestow on the Russian heir-apparent the title of "Ataman" of the Don Cossacks. The last investiture with Cossack *bâton* took place in 1887, when also the reigning Emperor confirmed, at a "circle," or open-air assemblage, all the ancient rights and privileges of the warlike Cossacks of the Don.

KHARKOF.

The chief town of the Kuban district is Ekaterinodar, a name which signifies, literally, "Catherine's gift," from having been founded by the sovereign of that name and bestowed, in 1792, together with the adjacent territory, on the Zaporogian, subsequently known as the Black Sea Cossacks. Catherine mistrusted their power and influence, and tempted them to the Kuban with grants of land and other privileges. The first service of some 20,000 of those new warrior settlers consisted in barring all egress from the mountains, by means of a "first fortified line" of stations that extended to Vladikavkas, where they united with the descendants of the Grebenski Cossacks, with whom they are not to be confounded. The predominant type amongst the Zaporogians is still that of the Little Russians, the Grebenski continuing to preserve their identity with the natives of Great Russia, whence their origin;

and although the whole of this imposing force, maintained at half a million, has long since adopted the dress of the Caucasian mountaineers, the Cossacks remain true to the orthodox faith and to the customs of their forefathers, whose vernacular tongue has never been forgotten by them. The dress so universally worn by the male sex, even from boyhood, in all parts of the Caucasus, consists of a single-breasted garment, like a frock-coat, but reaching almost to the ankles, tightened in closely at the waist, with a belt from which are suspended dagger, sword, and frequently a pistol, and having on either breast a row of ten or twelve sockets, each of a size to hold a cartridge. A rifle, which every man possesses, is slung across the back; and a tall sheep-skin hat finished off at its summit with a piece of coloured cloth completes the costume.

The number of Cossacks in Transcaucasia being very limited, for a few only are stationed in each principal town, chiefly as an escort to the governor of the province, their duties are performed by *Chapars*, an irregular force, equally dashing horsemen, and trained in like manner from early youth in those singular exercises and breakneck evolutions for which the Cossacks of the Caucasus have become so famous. Setting their horses at full gallop, they will stand on the saddle and fire all around at an imaginary enemy; or throw the body completely over to the right, with the left heel resting on their steed's hind quarter, and fire as if at an enemy in pursuit, or turn clean round, and sitting astride facing the horse's tail, keep up a rapid fire. A favourite feat, among many others, is to throw their hat and rifle to the ground, wheel, and pick them up whilst going at the horse's fullest speed.

Should the traveller elect to proceed eastward, but north of the great range, he will meet with the Kabardines, the first amongst the Circassians to enter into friendly relations with Russia; they are the "blood" of the Caucasus, a noble race, thoroughly domesticated, hospitable to strangers, and useful breeders of cattle. To the south of the Circassians, and occupying about one hundred miles of the coast in the Black Sea, are the Abkhases, who have enjoyed the reputation, from time immemorial, of being an indolent and lawless race, anciently given to piracy, now addicted to thieving when the opportunity is afforded them, for they are determinedly inimical to strangers. Their mountains abound in forests of magnificent walnut and box, where the enthusiastic sportsman will find the bear, hyena, and wolf, and plenty of smaller game, with seldom a roof to cover him other than the vault of heaven; but the ordinary traveller is likely to encounter difficulties and delays that he would prefer to avoid. Christianity was here introduced by Justinian, who constructed many churches that would have been notable specimens of Byzantine architecture, had the Abkhases not destroyed them in their struggles against the Russians, every such edifice being occupied and converted by the latter into a military post. One church, at Pitzunda on the coast, remarkable as being the place to which John Chrysostom was banished at the instance of Empress Eudoxia—although the exile never reached his destination—having escaped the general destruction, has been thoroughly restored of late years, and is a striking object to passing vessels. Being the mother church in the Caucasus, Pitzunda, then Pityus, continued to be the seat of the Catholics of Abkhasia until the Twelfth Century. Practically, the Abkhases are at present heathens.

Farther south, and extending some way inland from the sea, is the principality of Mingrelia, where we again tread classic ground, inasmuch as our wanderings have brought us to the Æa of Circe and the Argonauts. In a Mingrelian landscape we are struck at the aspect afforded by the numerous whitewashed cottages as they dot the well-wooded hills. The Mingrelians, too, like their neighbours whom we have just quitted, are incurably given to indolence, except in the making of wine from their abundant vineyards; otherwise they are content to live on the produce of their orchards, prolific through the interposition of a beneficent Providence rather than to any agricultural diligence on their part. They may certainly be included amongst the handsomest people in Transcaucasia, with their well-defined features and usually raven black hair. The Dadian, or prince, is the wealthiest of the dispossessed rulers: the foresight of his predecessor and his own European training having taught him the danger of disposing of land and squandering the proceeds, rather than preserving the property and contenting himself with a smaller income.

Between Mingrelia and Abkhasia courses the Ingur, and if we ascend to near its water-shed—a journey easily accomplished on horse-back, say from Sougdidi, the well-known military station—we should find ourselves amongst a very wild and singular people, the Svanni, whose complete subjugation dates back no farther it may be said than 1876, although they made a formal submission in 1833. They occupy some forty or fifty miles of the upper valley of the Ingur, at no part exceeding ten miles in width, and are cut off from all outside communication between the beginning of September and the end of May, in consequences of the passes being blocked with snow. "The scenery in this valley," writes a recent traveller, "is of great beauty and wildness, and grand beyond description; amid the most profuse vegetation, every imaginable flower is seen in its wild state, and bank, meadow, hill-side and grass plot are literally covered with all that is most lovely; in every forest and grove, and all undergrowth even, indeed wherever the pure air of heaven and its divine light is not obstructed, the earth is thus gorgeously arrayed."

IN THE CAUCASUS

J. BUCHAN TELLER

Returning to Mingrelia, we find it bounded on the south by the river Rion, the ancient Phasis, which flows through the country whence was introduced into Europe the Phasian bird—our pheasant. The Rion divides Mingrelia from Guria, another principality, where is situated Batoum, a somewhat pestiferous but important military station and commercial port, that has tended in no small degree, since its annexation to Russia in 1878, towards the development of the resources of this beautiful country, intersected with good roads through valleys highly cultivated with maize, corn, and barley, the hills and their declivities being overspread with the oak and box, exported in large quantities, and yielding handsome returns. Ozurgheti, the chief town, attractively situated, was the residence of the rulers who lie interred at the ancient monastery and episcopal church, Chemokmedy, about six miles distant.

Passengers from Odessa and the Crimea landing at Batoum find the train in readiness to convey them to Tiflis, the capital of the whole Transcaucasia, reached in about fifteen hours, the train travelling slowly enough, but through a land of much interest, historically and pictorially. On the right, in the distance, are the highlands of the old kingdom of Armenia, to the left is Imeritia, a glory, like Mingrelia and Guria, of the past. If so inclined, the traveller may exchange, at Rion station, the main for a branch line, which will take him to Kutaïs, the chief town of the old kingdom of Imeritia, where he may tarry for a while to great advantage. It is the ancient Khytæa, the residence of Ætes; at any rate a city of great antiquity, beautifully situated on the banks of the Rion.

Between Kutaïs and Tiflis is the Pass of Suram, at an altitude of three thousand and twenty-seven feet, over which are laid the lines of rail by gradients of one in twenty-two feet over a distance of about eight miles; a triumph of engineering skill due, as is the entire railway, to British capital and enterprise. Beyond this Pass the train stops at Gori, situated at the limits of a glorious plain, watered by the Kur and its tributaries. Since fairly good accommodation is obtainable, it were well to halt at this station for the purpose of visiting the unique rock-cut town, Uplytztzykhé, some eight miles off. Here is a town—there can be no other designation for it—consisting of public edifices—if such a term may be employed—of large habitations, presumably for the great, smaller dwellings for others, each being conveniently divided, and having doorways, openings for light, and partitions, while many are ornamented with cornices, mouldings, beams and pillars. The groups are separated by streets and lanes, and grooves have been cut, unquestionably for water-courses, and yet the whole has been entirely hewn and shaped out of the solid rock. Tradition is replete with incidents in the history of these remarkable excavations, but faithful historiographers have hitherto refrained from endorsing any of the tales that have been handed down by romancers of Georgia.

Tiflis, the chief seat of Government and residence of the Governor-General, having a population of about one hundred thousand souls, is unpleasantly situated between ranges of perfectly barren hills, and but for the River Kur, on the banks of which it is built, would be almost uninhabitable. Having driven through the suburbs on his way from the railway terminus, the traveller crosses the Kur over the Woronzoff Bridge, which at once brings him to the principal street, where he passes in succession the public gardens, gymnasium, law-courts, palace of the Governor-General, the main guard-house, public library, museum, etc.; by which time he will have reached Palace Street and Erivan Square, where are situated the best hotels and restaurants, and the National Theatre. From the square three main thoroughfares lead to as many separate quarters, viz.: the European, where the wealthy live in well-built houses of elegant construction; the native bazaars, and the marketplace and Russian bazaar. An extensive view of the city and an interesting sight is obtained from the eminence crowned by the old fortress which immediately overlooks the Asiatic quarter and bazaars, whence rise the confused sounds of human cries and the din from the iron, brass, and copper-workers. As is the custom elsewhere in the East, those of one trade congregate together, apart from the other trades, and so are passed a succession of silversmiths in their stalls, of furriers, armourers, or eating and wine-shops, the wine of the country being kept in buffalo, goat, or sheep-skins laid on their back, and presenting the disagreeable appearance of carcases swollen after lengthened immersion in water. The Georgians are merry folk, rarely allowing themselves to be depressed by the troubles of life. They love wine and music, and ever seek to drive away dull care by indulging in their favourite Kakhety—two bottles being the usual allowance to a man's dinner, an allowance, however, greatly exceeded when, of an evening, friends meet together to join in the national dance, called the Lezghinka.

The Cathedral of Zion was formerly the church of the Patriarch of Georgia. It dates from the Fifth Century, and encloses that most precious relic, with which the nation was converted to Christianity in the Fourth Century—nothing less than a cross of vine stems bound with the hair of St. Nina, the patron saint, who first preached the truth! The patriarchate has long been suppressed, and is replaced by a Russian Exarch, so that the Georgian Church may be considered in all respects identical with that of Russia. The palace of the kings has entirely disappeared, for not a vestige remains. George XIII. signed his renunciation of the crown in favour of the Emperor Paul in

1800, and died shortly afterwards amid the execrations of his subjects, for having ignominiously betrayed them. Many of his descendants are in the service of Russia, and are the representatives of one of the most ancient monarchies of the world—for the Bagrations first rose to power in 587; and if allowance be made for interregnums it will be found that their reign extended over 1092 years, during the twelve centuries that elapsed from their earliest election.

As Georgia is the land of wine and song, so is Armenia essentially the land of legend and tradition, for which must be held in great part responsible the magnificent mountain that exhibits itself suddenly at a dip in the road long before the plains are in sight. Well may the Armenians glory in "their" Ararat, peerless among the mighty works of the Creator, almost symmetrical in its outlines, and rising to an altitude of 16,916 feet above the sea, Lesser Ararat, 12,840 feet, looking almost dwarfed by the side of its mighty neighbour.

At Erivan, the largest city in Russian Armenia, the traveller will find fairly good accommodation, but the place is dull enough, whether in the Persian quarter, where crooked lanes are lined with high walls, that mask the dwellings within like the defences of a fortress, or in the broad streets and unpaved quarter laid out by the Russians since their occupation of the province in 1829, even though enlivened by a boulevard and gardens fair to look upon. The population is Armenian and Persian, for Persia ruled here during a considerable period until vanquished by Russia; but at the bazaar one meets with other nationalities, such as Tartars from the Steppes, Kurds, Greeks, and Turkish dealers in search of good horses, upon which they will fly across the frontier, defying Cossacks and custom officers alike.

Within a short distance of Erivan, and the post-station nearest to the Persian frontier, is Nahitchevan, the first abode of Noah after he came forth from the ark, and probably also his last, since his tomb is reverently shown by the inhabitants, who eagerly escort strangers to see it. Other still more important towns in Armenia, available by carriage-road, are Alexandropol and Kars, the former being the largest and most powerful fortress and the principal arsenal in Transcaucasia; the latter, long a Turkish fortress town, was gallantly defended in 1855 by Sir Fenwick Williams and a few British officers, until the garrison was starved into surrender by General Mouravieff. Kars was finally ceded to Russia by the Treaty of Berlin in 1878.

TIFLIS.

A Tartar city brought into prominence of late years through the introduction of railways is Elizavetpol, on the line between Tiflis and the Caspian, where we must now pick ourselves up after having retraced our steps from the plains, to journey by rail to dismal looking Bakù—a town of recent creation, approached through a desert of sand and stones, where neither vegetable nor animal life can possibly find an existence. Viewed from the sea, Bakù presents a distinctly picturesque appearance, with its sombre citadel, numerous minarets, and the palace of the princes of bygone days towering above the old town, where the houses look as if they were piled the one above the other—the new or Russian quarter being at the base, and lining the shore of the pretty little bay. Modern Bakù contains some handsome residences and well-paved streets, the principal being the busy quay, constructed of massive blocks of greystone masonry, where the naphtha, the wealth of Bakù, is embarked for transport to the interior of Russia by the Volga, or for conveyance across the Caspian to Central Asia. Numerous refineries, worth inspecting, at the west end of Bakù compose the Black Town, so called from its begrimed condition, and from being ever enveloped in clouds of the densest smoke. Since a remote period has this neighbourhood been considered holy by fire-worshippers, because of the many naphtha springs that were constantly burning, some even perpetually; indeed, the fires at Surakan, a suburb of Bakù, continued to be guarded by fire-worshippers from Yezd in Persia, and even from India, until, with the connivance of the government, they were hustled away some ten years ago by the increasing number of speculators engaged in a trade which has now completely driven out of the market all American produce.

In Daghestan is Gunib, the last stronghold of the brave Shamyl, whom the strength of Russia was unequal to subdue during the space of thirty years. "Do the Russians say that they are numerous as the grains of sand? Then are we the waves that will carry away that sand," said the great Tartar chief addressing the numerous tribes who placed themselves under his leadership to repel the invader. The mountaineers posted themselves on the heights, and, hidden by trees, shot down their enemies in scores as they advanced in column up the narrow defiles.

The great thoroughfare between Transcaucasia and Russia is from Tiflis to Vladikavkaz, the terminus of the Moscow-Rostof railway, by way of the Dariel road, a stupendous engineering success completed in the reign of Nicholas. This road winds over a pass 7,977 feet above the sea, and is kept in repair and clear for traffic in winter by the Ossets, whose country it traverses, in return for which service they are exempt from all taxes.

When the traveller will have completed the journey from Tiflis to Vladikavkaz, he will have arrived at the dépôt and point of transit for all goods brought by rail from Russia, and there transferred, for conveyance to the Transcaucasian provinces, to clumsy, unwieldly carts or vans drawn by horses or oxen; those in charge of the caravans never being in a hurry, completely indifferent as to when they start, or when they arrive at their destination, and rejoicing in a lengthened stay at Mlety station, after having accomplished the most tiresome part of the distance—the ascent and descent of the pass. Vladikavkaz was founded in 1785 on the site of an Osset village, and became the headquarters and chief military dépôt of the Russians during their lengthened struggle for supremacy with the stout-hearted hillmen; it is now the chief town and seat of government for the province of Kuban, and still an important military station. The population is made up of Circassians, Armenians, and Russians, and a few Ossets at the bazaars, for the natives made off long ago. The chief industries are the manufacture of silver and gold lace, arms, *burkas*, the Caucasian's all-weathers cloak, silver ornaments, etc. The hotels are fairly good, but there being nothing at Vladikavkaz itself sufficiently inviting to encourage a longer stay than is absolutely necessary, the following choice of routes lays before the stranger. He may post through Eastern Caucasus and embark at Petrovsk for Astrakhan and the tedious voyage up the Volga; or take the railway to Rostof *en route* to Moscow; or travel by rail to Novorossisk on the Black Sea, and there embark; or, following that line as far as Ekaterinodar, post thence to Taman and cross the straits to Kertch.

KHIVA

FRED BURNABY

We were now fast nearing Khiva, which could be just discerned in the distance, but was hidden, to a certain extent, from our view by a narrow belt of tall, graceful trees; however, some richly-painted minarets and high domes of coloured tiles could be seen towering above the leafy groves. Orchards surrounded by walls eight and ten feet high, continually met the gaze, and avenues of mulberry-trees studded the landscape in all directions.

The two Khivans rode first; I followed, having put on my black fur pelisse instead of the sheep-skin garment, so as to present a more respectable appearance on entering the city. Nazar, who was mounted on the horse that stumbled, brought up the rear. He had desired the camel-driver to follow in the distance with the messenger and the caravan; my servant being of opinion that the number of our animals was not sufficient to deeply impress the Khivans with my importance, and that on this occasion it was better to ride in without any caravan than with the small one I possessed. We now entered the city, which is of an oblong form, and surrounded by two walls: the outer one is about fifty feet high: its basement is constructed of baked bricks, the upper part being built of dried clay. This forms the first line of defense, and completely encircles the town, which is about a quarter of a mile within the wall. Four high wooden gates, clamped with iron, barred the approach from the north, south, east, and west, while the walls themselves were in many places out of repair.

The town itself is surrounded by a second wall, not quite so high as the one just described, and with a dry ditch, which is now half filled with ruined *débris*. The slope which leads from the wall to the trench has been used as a cemetery, and hundreds of sepulchres and tombs were scattered along some undulating ground just without the city. The space between the first and second walls is used as a market-place, where cattle, horses, sheep, and camels are sold, and where a number of carts were standing, filled with corn and grass.

Here an ominous-looking cross-beam had been erected, towering high above the heads of the people with its bare, gaunt poles. This was the gallows on which all people convicted of theft are executed; murderers being put to death in a different manner, having their throats cut from ear to ear in the same way that sheep are killed. This punishment is carried out by the side of a large hole in the ground, not far from the principal street in the centre of the town. But I must here remark that the many cruelties stated to have been perpetrated by the present Khan previous to the capture of his city did not take place. Indeed, they only existed in the fertile Muscovite imagination, which was eager to find an excuse for the appropriation of a neighbour's property. On the contrary, capital punishment was only inflicted when the laws had been infringed; and there is no instance of the Khan having arbitrarily put any one to death.

The two walls above mentioned appear to have made up the defenses of the city, which was also armed with sixteen guns. These, however, proved practically useless against the Russians, as the garrison only fired solid shot, not being provided with shell. The Khan seemed to have made no use whatever of the many inclosed gardens in the vicinity of the city during the Russian advance, as, if he had, and firmly contested each yard of soil, I much doubt whether the Tsar's troops could have ever entered the city.

It is difficult to estimate the population of an Oriental city by simply riding round its walls; so many houses are uninhabited, and others again are densely packed with inhabitants. However, I should say, as a mere guess, that there are about 25,000 human beings within the walls of Khiva. The streets are broad and clean, while the houses belonging to the richer inhabitants are built of highly polished bricks and coloured tiles, which lend a cheerful aspect to the otherwise somewhat sombre colour of the surroundings. There are nine schools: the largest, which contains 130 pupils, was built by the father of the present Khan. These buildings are all constructed with high, coloured domes, and are ornamented with frescoes and arabesque work, the bright aspect of the cupolas first attracting the stranger's attention on his nearing the city.

Presently we rode through a bazaar similar to the one at Oogentch, thin rafters and straw uniting the tops of the houses in the street, and forming a sort of roof to protect the stall-keepers and their customers from the rays of a summer sun. We were followed by crowds of people; and as some of the more inquisitive approached too closely, the Khivans who accompanied me, raising their whips in the air, freely belaboured the shoulders of the multitude, thus securing a little space. After riding through a great number of streets, and taking the most circuitous course—probably in order to duly impress me with an idea of the importance of the town—we arrived before my companion's house. Several servants ran forward and took hold of the horses. The Khivan dismounted, and, bowing obsequiously, led the way through a high door-way constructed of solid timber. We next entered a square open court, with carved stone pillars supporting a balcony which looked down upon a marble fountain, or basin, the general appearance of the court being that of a *patio* in some nobleman's house in Cordova or Seville. A door of a similar construction to the one already described, though somewhat lower, gave access to a long, narrow room, a raised daïs at each end being covered with handsome rugs. There were no windows, glass being a luxury which has only recently found its way to the capital; but the apartment received its light from an aperture at the side, which was slightly concealed by some trellis-work, and from a space left uncovered in the ceiling, which was adorned with arabesque figures. The two doors which led from the court were each of them handsomely carved, and in the middle of the room was a hearth filled with charcoal embers. My host, beckoning to me to take the post of honour by the fire, retired a few paces and folded his arms across his chest; then, assuming a deprecatory air, he asked my permission to sit down.

Grapes, melons, and other fruit, fresh as on the day when first picked, were brought in on a large tray and laid at my feet, while the host himself, bringing in a Russian tea-pot and cup, poured out some of the boiling liquid and placed it by my side; I all this time being seated on a rug, with my legs crossed under me, in anything but a comfortable position.

He then inquired if I had any commands for him, as the Khan had given an order that everything I might require was instantly to be supplied.

In the afternoon two officials arrived from the Khan's palace, with an escort of six men on horseback and four on foot. The elder of the two dignitaries said that His Majesty was waiting to receive me, and my horse being brought round, I mounted, and accompanied him towards the palace. The six men on horseback led the way, then I came between the two officials, and Nazar brought up the rear with some attendants on foot, who freely lashed the crowd with their whips whenever any of the spectators approached our horses too closely.

The news that the Khan was about to receive me had spread rapidly through the town, and the streets were lined with curious individuals all eager to see the Englishman. Perhaps in no part of the world is India more talked of than in the Central Asian khanates; and the stories of our wealth and power, which have reached Khiva through Afghan and Bokharan sources, have grown like a snow-ball in its onward course, until the riches described in the garden discovered by Aladdin would pale if compared with the fabled treasures of Hindoostan.

After riding through several narrow streets, where, in some instances, the house-tops were thronged with people desirous of looking at our procession, we emerged on a small, flat piece of ground which was not built over, and which formed a sort of open square. Here a deep hole was pointed out to me as the spot where criminals who have been found guilty of murder had their throats cut from ear to ear.

The Khan's palace is a large building, ornamented with pillars and domes, which, covered with bright-coloured tiles, flash in the sun, and attract the attention of the stranger approaching Khiva. A guard of thirty or forty men armed with cimeters stood at the palace gates. We next passed into a small court-yard. The Khan's guards were all arrayed in long flowing silk robes of various patterns, bright-coloured sashes being girt around their waists, and tall fur hats surmounting their bronzed countenances. The court-yard was surrounded by a low pile of buildings, which are the offices of the palace, and was filled with attendants and menials of the court, while good-looking boys of an effeminate appearance, with long hair streaming down their shoulders, and dressed a little like the women, lounged about, and seemed to have nothing in particular to do.

A door at the farther end of the court gave access to a low passage, and, after passing through some dirty corridors, where I had occasionally to stoop in order to avoid knocking my head against the ceiling, we came to a large, square-shaped room. Here the treasurer was seated, with three moullahs, who were squatted by his side, while several attendants crouched in humble attitudes at the opposite end of the apartment. The treasurer and his companions were busily engaged in counting some rolls of ruble-notes and a heap of silver coin, which has been received from the Khan's subjects, and were now to be sent to Petro-Alexandrovsk as part of the tribute to the Tsar.

The great man now made a sign to some of his attendants, when a large wooden box, bearing signs of having been manufactured in Russia, was pushed a little from the wall and offered to me as a seat. Nazar was accommodated among the dependents at the other end of the room. After the usual salaams had been made, the functionary continued his task, leaving me in ignorance as to what was to be the next part of the programme; Nazar squatting himself as far as possible from one of the attendants, who was armed with a cimeter, and whom he suspected of being the executioner.

After I had been kept waiting for about a quarter of an hour, a messenger entered the room and informed the treasurer that the Khan was disengaged, and ready to receive me. We now entered a long corridor, which led to an inner court-yard. Here we found the reception-hall, a large tent, or *kibitka*, of a dome-like shape. The treasurer, lifting up a fold of thick cloth, motioned to me to enter, and on doing so I found myself face to face with the celebrated Khan, who was reclining against some pillows or cushions, and seated on a handsome Persian rug, warming his feet by a circular hearth filled with burning charcoal. He raised his hand to his forehead as I stood before him, a salute which I returned by touching my cap. He then made a sign for me to sit down by his side.

Before I relate our conversation, it may not be uninteresting if I describe the sovereign. He is taller than the average of his subjects, being quite five feet ten in height, and is strongly built: his face is of a broad, massive type, he has a low, square forehead, large dark eyes, a short straight nose with dilated nostrils, and a coal-black beard and mustache; while an enormous mouth, with irregular but white teeth, and a chin somewhat concealed by his beard, and not at all in character with the otherwise determined appearance of his face, must complete the picture.

He did not look more than eight-and-twenty, and has a pleasant, genial smile, and a merry twinkle in his eye, very unusual among Orientals; in fact, to me an expression in Spanish would better describe his face than any English one I can think of. It is very *simpatica*, and I must say I was greatly surprised, after all that has been written in Russian newspapers about the cruelties and other iniquities perpetrated by this Khivan potentate, to find the original such a cheery sort of fellow.

His countenance was of a very different type from his treasurer's. The hang-dog expression of the latter made me bilious to look at him, and it was said that he carried to great lengths these peculiar vices and depraved habits to which Orientals are so often addicted. The Khan was dressed in a similar sort of costume to that generally worn by his subjects, but it was made of much richer materials, and a jewelled sword was lying by his seat. His head was covered by a tall black Astrakhan hat, of a sugar-loaf shape; and on my seeing that all the officials who were in the room at the same time as myself kept on their fur hats, I did the same.

The sovereign, turning to an attendant, gave an order in a low tone, when tea was instantly brought, and handed to me in a small porcelain tea-cup. A conversation with the Khan was now commenced, and carried on through Nazar and a Kirghiz interpreter who spoke Russian, and occasionally by means of a moullah, who was acquainted with Arabic, and had spent some time in Egypt.

THE TRANS-SIBERIAN RAILWAY

WILLIAM DURBAN

The general characteristics of the Trans-Siberian Railroad may be described in a few words. It is by far the longest railway on earth. It is very much more solidly constructed, for the most part, than is generally supposed. The road bed is perfectly firm, and the track is well ballasted. Though in certain of the sections far to the east great engineering difficulties had to be contended with, the gradients on the greater part of the route are remarkably easy.

Uniformity of gauge is the keynote of Russian railway engineers. Accordingly in possessing a five-foot guage, the Great Siberian is uniform with all the railroads throughout the Russian Empire. Thus, the ample breadth of the cars harmonizes with the luxury which astonishes the traveller who visits Russia for the first time, no matter in what region of the Empire he happens to be touring. The great height of the carriages, proportionate with the width, adds to the imposing aspect of the trains. It is necessary to bear these considerations in mind, for the idea prevails throughout the world outside Russia that this colossal road was carried through, not only with great haste, but also on a flimsy and superficial system. The bridges are necessarily very numerous, for Siberia is a land of mighty rivers with countless tributaries. All the permanent bridges are of iron. Those which were temporarily made of timber are being in every case reconstructed, and the Great Siberian includes some of the most magnificent bridges in the world.

The bridge over the Irtish is unrivalled. Being nearly four miles long, it is on that account phenomenal; but its stupendous piers, designed specially to resist the fearful pressure of the ice, would alone convince any sceptic of the determination of the Russian administration to spare none of the resources of the Empire in order to make this railway absolutely efficient, alike for mercantile and military purposes. The Trans-Siberian Railway is intended to create a new Siberia. It is already fulfilling that aim, as I shall show. The most potent of the civilizing factors of the Twentieth Century is in this enterprise presented to the world, and in a very few years people will realize with astonishment what this railway means.

The Trans-Siberian nominally begins in Europe. It is inaugurated by the magnificent iron bridge which spans the Volga at Samara in East Russia. The Volga is here a giant river, and this noble bridge joins the European railway system with the new Asiatic line. But practically the Asian line commences in the heart of the Ural Mountains, if that long and broad chain of low and pretty hills ought to be dignified with the name of mountains. Here lies the little town of Cheliabinsk, which in 1894 was the terminus of the European system.

It is an interesting fact that Americans and Englishmen were the real authors of this splendid and romantic scheme for spanning the Asiatic continent with a railway from west to east. In 1857, an American named Collins came forward with a scheme for the formation of an Amur Railway Company, to lay a line from Irkutsk to Chita. Although his plan was not officially adopted, it was carefully kept in mind, and it actually forms the main and central part of the present line. An English engineer offered to lay a tramroad across Siberia, after Muravieff had carried Russia to the Pacific by his brilliant annexation of the mouths of the Amur. In 1858, three Englishmen offered to construct a railway from Moscow through Nijni-Novgorod to Tartar Bay. Though all proposals by foreigners have been courteously shelved, they have in reality formed the bases of native enterprise. It is to the credit of Russia that she has determined to depend on the energy and ability of her own sons to carry out this colossal undertaking.

One of the chronic troubles of the Russian Government arises from the uneven distribution of the population. It happens that those are the most thickly inhabited districts which are the least able to support a dense population. For instance, an immense number of villages are scattered through the vast forest regions of Central and Western Russia, where birch trees grow by millions, while the great wheat-growing plains of the west centre and south-west are but sparsely inhabited. Then again, the infatuation of the military oligarchy has been evidenced in the plan by which all the railways except this new Siberian line have been designed for purely military purposes. The Emperor Nicholas insisted on all the lines being developed without the slightest regard to the wants of the towns and the conveniences of commerce. Even the natural facilities for engineering operations were not allowed by that autocrat to be for a moment taken into consideration. His engineers were once consulting him as to the expediency of taking the line from St. Petersburg to Moscow by a slight detour, to avoid some very troublesome obstacles. The Tsar took up a ruler, and with his pencil drew a straight line from the old metropolis. Handing back the chart, he peremptorily said: "There, gentlemen, that is to be the route for the line!" And certainly there is not a straighter reach of 600 miles on any railroad in the world, as every tourist knows who has journeyed between the two chief cities of the Russian Empire. For instance, not very far beyond the Urals there is one magnificent stretch of perfectly straight road for 116 versts, or nearly eighty miles.

The traveller who expects that on the great Siberian route he will speedily find himself plunged into semi-savagery, or that he will on leaving Europe begin to realize the solitude of a vast forlorn wilderness, will be agreeably disappointed. This great line is intended to carry forward in its progress all the comforts of modern civilization. Every station is picturesque and even artistic. No two stations are alike in style, and all are neat, substantial, comfortable, and comparable to the best rural stations anywhere in Europe or America. In one respect Russian provision for travellers is always far in advance of that in other countries. Those familiar with the country will know at once that I refer to the railway restaurants. The Great Siberian follows the rule of excellence and abundance. There, at every station, just as on the European side of the Urals, the traveller sees on entering the handsome dining-room the immense buffet loaded with freshly cooked Russian dishes, always hot and steaming, and of a variety not attempted in any other land excepting at great hotels. You select what fancy and appetite dictate, without any supervision. To dine at a railway restaurant anywhere in the Russian Empire is one of the luxuries of travel. Your dinner costs only a rouble— about two shillings, and what a dinner you secure for the money! Soup, beef, sturgeon, trout, poultry, game, bear's flesh, and vegetables in profusion are supplied *ad libitum*, the visitor simply helping himself just as he pleases. I mention these little details to prove that the longest railway in the world is to push civilization with it as it goes forward.

Readers who will glance at any map of the new line will notice that the track runs across the upper waters of the great rivers, just about where they begin to be navigable. All through the summer, at any rate, America and England will, by the Arctic passage and by these mighty rivers, communicate with the heart of Asia, the railway in the far interior completing the circle of commerce. Other results will follow. Siberia at present contains a population of four million—less by more than a million than London reckons within its borders. Millions of the Russian peasantry in Europe are in a condition of chronic semi-starvation. Ere long thousands of these will weekly stream to the new Canaan in the East. Within the borders of Siberia, the whole of the United States of America could be enclosed, with a great spare ring around for the accommodation of a collection of little kingdoms. In the wake of the new line towns are springing up like mushrooms. Many of these will become great cities. There are several reasons for this development. The first is that the railway runs through South Siberia, where the climate is delightfully mild compared with the rigorous conditions of the atmosphere further north. The next reason is that all the chief gold-fields are in this southern latitude.

One characteristic worthy of note is the absolute security aimed at by the administration of the line. Train and track are protected by an immense army of guards. The road is divided into sections of a verst each, a verst being about two-thirds of a mile. Every section is marked by a neat cottage, the home of the guard and his family. Night and day the guard or one of his household must patrol the section. A train is never out of sight of the guards, several of whom are employed wherever there are heavy curves. There are nearly 4,000 of these guards on the stretch between the Urals and Tomsk.

All sense of solitude is thus removed from the mind of the traveller. The old post road through Siberia is one of the most dangerous routes in the world, being infested by murderous "brodyags," or runaway convicts; but the Siberian line is as safe as Cheapside or Oxford Street. With the fact of perfect safety is soon blended in the mind of the observer that of plenty. All along this wonderful route grass is seen growing in rank luxuriance that can hardly be equalled in any other part of the globe, Siberia being emphatically a grass-growing country. It is the original home of the whole graniferous stock. Wheat is indigenous to Siberia. Here is the largest grazing region in existence. Through this the train rolls on hour after hour, as in European Russia it goes on and on through interminable birch forests. Countless herds of animals in superb condition are everywhere seen roaming over these magnificent flowering Steppes, over which the Muscovite Eagle proudly floats.

Parts of the great railway, however, traverse regions other than these. To make the reader understand the general characteristics of Siberia and the importance of the railway in the light of these characteristics, a few words must be said about the three great zones which mainly make up the country. The first is the *tundra*, the vast region which stretches through the northern sub-arctic latitudes. This desolate belt is not less than 5,000 miles in extent. In breadth it varies from 200 to 500 miles. In winter the *tundra* is, of course, one vast frozen sheet. In the brief summer it is swampy, steaming, and swarming with mosquitoes. Treeless and sterile, the *tundra* is the home of strange uncouth tribes, but it is a valuable training ground for hardy hunters. To the minds of most people the *tundra* is Siberia. This mischievous fallacy is difficult to dispel. In a few years the Siberian railway will have completely dissipated it. Much more valuable is the far wider zone called the *taiga*, the most wonderful belt of forest on the surface of the earth. I can testify to the profound impression of mingled mystery and delight produced on the mind by riding a thousand miles through Russian forests as they still exist in European Russia, where myriads of square miles in the north and centre of the land are covered by birch, spruce, larch, pine, and oak plantations. Where do these forests begin and where do they have an end? That is the traveller's thought. He finds that they thicken and broaden, and deepen as they sweep in their majestic gloom across the Urals, and make up for thousands of miles the grand Siberian arboreal belt. In this *taiga* the Tsar possesses wealth beyond all computation; and the railway will put it actually at his disposal. The third zone, the most valuable of all, is that which mainly constitutes Southern Siberia. It is the region of the Steppes, that endless natural garden which again makes Siberia an incomparable land. Sheeted with flowers, variegated by woodlands, it holds in its lap ranges of mountains, all running with fairly uniform trend from north to south, while in its heart lies the romantic and mysterious Baikal, the deepest of lakes. Through the spurs of the *taiga*, running irregularly through the lovely Steppes, passes the new railroad, which thus taps the chief resources of the land. It will open up the forests, the arable country land, the cattle-breeding districts, and, above all, the mineral deposits. Here is a fine coming opportunity for the capitalists of the world.

The Siberian railway starts at Cheliabinsk, just across the Ural Mountains, which it reaches through Samara on the Volga from the European side, coming over the boundary hills through Ufa, Miass and Zlatoust. Shortly after leaving the latter town, which is the centre of the Uralian iron industry, the train passes that pathetic "Monument of Tears," which marks the boundary between Europe and Asia. The triangular post of white marble, which thousands of weeping exiles every year embrace as they pay their sad farewell to Europe, is simply inscribed on one of its three sides, "Asia," on another, "Europe." Passing down the eastern slopes of the Urals the train soon reaches Cheliabinsk, running beside the Isset, a tributary of the Irtish, one of the main branches of the grand Obi river. On leaving Cheliabinsk, the traveller begins to realize that he is in Siberia. In the near future this section of the line will be traversed by many an explorer and many a hunter, who will in summer come to seek fresh fields on the course of the Obi, to track out towards the north the haunts of the seal, the walrus, and the white bear. The line crosses the Tobol at Kurgan, the Ishim at Patropavlosk, and the Irtish at Omsk, where the majestic new bridge spans a stream of two hundred yards. The three fine rivers are confluents of the Obi. Kurgan lies embosomed in the finest and richest, as well as the largest pasturage in the world. The magnitude of this undertaking may be imagined from the fact that the Yenisei river is only reached after a ride of 2,000 miles from Cheliabinsk, and then the traveller has not traversed half the distance across the continent which this railroad spans.

We arrive at the main stream of the Obi when the train rolls into the station at Kolivan. Thus Tomsk, one of the chief cities of Siberia, is missed, for it lies further north on the Obi. In the same way does the line ignore Tobolsk, the Siberian capital, as it touches the Irtish far south of the city. These important places will be served by branch lines. Indeed, the branch to Tomsk is already finished. It is eighty miles long, and runs down the Tom valley northward to the city, which is the largest and most important in all Siberia. Tomsk will become the "hub" of Asia. It lies near the centre of the new railway system. It has a telephone system, is lighted by electricity, and possesses a flourishing university with thirty professors and 300 students. Tomsk, Tobolsk, and Yeniseisk would be difficult to reach by the main line as they are surrounded by vast swamps, and therefore the line is thus laid considerably south of these great towns. They are accessible with ease by side lines down their respective rivers.

The Siberian line is designed to run through the arable lands of the fertile zone. The adjacent land will be worth countless millions of roubles to a Government which has not had to pay a single copeck for it. On for many hundreds of versts rolls the train through the pasture lands of the splendid Kirghiz race. The Kirghiz are by far the finest of the Tartars. They are a purely pastoral people, frugal, cleanly, and hospitable, living mainly on meats, and milk and cheese, the products of their herds. Both for pasture and for the culture of cereals, the vast territory between the Obi and the Yenisei will be unrivalled in the whole world. Kurgan is the capital. It will become an Asiatic Chicago.

On the Shim river, a fairly important though minor tributary of the Obi, is Patropavlosk, with a population already of 20,000. It is growing rapidly, and fine buildings are springing up, in attestation of the immense influence of the new line. This city was once the frontier fortress erected by Russia against the Kirghiz. It was of commercial importance before the railroad was thought of, as the emporium of the brisk trade with Samarkand and Central Asia; great camel caravans constantly reaching it. All the old towns which are traversed by the Great Siberian are being transformed as if by magic. From Patropavlosk to Omsk is a distance equal to that between London and Edinburgh, about 400 miles. New and promising villages are frequently espied in the midst of the level, fertile flowery plains, varied by great patches of cultivated land. All along the track the land is being taken up on each side, and crops are being raised. We are in the midst of the great future granary of the whole Russian Empire, and not of that Empire alone.

Reaching the Yenisei river, the grandest stream in Siberia, the train crosses a bridge 1,000 yards in length. But some time before this a stoppage is made at the town of Obb, which is a striking sample of the magical results of the railway. The whole country was till recently a scene of wild desolation. The thriving community, busy with a prosperous trade, is typical of the coming transformation of Siberia.

A short distance beyond Irkutsk the line reaches one of the most remarkable places in the world—Lake Baikal. This grand lake is as long as England. It is nearly a mile deep, and covers an area of 13,430 square miles. Its surface is 1,500 feet above the level of the sea. On every side it is hemmed in by lofty mountains, covered with thick forest. Only a few tiny villages relieve its dreary solitude. The early Russian settlers, impressed by the mystic silence and gloomy grandeur of Baikal, named it the "Holy Sea." It abounds in fish of many species, and every season thousands of pounds' worth of salmon are caught and dried. At the north end great numbers of seals have their habitat, the Buriat hunters sometimes taking as many as 1,000 in a single season. Baikal is the only fresh-water sea in the world in which this animal is found.

The Transbaikalian section takes the line from Lake Baikal to the great Amur River. The line gradually ascends to the crest of the Yablonoi Mountains, reaching a height of 3,412 feet above the sea level. This is the greatest altitude of the Siberian Railway. In this province of Transbaikalia lies the interesting city of Chita, the far-off home of the most famous and estimable Socialist exiles sent from Russia. From this point to the Amur, where Manchuria is reached, the line is carried down the Pacific slope, through one of the wildest and most romantic tracks ever penetrated by railway engineers. It is not generally remembered that the Great Siberian Railway was begun at the Pacific end, and that the present Tsar Nicholas II., when Tsarevitch, inaugurated the colossal enterprise by laying the first stone of the eastern terminus at Vladivostock, on May 12, 1891.

HIGH LIFE IN RUSSIA

THE COUNTESS OF GALLOWAY

The Russian aristocracy and plutocracy have few powers or privileges beyond that of serving their sovereign, and their position depends entirely on the will of the emperor. Official rank is the only distinction, and all ranks or "tchin," as it is called, is regulated according to the army grades. By this "tchin" alone is the right of being received at Court acquired. Society is, therefore, subservient to the Court, and occupies itself more with those whose position can best procure them what they desire than with any other ideas. The Court itself is very magnificent, and its entertainments display unbounded splendour, taste, and art. In the midst of winter the whole palace is decorated for the balls with trees of camellias, dracænas and palms. The suppers seem almost to be served by magic. Two thousand people sup at the same moment: they all sit down together, and all finish together in an incredibly short space of time. The palace is lit by the electric light, the tables are placed under large palm-trees, and the effect is that of a grove of palms by moonlight. At these Court balls, besides the Royal Family of Grand Dukes and Duchesses, with gorgeous jewels, may be seen many of the great generals and governors of the provinces who come to St. Petersburg to do homage to their sovereign; a splendid-looking Circassian Prince, whose costume of fur and velvet is covered with chains of jewels and gold; the commander of the Cossack Guard, Tchérévine, who watches over the Emperor's safety, dressed in what resembles a well-fitting scarlet dressing-gown, with a huge scimitar in his belt sparkling with precious stones; Prince Dondoukoff Korsakoff, the Governor of the Caucasus, also in Cossack attire, with the beard which is the privilege of the Cossack birth. M. de Giers, whose civilian blue coat with gold buttons is remarkable among the numberless brilliant uniforms, talks to the Ambassadors with the wearied anxious expression habitual to his countenance. The Empress dances, but not the Emperor; he does not sit down to supper either, but walks about, after the Russian fashion of hospitality, to see that all his guests are served.

THE WINTER PALACE, ST. PETERSBURG

If, to the outsider, society seems to lack the serious side, science, learning, and politics, it gains energy from its contact with men who are continually engaged in distant provinces, carrying Russian rule and civilization to the conquered Eastern tribes. Notwithstanding the great ease and luxury, the fact that so much of the male portion is composed of officers, who wear no other clothes than their uniforms, gives something of a business-like air, and produces a sense of discipline at the entertainments. Individually, the Russians have much sympathy with English ways and habits, and the political antagonism between the two nations does not appear to affect their social intercourse. They are exceedingly courteous, hospitable, and friendly, throwing themselves with much zest into the occupation or amusement of the moment. In these days of rapid communication social life is much the same in every great capital. St. Petersburg is a very gay society, and the great troubles underlying the fabric do not come to the surface in the daily life. There are of course representatives of all the different lines of thought and policy, and because they cannot govern themselves, it must not be supposed that they have not predilections in favour of this or that line of action.

The season in St. Petersburg begins on the Russian New Year's Day, which is thirteen days late, for they adhere to what the Western nations now call the Old Style. It lasts till Lent, which the Eastern Church fixes also by a different calculation from the Western, and during that time there are Court balls twice a week and dancing at private houses nearly every other night, Sundays included. Private balls begin, as in London, very late and end very late. The dancing is most vigorous and animated. The specially Russian dance is the Mazurka, of Polish origin, and very pretty and graceful. Like the Scotch reel, it is a series of different figures with numerous and varied steps. The music, too, is special and spirited. The supper, which is always eaten sitting down, is a great feature of the evening, and there is invariably a cotillon afterwards. The pleasantest and most sociable entertainments are the little suppers every evening, where there is no dancing, and where the menu is most *recherché* and the conversation brilliant. The houses are well adapted for entertainments, and those we saw comfortable and luxurious as far as the owners are concerned. The bedrooms were prettily furnished, and the dressing-rooms attached fitted up with a tiled bath, hot and cold water, and numberless mirrors. The wives of the great Court and State officials, as well as many other ladies, have one afternoon in the week on which they sit at home and receive visitors. There is always tea and Russian bonbons, which are most excellent. What strikes an English-woman is the number of men, officers of the army, and others, who attend these "jours," as they are called in French. Many of noted activity, such as General Kaulbars, may be seen quietly sipping their tea and talking of the last ball to the young lady of the house. A fête given by Madame Polovtsoff, wife of the Secrétaire de l'Empire, was wonderfully conducted and organized. It took place at a villa on the Islands, as that part of St. Petersburg which lies between the two principal branches of the Neva is called. It is to villas here that the officials can retire after the season when obliged to remain near the capital. The rooms and large conservatories were lit by electricity. At the further end of the conservatory, buried in palm-trees were the gipsies chanting and wailing their savage national songs and choruses, while the guests wandered about amongst groves of camellias, and green lawns studded with lilies-of-the-valley and hyacinths; rose-bushes in full flower at the corners. When the gipsies were exhausted, dancing began, and later there was an excellent supper in another still more spacious conservatory. The entertainment ended with a cotillon, and for the stranger its originality was only marred by the fact that it had been thawing, and the company could not arrive or depart in "*troikas*,"— sleighs with three horses which seem to fly along the glistening moonlit snow. A favourite amusement, even in winter, is racing these "*troikas*," or sleighs, with fast trotters. The races are to be seen from stands, as in England, and are only impeded by falling snow. The pretty little horses are harnessed, for trotting races, singly, to a low sleigh (in summer to a drosky) driven by one man, wearing the colours of the owner. Two of these start at once in opposite directions on a circular or oblong course marked out on a flat expanse of snow and ice, which may be either land or water, as is found most convenient. It is a picturesque sight, and reminds one of the pictures of ancient chariot races on old vases and carved monuments.

The character of a nation can scarcely fail to be affected by the size of the country it inhabits, and a certain indifference to time and distance is produced by this circumstance. There is also a peculiar apathy as regards small annoyances and casualties. Whatever accident befalls the Russian of the lower orders, his habitual remark is "*Nitchivo*" ("It is nothing"). Nevertheless, Northern blood and a Northern climate have mixed a marvellous amount of energy and enterprise with this Oriental characteristic. Take for example the Caspian railway, undertaken by General Annenkoff. This general completes fifteen hundred miles of railway in the incredibly short space of time of a year and a half, and almost before the public is aware of its having been commenced, he is back again in St. Petersburg dancing at a Court ball in a quadrille opposite the Empress. The railway made by him runs at present from the Caspian Sea to the Amou-Daria River, and will be continued to Bokhara, Samarkand, and Tashkend, in a northerly direction, while on the south it is to enter Persia. Should European complications, by removing the risk of foreign interposition, make it possible for a Russian army to reach the Caspian by way of the Black Sea and the Caucasus, this railway gives it the desired approach to India. By attacking us in India, which they possibly do not desire to conquer, the Panslavists and Russian enthusiasts believe they would establish their empire at Constantinople, and unite the whole Sclav race under the dominion of the Tsar.

The one preponderating impression produced by a short visit to Russia is an almost bewildering sense of its vastness, with an equally bewildering feeling of astonishment at the centralization of all government in the hands of the Emperor. This impression is perhaps increased by the nature of the town of St. Petersburg. Long, broad streets, lit at night by the electric light, huge buildings, public and private, large and almost deserted places or squares, all tend to produce the reflection that the Russian nation is emerging from the long ages of Cimmerian darkness into which the repeated invasions of Asiatic hordes had plunged it, and that it is full of the energy and aspirations belonging to a people conscious of a great future in the history of mankind.

RURAL LIFE IN RUSSIA

LADY VERNEY

The amount of territory given up to the serfs by the Emancipation Act of 1861 was about one-half of the arable land of the whole empire, so that the experiment of cutting up the large properties of a country, and the formation instead of a landed peasantry, has now been tried on a sufficiently large scale for a quarter of a century to enable the world to judge of its success or failure. There is no doubt of the philanthropic intentions of Alexander the First, but he seems to have also aimed (like Richelieu) at diminishing the power of the nobles, which formed some bulwark between the absolute sway of the Crown and the enormous dead level of peasants.

The serfs belonged soul and body to the landowner: even when they were allowed to take service or exercise a trade in distant towns, they were obliged to pay a due, "*obrok,*" to their owner, and to return home if required; while the instances of oppression were sometimes frightful, husbands and wives were separated, girls were sold away from their parents, young men were not allowed to marry. On the other hand, when the proprietor was kind, and rich enough not to make money of his serfs, the patriarchal form of life was not unhappy. "See now," said an old peasant, "what have I gained by the emancipation? I have nobody to go to to build my house, or to help in the ploughing time; the Seigneur, he knew what I wanted, and he did it for me without any bother. Now if I want a wife, I have got to go and court her myself; he used to choose for me, and he knew what was best. It is a great deal of trouble, and no good at all!" Under the old arrangements three generations were often found living in one house, and the grandfather, who was called "the Big One," bore a very despotic sway. The plan allowed several of the males of the family to seek work at a distance, leaving some at home to perform the "*corvée*" (forced labour) three days a week; but the families quarrelled among themselves, and the effect of the emancipation has been to split them up into different households. A considerable portion of the serfs were not really serfs at all. They were coachmen, grooms, gardeners, gamekeepers, etc., while their wives and daughters were nurses, ladies'-maids, and domestic servants. Their number was out of all proportion to their work, which was always carelessly done, but there was often great attachment to the family they served. The serfs proper lived in villages, had houses and plots of land of their own, and were nominally never sold except with the estate. The land, however, was under the dominion of the "*Mir*"; they could neither use it nor cultivate it except according to the communal obligations.

The outward aspect of a Russian village is not attractive, and there is little choice in the surrounding country between a wide grey plain with a distance of scrubby pine forest, or the scrubby pine forest with distant grey plains. The peasants' houses are scattered up and down without any order or arrangement, and with no roads between, built of trunks of trees, unsquared, and mortised into each other at the corners, the interstices filled with moss and mud, a mode of building warmer than it sounds. In the interior there is always an enormous brick stove, five or six feet high, on which and on the floor the whole family sleep in their rags. The heat and the stench are frightful. No one undresses, washing is unknown, and sheepskin pelisses with the wool inside are not conducive to cleanliness. Wood, however, is becoming very scarce, the forests are used up in fuel for railway engines, for wooden constructions of all kind, and are set fire to wastefully—in many places the peasants are forced to burn dung, weeds, or anything they can pick up—fifty years, it is said, will exhaust the peasant forests, and fresh trees are never planted.

The women are more diligent than the men, and the hardest work is often turned over to them, as is generally the case in countries where peasant properties prevail. "They are only the females of the male," and have few womanly qualities. They toil at the same tasks in the field as the men, ride astride like them, often without saddles, and the mortality is excessive among the neglected children, who are carried out into the fields, where the babies lie the whole day with a bough over them and covered with flies, while the poor mother is at work. Eight out of ten children are said to die before ten years old in rural Russia.

In the little church (generally built of wood) there are no seats, the worshippers prostrate themselves and knock their heads two or three times on the ground, and must stand or kneel through the whole service. The roof consists of a number of bulbous-shaped cupolas; four, round the central dome, in the form of a cross is the completed ideal, with a separate minaret for the Virgin. These are covered with tiles of the brightest blue, green, and red, and gilt metal. The priest is a picturesque figure, with his long unclipped hair, tall felt hat largest at the top, and a flowing robe. He must be married when appointed to a cure, but is not allowed a second venture if his wife dies. Until lately they formed an hereditary caste, and it was unlawful for the son of a pope to be other than a pope. They are taken from the lowest class, and are generally quite as uneducated, and are looked down upon by their flocks. "One loves the Pope, and one the Popess" is an uncomplimentary proverb given by Gogol. "To have priests' eyes," meaning to be covetous or extortionate, is another. The drunkenness in all classes strikes Russian statesmen with dismay, and the priests and the popes, are among the worst delinquents. They are fast losing the authority they once had over the serfs, when they formed part of the great political system, of which the Tsar was the religious and political head. A Russian official report says that "the churches are now mostly attended by women and children, while the men are spending their last kopeck, or getting deeper into debt, at the village dram shop."

Church festivals, marriages, christenings, burials and fairs, leave only two hundred days in the year for the Russian labourer. The climate is so severe as to prevent out-of-door work for months, and the enforced idleness increases the natural disposition to do nothing. "We are a lethargic people," says Gogol, "and require a stimulus from without, either that of an officer, a master, a driver, the rod, or *vodki* (a white spirit distilled from corn); and this," he adds in another place, "whether the man be peasant, soldier, clerk, sailor, priest, merchant, seigneur or prince." At the time of the Crimean War it was always believed that the Russian soldier could only be driven up to an attack, such as that of Inkermann, under the influence of intoxication. The Russian peasant is indeed a barbarian at a very low stage of civilization. In the Crimean hospitals every nationality was to be found among the patients, and the Russian soldier was considered far the lowest of all. Stolid, stupid, hard, he never showed any gratitude for any amount of care and attention, or seemed, indeed, to understand them; and there was no doubt that during the war he continually put the wounded to death in order to possess himself of their clothes.

The Greek Church is a very dead form of faith, and the worship of saints of every degree of power "amounts to a fetishism almost as bad as any to be found in Africa." I am myself the happy possessor of a little rude wooden bas-relief, framed and glazed, of two saints whose names I have ungratefully forgotten, to whom if you pray as you go out to commit a crime, however heinous, you take your pardon with you—a refinement upon the whipping of the saints in Calabria and Spanish hagiolatry. The icons, the sacred images, are hung in the chief corner, called "The Beautiful," of a Russian *izba*. A lamp is always lit before them, and some food spread "for the ghosts to come and eat." The well-to-do peasant is still "strict about his fasts and festivals, and never neglects to prepare for Lent. During the whole year his forethought never wearies; the children pick up a number of fungi, which the English kick away as toadstools, these are dried in the sun or the oven, and packed in casks with a mixture of hot water and dry meal in which they ferment. The staple diet of the peasant consists of buckwheat, rye meal, sauerkraut, and coarse cured fish" (little, however, but black bread, often mouldy and sauerkraut, nearly putrid, is found in the generality of Russian peasant homes). No milk, butter, cheese, or eggs are allowed in Lent, all of which are permitted to the Roman Catholic, and the oil the peasant uses for his cooking is linseed instead of olive oil, which last he religiously sets aside for the lamps burning before the holy images. "To neglect fasting would cause a man to be shunned as a traitor, not only to his religion, but to his class and country."

RUSSIAN FARM SCENE.

In a bettermost household, the samovar, the tea-urn, is always going. If a couple of men have a bargain to strike, the charcoal is lighted inside the urn, which has a pipe carried into the stone chimney, and the noise of the heated air is like a roaring furnace. They will go on drinking boiling hot weak tea, in glasses, for hours, with a liberal allowance of *vodki*. The samovar, however, is a completely new institution, and the old peasants will tell you, "Ah, Holy Russia has never been the same since we drank so much tea."

The only bit of art or pastime to be found among the peasants seems to consist in the "circling dances" with songs, at harvest, Christmas, and all other important festivals, as described by Mr. Ralston. And even here "the settled gloom, the monotonous sadness," are most remarkable. Wife-beating, husbands' infidelities, horrible stories of witches and vampires, are the general subjects of the songs. The lament of the young bride who is treated almost like a slave by her father and mother-in-law, has a chorus: "Thumping, scolding, never lets his daughter sleep"; "Up, you slattern! up, you sloven, sluggish slut!" A wife entreats: "Oh, my husband, only for good cause beat thou thy wife, not for little things. Far away is my father dear, and farther still my mother." The husband who is tired of his wife sings: "Thanks, thanks to the blue pitcher (*i. e.*, poison), it has rid me of my cares; not that cares afflicted me, my real affliction was my wife," ending, "Love will I make to the girls across the stream." Next comes a wife who poisons her husband: "I dried the evil root, and pounded it small;" but in this case the husband was hated because he had killed her brother. The most unpleasant of all, however, are the invocations to *vodki*. A circle of girls imitate drunken women, and sing as they dance: "*Vodki* delicious I drank, I drank; not in a cup or a glass, but a bucketful I drank.... I cling to the posts of the door. Oh, doorpost, hold me up, the drunken woman, the tipsy rogue."

The account of the Baba Zaga, a hideous old witch, is enough to drive children into convulsions. She has a nose and teeth made of strong sharp iron. As she lies in her hut she stretches from one corner to the other, and her nose goes through the roof. The fence is made of the bones of the people she has eaten, and tipped with their skulls. The uprights of the gate are human legs. She has a broom to sweep away the traces of her passage over the snow in her seven-leagued boots. She steals children to eat them.

Remains of paganism are to be found in some of the sayings. A curse still existing says, "May Perun (*i. e.*, the lightning) strike thee." The god Perun, the Thunderer, resembles Thor, and like him carries a hammer. He has been transformed into Elijah, the prophet Ilya, the rumbling of whose chariot as he rolls through heaven, especially on the week in summer when his festival falls, may be heard in thunder. There is a dismal custom by which the children are made to eat the mouldy bread, "because the Rusalkas (the fairies) do not choose bread to be wasted." Inhuman stories about burying a child alive in the foundation of a new town to propitiate the earth spirit; that a drowning man must not be saved, lest the water spirit be offended; that if groans or cries are heard in the forest, a traveller must go straight on without paying any attention, "for it is only the wood demon, the lyeshey," seem only to be invented as excuses for selfish inaction. Wolves bear a great part in the stories. A peasant driving in a sledge with three children is pursued by a pack of wolves: he throws out a child, which they stop to devour; then the howls come near him again, and he throws out a second; again they return, when the last is sacrificed; and one is grieved to hear that he saves his own wretched cowardly life at last.

The Emancipation was doubtless a great work. Twenty million serfs belonging to private owners, and 30,000,000 more, the serfs of the Crown were set free. They had always, however, considered the communal land as in one sense their own. "We are yours but the land is ours," was the phrase. The Act was received with mistrust and suspicion, and the owners were supposed to have tampered with the good intentions of the Tsar. Land had been allotted to each peasant family sufficient, as supposed, for its support, besides paying a fixed yearly sum to Government. Much of it, however, is so bad that it cannot be made to afford a living and pay the tax, in fact a poll tax, not dependent on the size of the strip, but on the number of the souls. The population in Russia has always had a great tendency to migrate, and serfdom in past ages is said to have been instituted to enable the lord of the soil to be responsible for the taxes. "It would have been impossible to collect these from peasants free to roam from Archangel to the Caucasus, from St. Petersburg to Siberia." It was therefore necessary to enforce the payments from the village community, the Mir, which is a much less merciful landlord than the nobles of former days, and constantly sells up the defaulting peasant.

The rule of the Mir is strangely democratic in so despotic an empire. The Government never interferes with the communes if they pay their taxes, and the ignorant peasants of the rural courts may pass sentences of imprisonment for seven days, inflict twenty strokes with a rod, impose fines, and cause a man who is pronounced "vicious or pernicious" to be banished to Siberia. The authority of the Mir, of the Starosta, the Whiteheads, the chief elders, seems never to be resisted, and there are a number of proverbs declaring "what the Mir decides must come to pass"; "The neck and shoulders of the Mir are broad"; "The tear of the Mir is cold but sharp." Each peasant is bound hand and foot by minute regulations; he must plough, sow and reap only when his neighbours do, and the interference with his liberty of action is most vexatious and very injurious.

The agriculture enforced is of the most barbarous kind. Jensen, Professor of Political Economy at Moscow, says: "The three-field system—corn, green crops and fallow—which was abandoned in Europe two centuries ago, has most disastrous consequences here. The lots are changed every year, and no man has any interest in improving property which will not be his in so short a time. Hardly any manure is used, and in many places the corn is threshed out by driving horses and wagons over it. The exhaustion of the soil by this most barbarous culture has reached a fearful pitch."

The size of the allotments varies extremely in the different climates and soils, and the country is so enormous that the provinces were divided into zones to carry out the details of the Emancipation Act—the zone without black soil; the zone with black soil; and, third, the great steppe zone. In the first two the allotments range from two and two-thirds to twenty acres, in the steppes from eight and three-quarters to thirty-four and one-third. "Whether, however," says Jensen, "the peasants cultivate their land as proprietors at 1*s.* 9*d.* or hire it at 18*s.* 6*d.* the result is the same—the soil is scourged and exhausted, and semi-starvation has become the general feature of peasant life."

Usury is the great nightmare of rural Russia, at present, an evil which seems to dog the peasant proprietor in all countries alike. The "Gombeen Man" is fast getting possession of the little Irish owners. A man who hires land cannot borrow on it; the little owner is tempted always to mortgage it at a pinch. In Russia he borrows to the outside of its value to pay the taxes and get in his crop. "The bondage labourers," *i. e.*, men bound to work on their creditor's land as interest for money lent, receive no wages and are in fact a sort of slaves. They repay their extortioners by working as badly as they can—a "level worst," far inferior to that of the serfs of old, they harvest three and a half or four stacks of corn where the other peasants get five. The Koulaks and Mir-eaters, and other usurers, often of peasant origin, exhaust the peasant in every way; they then foreclose the mortgages, unite the small pieces of land once more, and reconstitute large estates. A Koulak is not to be trifled with; he finds a thousand occasions for revenge; the peasant cannot cheat the Jew as he does the landlord, and is being starved out—the mortality is enormous.

The peasant class comprises five-sixths of the whole population—a stolid, ignorant, utterly unprogressive mass of human beings. They have received in gift nearly half the empire for their own use, and cling to the soil as their only chance of existence. They consequently dread all change, fearing that it should endanger this valuable possession. A dense solid stratum of unreasoning conservatism thus constitutes the whole basis of Russian society backed by the most corrupt set of officials to be found in the whole world. The middle and upper classes are often full of ardent wishes for the advancement of society and projects for the reform of the State. These are generally of the wildest and most terrible description, but their objects are anything but unreasonable. They desire to share in political power and the government of their country, as is the privilege of every other nation in Europe, and they hope to do something for the seething mass of ignorance and misery around them. The Nihilists have an ideal at least of good, and the open air of practical politics would probably get rid of the unhealthy absurdities and wickedness of their creeds. But the Russian peasant cares neither for liberty nor politics, neither for education, nor cleanliness, nor civilization of any kind. His only interest is to squeeze just enough out of his plot of ground to live upon and get drunk as many days in the year as possible.[1] With such a base to the pyramid as is constituted by the peasant proprietors of Russia, aided by the enormous army, recruited almost to any extent from among their ranks, whose chief religion is a superstitious reverence for the "great father," the Tsar is safe in refusing all concessions, all improvements; and the hopeless nature of Russian reform hitherto, mainly hangs upon the conviction of the Government that nothing external can possibly act upon this inert mass. "Great is stupidity, and shall prevail." But surely not forever!

[Footnote 1: "When God created the world He made different nations and gave them all sorts of good things—land, corn and fruit. Then He asked them if they were satisfied, and they all said 'Yes' except the Russian, who had got as much as the rest, but simpered 'Please Lord, some *vodki*.'"— *Russian Popular Tale.*]

FOOD AND DRINK

H. SUTHERLAND EDWARDS

The essential point in the service of the Russian dinner is—as is now generally known throughout Europe—that the dishes should be handed round instead of being placed on the table, which is covered throughout the meal with flowers, fruit, and the whole of the dessert. One advantage of this plan is, that it makes the dinner-table look well; another, that it renders the service more rapid, and saves much trouble to the host. The dishes are brought in one by one; or two at a time, and of the same kind, if a large number are dining. The ordinary wines are on the table, and nothing has to be changed except the plates. At the end of dinner, as the cloth is not removed, the dessert is ready served; and this has always been one of the great glories of a Russian banquet.

"I was particularly struck," says Archdeacon Coxe, "with the quantity and quality of the fruit which made its appearance in the dessert. Pines, peaches, apricots, grapes, pears, and cherries, none of which can in this country be obtained without the assistance of hot-houses,[1] were served," he tells us, "in the greatest profusion. There was a delicious species of small melon, which had been sent by land-carriage from Astrakhan to Moscow—a distance of a thousand miles. These melons," he adds, "sometimes cost five pounds apiece, and at other times may be purchased in the markets of Moscow for less than half-a-crown apiece." One "instance of elegance" which distinguished the dessert, and which appears to have made an impression on the Archdeacon, is then mentioned. "At the upper and lower ends of the table were placed two china vases, containing cherry-trees in full leaf, and fruit hanging on the boughs which was gathered by the company." This cherry-tree is also a favourite, and certainly a very agreeable ornament, in the present day. At the conclusion of the dessert coffee is served as in France and England. Men and women leave the table together, and after dinner no wine is taken. Later in the evening tea is brought in, with biscuits, cakes, and preserved fruits.

[Footnote 1: That is to say, not in the winter. In the summer, pears and cherries abound in Moscow, and every kind of fruit ripens in the south.]

The reception-rooms in Russian houses are all *en suite*; and instead of doors you pass from room to room through arches hung with curtains. The number of the apartments in most of the houses I remember varied from three to six or seven; but in the clubs and in large mansions there are more. Grace before or after dinner is never said under any circumstances; but all the guests make the sign of the cross before sitting down to table, usually looking at the same time towards the eastern corner of the room, where the holy image hangs.

This ceremony is never omitted in families, though in the early part of the century, when the Gallomania was at its height, it is said to have been much neglected. In club dinners, when men are dining alone, it will be easily believed that the same importance is not attached to it; but the custom may be described as almost universal among the rich, and quite universal among the poor. Indeed, a peasant or workman would not on any account eat without first making the sign of the cross. In Russia, with its "patriarchal" society (as the Russians are fond of saying), it is usual to thank the lady of the house, either by word or gesture, after dining at her table; and those who are sufficiently intimate kiss her hand.

THE TSAR'S DINING-ROOM, MOSCOW.

We now come to the composition of the Russian dinners; and here I must repeat with Archdeacon Coxe, that although the Russians have adopted many of the delicacies of French cookery, they "neither affect to despise their native dishes nor squeamishly reject the solid joints which characterize our own repasts." I was astonished, at one Russian dinner, which I was assured was thoroughly national in style, to meet with the homely roast leg of mutton and baked potatoes of my native land. Like the English, the Russians take potatoes with nearly every dish—either plain boiled, fried, or with parsley and butter over them. Plum-pudding, too, and boiled rice-pudding with currants in it, and with melted butter, are known in Russia—at all events in Moscow and St. Petersburg; and goose is not considered complete without apple-sauce. As in France, every dinner begins with soup; but this custom has not been borrowed from the French. It seems to date from time immemorial, for all the Russian peasants, a thoroughly stationary class, take

- 155 -

their soup daily. The Russians are very successful with some kinds of pickles, such as salted cucumbers and mushrooms; and they excel in salads, composed not only of lettuce, endive, and beetroot, but also of cherries, grapes, and other fruits, preserved in vinegar. The fruit is always placed at the top, and has a very picturesque effect in the midst of the green leaves. Altogether it may be said that the Russian *cuisine* is founded on a system of eclecticism, with a large number of national dishes for its base. Of course, in some Russian houses, as in some English ones, the cooking is nearly all in the French style; but even then there are always a few dishes on the table that might easily be recognized as belonging to the country. We need scarcely remark, that only very rich persons dine every day in the sumptuous style described by Archdeacon Coxe, though the rule as to service may be said to be general—one dish at a time, and nothing on the table but flowers and the dessert. In the winter, when it is difficult and expensive to get dessert, those who are rich send for it where it *can* be obtained—perhaps to their own hot-houses; and those who are not rich, as in other countries, go without. At the *traktirs*, or *restaurants*, the usual dinner supplied for three-quarters of a rouble consists of soup, with a pie of mince-meat, or minced vegetables, an *entrée*, roast meat, and some kind of sweet. That, too, may be considered the kind of dinner which persons of moderate means have every day at home. Rich proprietors, who keep a head-cook, a roaster, a pastry-cook, and two or three assistant-cooks, would perhaps despise so moderate a repast; but from a little manual of cookery which a friend has been kind enough to send me from Russia, it would appear that the generality of persons do not have more than four dishes at each meal.

The most ancient and popular drinks in Russia are hydromel or mead (called by the same name in Russia), beer, and *kvass*. Mead, the fine old Scandinavian drink, is mentioned as far back as the Tenth Century; and in a chronicle of Novgorod of the year 989, it is stated that "A great festival took place, at which a hundred and twenty thousand pounds of honey were consumed." Hydromel is flavoured with various kinds of spices and fermented with hops. Gerebtzoff states that beer is mentioned (under the name of *oloul*—the present word being *pivo*) in the *Book of Ranks*, written in the Eleventh and Twelfth Centuries. But no drink is so ancient as *kvass*, which, according to the chronicle of Nestor, was in use among the Sclavonians in the first century of our era. Among the laws of Yaroslaff there is an old edict determining the quantity of malt to be furnished for making *kvass* to workmen engaged in building a town.

The Russians learnt to drink wine from the Greeks, during their frequent intercourse with the Eastern Empire, long before the Mongol invasion. During the Tartar domination there was less communication with Constantinople and the consumption of wine decreased, but it became greater again during the period of the Tsars. In the beginning of the Seventeenth Century wine was supplied to ambassadors, but the Russians for the most part still preferred their native drinks. The cultivation of the vine was introduced at Astrakhan in 1613, and a German traveller named Strauss, who visited the city in 1675, found that it had been attended with great success; so much so, that, without counting what was sold in the way of general trade, the province supplied to the Tsar alone every year two hundred tuns of wine, and fifty tuns of grape brandy. The wines of Greece were at the same time replaced by those of Hungary, which were in great demand when Peter came and introduced the vintage of France. This by many persons will be considered not the least of his reforms.

The Russians acquired the art of distilling from grain in the Fourteenth Century from the Genoese established in the Crimea, and seem to have lost no time in profiting by their knowledge. They soon began to invent infusions of fruit and berries, which under the name of "*nalivka*" have long been known to travellers, and which I for my part found excellent. "*Raki*," about the consumption of which by the Russian soldiers so much was written during the Crimean war, is a Turkish spirit, and is unknown in Russia. The Russian grain-spirit is called "*vodka*." The best qualities are more like the best whiskey than anything else, only weaker; but it is of various degrees of excellence as of price. The new common *vodka*, like other new spirits, is fiery; but when purified, and kept for some time, it is excellent and particularly mild. Travellers to Moscow who are curious on the subject of *vodka* may visit a gigantic distillery in the neighbourhood, to which it is easy to gain admission, and where they can obtain information and samples in abundance. *Vodka* is sometimes made in imitation of brandy, and there are also sweet and bitter *vodkas*; and, indeed, *vodka* of all flavours. But the British spirit which the ordinary *vodka* chiefly resembles is whiskey. There is one curious custom connected with drinking in Russia which, as far as I am aware, has never been noticed. The Russians drink first and eat afterwards, and never drink without eating. If wine and biscuits are placed on the table, everyone takes a glass of wine first, and then a biscuit; and at the *zakouska* before dinner, those who take the customary glass of *vodka* take an atom of caviare or cheese after it, but not before. It may also be remarked that, as a general rule, the Russians, like the Orientals, drink only at the beginning of a repast.

A hospitable Englishman entertaining a Russian, on seeing him eat after drinking, would press him to drink again, and having drunk a second time, the Russian would eat once more on his own account; which would involve another invitation to drink on the part of the Englishman. As a hospitable Russian, on the other hand, entertaining an Englishman, would endeavour to prevail upon him to eat after drinking, and as it is the Englishman's habit to drink after eating, it is easy to see that too much attention on either side might lead to very unfortunate results.

A great deal is said about the enormous quantity of champagne consumed in Russia. Champagne, however, costs five roubles (from sixteen to seventeen shillings) a bottle—the duty alone amounting to one rouble a bottle—and is only drunk habitually by persons of considerable means. Nor does the champagne bottle go round so frequently at Russian as at English dinners. It is usually given, as in France, with the pastry and dessert, and no other wine is taken after it. The rich merchants are said to drink champagne very freely at their evening entertainments; but the only merchant at whose house I dined had, unfortunately, adopted Western manners, and gave nothing during the evening but tea. However, at festivals and celebrations of all kinds—whether of congratulation, of welcome, or of farewell—champagne is indispensable. What Alphonse Karr says of women and their toilette—that they regard every event in life as an occasion for a new dress—may certainly be paraphrased and applied to the Russians in connection with champagne. Besides the champagne which is given as a matter of course at dinner-parties and balls, there must be champagne at birthdays, champagne at christenings, champagne at, or in honour of, betrothals, champagne in abundance at weddings, champagne at the arrival of a friend, and champagne at his departure. For those who cannot afford veritable champagne, Russian viniculture supplies an excellent imitation in the shape of "*Donskoi*" and "*Crimskoi*,"—the wines of the Don and of the Crimea. As "*Donskoi*" costs only a fifth of the price of real champagne, it will be understood that it is not seldom substituted for the genuine article, both by fraudulent wine merchants and economic hosts. However, it is a true wine, and far superior to the fabrications of Hamburg, which, under the name of champagne, find their way all over the north of Europe. It has often been said that the Russians drink champagne merely because it is dear. But the fact is, they have a liking for all effervescing drinks, and naturally, therefore, for champagne, the best of all. Among the effervescing drinks peculiar to Russia, we may mention apple *kvass, kislya shchee*, and *voditsa. Kislya shchee* is made out of two sorts of malt, three sorts of flour, and dried apples; in apple *kvass* there are more apples and less malt and flour. *Voditsa* (a diminutive of *voda*, water), is made of syrup, water, and a little spirit. All these summer-drinks are bottled and kept in the ice-house.

CARNIVAL-TIME AND EASTER

A. NICOL SIMPSON

Lent is heralded by carnival, called by Russians "Maslanitza"—the "*Butter Wochen*" of the Germans. *Maslanitza* is held during the eighth week preceding Easter, the fast proper is observed during the intervening seven weeks. During Maslanitza every article of diet, flesh excepted, is allowed to be partaken of, but over-indulgence in other articles, including drinks, is not forbidden.

Carnival commences on Sunday at noon and continues till the close of the succeeding Sunday. The salutation during the week is "*Maslanitza*," or "*Sherokie Maslanitza*," "*Sherokie*" meaning, literally "broad," indicating a full amount of pleasure, and the facial expression accompanying this salutation shows plainly that unrestrained enjoyment is the aim and object for the week. Upon the discharge of the time gun at noon, there emerge from all parts of the city tiny sleighs driven by peasants, chiefly Finns, who for the time are allowed to ply for hire by the payment of a nominal tax imposed by the police or city corporation. Most of these Finns are unable to speak Russian intelligibly, although living at no great distance from the capital. It is said that from 5,000 to 10,000 of these jehus come annually to St. Petersburg for *Maslanitza*, and they add materially to the gaiety of the city as they drive along the streets. These Finns are mostly patronized by the working-classes, for the simple reason that their charges are lower than the ordinary *isvozchick*, or cabby.

During the festivities the great centre of attraction for the working population is the "Marco Polo," or "Champ de Mars," an immense plain on the banks of the Neva. Here a huge fair is held, with the usual assortment of stalls, loaded with sweetmeats and similar dainties. Actors from the city theatres are upon the ground, with smaller booths where the stage-struck hero acts the leading part. There are dwarfs, fat women, giants, and the renowned ubiquitous Punch and Judy, merry-go-rounds, card-sharpers, cheap-jacks, and a medley crowd of men and women all catering for the roubles of the crowd. What are termed the "ice-hills" are perhaps the most attractive feature of the gathering.

In the city feasting and visiting are the order of the day. There is no limit to the consumption of "*bleenies*," a kind of pancake made of buckwheat flour, and eaten with butter sauce or fresh caviare, according to the circumstances of the families. Morn, noon, and night *bleenies* are cooked and eaten by the dozen, moistened, of course, with the indispensable *vodka* or native gin, which is distilled from rye.

When midnight of the second Sunday arrives, all gaieties are supposed to vanish, and a subdued and demure aspect must be assumed, and the form of congratulation between friends and acquaintances is—"*Pozdravlin vam post,*" or "I congratulate you on the fast." The church bells toll mournfully at brief intervals from 4 or 5 A. M., when early mass is celebrated until about 8 P. M., when evening service closes.

Before the Passion—like the Jews, who at Passover search diligently for and cast out the old leaven—the Russian housewife likewise searches out every corner, most remorselessly sweeps from its hiding-place every particle of dust. Everything is done to make the house and its contents fit to meet a risen Saviour. The streets, always very clean, receive special attention, even the lamp-posts are carefully washed down and the kerbs sanded. Everything that will clean has brush and soap-and-water applied to it. The reason of this is the belief that our Saviour invisibly walks about the earth for forty days after Easter, that is, until Ascension Day.

On the Thursday of Passion Week "*Strashnaya Nedelli,*" *i. e.,* "*Terrible Week,*" is enacted in a very realistic fashion one of the last acts of our Saviour—"the washing of the Disciples' feet." After the close of the second diet of worship at St. Isaac's Cathedral this ceremony is performed.

The most important day of the week is that of "*Strashnaya Piatnitsa,*" or Good Friday, when the burial of our Lord is enacted before the people in a truly solemn and impressive manner. In every church there is a sarcophagus in imitation of our Saviour's tomb, and many of these sarcophagi are of elaborate workmanship with gorgeous gilt and otherwise ornamented. The lid is adorned with a painting representing our Saviour in death. At dawn this lid is carried into the chapel, and by 3 P. M. the sarcophagus is in its place on the daïs ready to receive the body of our Lord. Shortly before the service is concluded, all the worshippers have their tapers lighted, the flame being procured from a candelabrum in front of the sacred icon. This is done by those nearest to the candelabrum lighting their tapers, while those behind them get the sacred flame from them, and in this way all get their tapers lit. Many endeavour to carry their burning tapers home, so that they may have the holy flame in their dwellings.

ST. ISAAC'S CATHEDRAL, ST. PETERSBURG.

Leaving the chapel the crowd musters in the street. Then there emerges a church dignitary bearing a large brightly-burnished crucifix, followed by others bearing bannerettes and other symbols, the names and uses of which are to us a mystery. Last of all come forth four priests, clad in their gorgeous canonical vestments, bearing the lid of the sarcophagus which is supported on brass rods. Under the lid walks an aged priest clad in his clerical vestments, representing the dead Christ being carried to his tomb. Slowly, sadly, and reverently he is borne to the tomb, the worshippers crossing themselves most devoutly. A sudden rush is made for the church to witness the interment, the big bell meanwhile tolling mournfully as the procession moves on. The sad procession enters the church, and, going up to where the sarcophagus is placed with all the external appearances of love, mourning, and lamentation, the lid is placed on the sarcophagus and the last obsequies of the crucified "Christ" are over.

Preparations are now industriously made for the due celebration of the Resurrection morn. Shopping, shopping, shopping goes on without intermission. Those who can, prepare to adorn their bodies with one or more articles of new clothing, but all make preparations for a sumptuous feast. It is interesting to watch the shops, especially in the public markets, to see the avidity with which every article of food is bought up. The butchers come in, perhaps, for the largest share of custom, as flesh, especially smoked ham, is in universal demand. Ham among all classes of the community is indispensable for the breaking of the fast and the due celebration of the feast. Dyed eggs are in universal request. The exchange of eggs, accompanied with kissing on the lips and cheeks in the form of the cross, accompanies all gifts or exchange. The *koolitch* and *paska* have also to be bought. The *koolitch* is a sweet kind of wheaten bread, circular in form, in which there are raisins. It is ornamented with candied sugar and usually has the Easter salutation on it: "*Christos vozkress*"—"Christ is risen"—the whole surmounted with a large gaudy red-paper rose. The *paska* is made of cords, pyramidal in shape, and contains a few raisins, and, like the former, has also a paper rose inserted on the top. These are the *sine qua non* for the due observance of Easter, but what relation they may have, if any, to the Jewish Feast of the Passover, it is difficult to see, although in many other respects there is a striking resemblance to the service of the Temple in Jerusalem in the ritual of the Russo-Greek Church. The *koolitch* and *paska* and dyed eggs are brought to, but not into, the church on the Saturday evening. Some have burning tapers inserted into them, while a pure white table napkin is spread on the ground, or on benches specially provided for the purpose, awaiting the priests' blessing. The hours for this purpose are six, eight, and ten o'clock. The priests sprinkle the *koolitch, paska*, and dyed eggs at these hours, those to whom they belong slipping a silver or copper coin into his hand as a reward for his services. These articles are then carried home, and along with the other necessities for the feast are laid out on a table, there to lie untouched till the resurrection of the "Saviour" is an accomplished fact. Meanwhile the lessons are being read over the tomb of "Christ," and the devotees, still in large numbers, kiss His face and feet. About 11 P. M. the sarcophagus is wheeled to its usual place in the church, where it remains until the following Easter.

All the churches by this time are densely packed with worshippers, silently waiting with eager expectancy the time when their "Saviour" will break the bonds of death and rise from the tomb in which he has now lain for three days.

As if by magic, everyone has lighted his or her taper, and looks anxiously towards the altar-screen, where preparations are being made by the priests to go to Joseph of Arimathea's garden, as the disciples and women did of old to visit the tomb where Christ was buried. This they do by forming a procession with the crucifix, bannerettes, etc., each carrying a lighted candle in his hand. There is a rush among the worshippers to join the procession. They walk thrice round the church, searching diligently by the aid of their candles for "Christ," and not finding Him, they go to bring the disciples word that He is risen from the dead.

When the procession enters the threshold of the church, the royal gates are thrown back, suddenly displaying a marvellously beautiful stained glass window, and all eyes behold an enchanting representation of the Saviour in the act of rising from the cold grave.

The priests with the choristers, as they enter the church, proclaim in joyful tones, "*Christos vozkress*" ("Christ is risen"), the response being "*Voestenno vozkress*" ("Truly He is risen"). It is really a jubilant song of praise they sing—the finely trained voices of the choir and priests, joined with those of the worshippers, making it most impressive. Every face in the vast crowd bears the joyous expression of gladness, for to these men and women a really dead Christ has risen, and is now invisibly in their midst. Relatives and friends kiss each other and shake hands, and the salutation, "*Christos vozkress*," with the refrain, "*Voestenno vozkress*," is heard on every side. The officiating priest begins the usual early morning service (celebrated on ordinary Sundays at 5 A. M.), which continues until nearly three o'clock, when the churches are closed for the day.

Immediately after midnight a salute of one hundred and one guns is given from the fortress to greet the sacred morn. The whole city is stirred as the loud peal of cannon reverberates, proclaiming to the faithful that Christ is indeed risen from the dead. Some few worshippers remain in church until the early service is over, but the majority retire to their homes to tender the greetings of the day.

Then families and friends assemble at the domestic board that groans under a load of the good things of this life, according to their circumstances, and to make reparation to their stomachs for the privation they have endured during the seven weeks of Lent. And full compensation their stomachs get, as the feast is a literal gorge of meat and drink. Ham is on the table of prince and peasant alike, and it is first partaken of. The table of the rich is spread with all gastronomical luxuries, *vodka* and wines, cold roast beef, eggs, etc. These dainties remain on the table for several days; indeed a free table is kept, and all who call to congratulate are expected to partake of the hospitality. Not to do so is regarded in the light of an insult.

On Easter Sunday only gentlemen pay visits of congratulation; ladies remain at home for that day to receive and entertain visitors. Presents are dispensed to domestic and other servants. A good drink is as indispensable to the feast among the peasant class as a good feed, and they neither deny themselves the one nor the other, their potations lasting for several days.

To the Western mind the continual kissing and giving of eggs on the streets appear strangely out of keeping with the solemnity of the hour. To see a couple of bearded men hugging and kissing each other and each other's wives on the public streets, with the salutation, "*Christos vozkress*," is indeed peculiar. But use and wont justify this, and it would be a breach of courtesy to withhold the lips and cheeks, and would be regarded as indicating indifference to the great feast of the Church. Present-giving, although on somewhat similar lines to our Christmas greetings, is a much heavier tax on a Russian household than Christmas gifts are with us. In the ordinary house in St. Petersburg, the master, on gaining his breakfast-room, is saluted by his domestic servant with "*Prazdnik* (holiday), *Christos vozkress*," which involves a new dress for the female, or a money equivalent. Then the *dvorniks*, or house-porters, resplendent in clean white aprons, make their appearance, giving the usual salutation, and one or two roubles must be given. They have scarcely vanished when a couple of chimney-sweepers put in an appearance, necessitating another appeal to the purse; postmen follow, and in their rear come the juvenile representatives of your butcher, greengrocer, etc., all bent upon testing your liberality. You go to church and the doorkeeper gravely says, "*Christos vozkress*," while he of the cloak-room echoes the sentiment to the impoverishment of one's exchequer. But this seeming mendicancy is not confined to these classes, for even the reverend fathers and brethren walk in the same footsteps unblushingly. Either on foot or by carriage they call upon the well-to-do of their church, give the usual salutation, "*Christos vozkress*," and the kiss, partake of the general hospitality, and get their gratuity or "*Na Chai*," as it is called, and retire. They are scarcely gone when the "*Staroste*," or elders, put in an appearance, followed by the "*Pyefche*," or choristers, all of whom share in the bounty and hospitality of those on whom they call. The priests, of course, come in for the largest share, and, generally speaking, they know the value of the adage, "First come first served."

At mid-day of Easter Sunday a salute is fired from the fortress, and carnival begins again. It is a repetition of the same amusements as in carnival before Lent, and continues until the following Sunday evening.

RUSSIAN TEA AND TEA-HOUSES

H. SUTHERLAND EDWARDS

A true Russian *restaurant*, or *traktir* (probably from the French *traiteur*), is not to be found in St. Petersburg, whose *cafés* and *restaurants* are either German or French, or imitated from German or French models. One of the large Moscow *traktirs* is not only very much larger, but at least twelve times larger than an ordinary French *café*. The best of them is the Troitzkoi *traktir*, where the merchants meet to complete the bargains they have commenced on the Exchange—that is to say—in the street beneath, where all business is carried on, summer and winter, in the open air. St. Petersburg is more fortunate, and has a regular bourse, with a chapel attached to it. The merchants always enter this chapel before commencing their regular afternoon's work ('Change is held at four o'clock in St. Petersburg), and remain for several minutes at their devotions, occasionally offering a candle to the Virgin or some saint. Now and then it must happen that a speculator for the rise and a speculator for the fall enter the chapel and commence their orisons at the same time. Probably they pray that they may not be tempted to cheat one another.

There is no special chapel for the Moscow merchants, nor is there one attached to the Troitzkoi *traktir*, which I am inclined to look upon after all as the real Moscow Exchange. But in each of the rooms, of which the entrances as usual are arched, and which together form an apparently interminable suite, the indispensable holy picture is to be seen; and no Russian goes in or out without making the sign of the cross. No Russian, to whatever class he may belong, remains for a moment with his hat on in any inhabited place; whether out of compliment to those who inhabit it, or from respect to the holy pictures, or from mixed reasons. The waiters, of whom there are said to be a hundred and fifty at the Troitzkoi *traktir*, are all dressed in white, and it is facetiously asserted that they are forbidden to sit down during the day for fear of disturbing the harmony and destroying the purity of their spotless linen. The service is excellent. The waiters watch and divine the wishes of the guests, instead of the guests having to watch, seek, and sometimes scream for the waiters, as is too often the case in England. Here the attendants do everything for the visitor; cut up his *pirog* (meat, or fish patty), so that he may eat it with his fork; pour out his tea, fill his *chibouk*, and even bring it to him ready lighted. The reader perceives that there is a certain Oriental style about the Russian *traktirs*. The great article of consumption in them is tea. Every one orders tea, either by itself, or to follow the dinner; and the majority of those who come into the place take nothing else. You can have a tumbler of tea, or a pot of tea; but in ordering it you do not ask for tea at all, but for so many portions of sugar. The origin of this curious custom it is scarcely worth while to consider; but it apparently dates from the last European war, when, during the general blockade, the price of sugar in Russia rose to about four shillings a pound.

All sorts of stories have been told about the quantity of tea consumed by Russian merchants, nor do I look upon any of them as exaggerated. From twelve to twenty cups are thought nothing of. I have seen two merchants enter a *traktir*, order so many portions of sugar, and drink cup after cup of tea, until the tea-urn before them is empty; yet the ordinary tea-urn of the *traktir* holds at least a gallon, or a gallon and a half.

"Tea," says M. Gerebtzoff, "has become, for every one, an habitual article of consumption, and replaces, advantageously for morality, brandy and beer; for on all occasions when a bargain has to be concluded, or when a companion has to be entertained, or on receiving or taking leave of a friend, tea is given instead of wine or brandy." Indeed, I not only observed that in the Moscow *traktirs* nearly every one drank tea, but that it was a favourite beverage with all classes on all occasions. The middle and upper classes take tea twice or three times a day,—always in the morning, and often twice in the evening. The *isvostchik*, who formerly had a reputation for drunkenness, which travellers of the present day continue to ascribe to him, appears to prefer tea to every other drink. Such, at least, was my experience; and his mode of asking for a *pour boire* seems to confirm it. Some years since travellers used to tell us of the *isvostchik* asking at the end of his drive for *vodka* money ("*na votkou*"); at present the invariable request is for tea-money ("*na tchai*"). Even in roadside inns, where I have seen from twelve to twenty coachmen and postilions sitting down together, nothing but tea was being drunk. A well-known tourist has told us that every Russian peasant possesses a tea-urn, or *samovar*; but this is not the case. The majority of the peasants are too poor to afford such a luxury as tea, except on rare occasions, but a tea-urn is one of the first objects that a peasant who has saved a little money buys; and it is true, that in some prosperous villages there is a samovar in every hut; and in all the post-houses and inns each visitor is supplied with a separate one.

ST. ANNE RESTAURANT, WIBORG.

The samovar, which, literally, means "self-boiler," is made of brass lined with tin, with a tube in the centre. In fact, it resembles the English urn, except that in the centre-tube red-hot cinders are placed instead of the iron heater. Of course, the charcoal, or *braise*, has to be ignited in a back kitchen or court-yard; for in a room the carbonic acid proceeding from it would prove injurious. It has no advantage then, whatever, over the English urn, except that it can be heated with facility in the open air, with nothing but some charcoal, a few sticks of thin dry wood, and a lucifer; hence its value at picnics, where it is considered indispensable. In the woods of Sakolniki, in the gardens of Marina Roschia, and in the grounds adjoining the Petrovski Palace, all close to Moscow, large supplies of samovars are kept at the tea-houses, and each visitor, or party of visitors, is supplied with one. Indeed, the quantity of tea consumed at these suburban retreats in the spring and summer is prodigious. In Russia there is no interval between winter and spring. As soon as the frost breaks up the grass sprouts, the trees blossom, and all nature is alive. In that country of extremes there is sometimes as much difference between April and May as there is in England between January and June. The summer is celebrated by various promenades to the country, which take place at Easter, on the first of May, Ascension Day, Trinity Sunday, and other occasions. The great majority of these promenades are of a festive nature, but some, like that which is made on the 19th of May to the monastery and cemetery of the Don, have a penitential, or, at least, a mournful character. The samovar, however, is present even in the churchyard. I never joined in one of the funeral pilgrimages to the Donskoi convent; but in other cemeteries outside Moscow and St. Petersburg (intramural burial not being tolerated), I noticed that the custodians kept in their lodges a supply of samovars for the benefit of visitors. And, after all, what can be more appropriate than an urn in a cemetery?

Between St. Petersburg and Kovno or Tauroggen, there are upwards of fifty "stations," at each of which tea can be procured. Travellers whose route does not lie along the government post-roads, take samovars with them in their carnages; and small samovars that can be packed into the narrowest compass are made for the use of officers starting on a campaign, and other persons likely to find themselves in places where it may be difficult to procure hot water. Small tea-caddies are also manufactured with a similar object. Each caddy contains one or more glasses; for men among themselves usually drink their tea, not out of tea-cups, but out of tumblers. Not many years since it was the fashion to give cups to women and tumblers to men in the evening; but the tumbler is gradually being banished, at least from the drawing-room.

The Russians never take milk in their tea; they take either cream, or a slice of lemon or preserved fruit, or simply sugar without the addition of anything else. They hold that milk spoils tea, and they are right. Tea with lemon or preserves (forming a kind of tea-punch, well worthy the attention of tea-totallers), is only taken in the evening. Sometimes the men add rum.

HOW RUSSIA AMUSES ITSELF

FRED WHISHAW

If I were asked to state what a Russian schoolboy does with his spare time after working hours are over, I should be much puzzled what to say.

Unfortunately young Russia has not the faintest glimmering of knowledge of the practice or even of the existence of such things as football, cricket, fives, rackets, golf, athletic sports, hockey, or any other of the numerous pastimes which play so important a part in the life of every schoolboy in this merry land of England. Therefore there is no question, for him, of staying behind at the school premises after working hours, in order to take part in any game. He goes home; that much is certain; most of his time is loafed away—that, too, is beyond question. He may skate a little, perhaps, in the winter, if he happens to live near a skating ground, but he will not go far for it; and in the summer, which is holiday time for him, from June to September, he walks up and down the village street clothed in white calico garments, or plays cup and ball in the garden; fishes a little, perhaps, in the river or pond if there happen to be one, and lazies his time away without exertion. Of late years "lorteneece," as lawn-tennis is called in the Tsar's country has been slightly attempted; but it is not really liked: too many balls are lost and the rules of the game have never yet been thoroughly grasped. A quartette of men will occasionally rig up their net, which they raise to about the height of a foot and a half, and play a species of battledore and shuttlecock over it until the balls disappear; but it is scarcely tennis. As a matter of fact, a Russian generally rushes at the ball and misses it; on the rare occasions when he strikes the object, he does so with so much energy that the ball unless stopped by the adversary's eye, or his partner's, disappears forever into "the blue."

Croquet is a mild favourite, too; but it is played very languidly and unscientifically.

Most gardens in Russian country houses contain a swing, a rotting horizontal bar for the gymnastically (and suicidally) inclined, and a giant stride. Occasionally there is a flower-bed in the centre, in which our dear old British friend the rhubarb, monopolizes the space, and makes a good show as an ornamental plant; for he is not known in that benighted country as a comestible, though, of course, children are acquainted with and hate him in his medicinal capacity. Besides the swings and the rhubarb, there are sand or gravel paths; and built out over the dusty road is an open summer-house, wherein the Muscovitish householder and his ladies love to sit and sip their tea for the greater part of each day—this being their acme of happiness. The dust may lie half-an-inch thick over the surface of their tea and bread and butter, but this does not detract from the delights of the fascinating occupation.

I should point out that in all I have said above, I refer not so much to the highest or to the lowest classes of Russian society, as to that middle stratum to which belong the families of the *Chinovnik*, of the infantry officer, or the well-to-do merchant. The aristocracy amuse themselves very much in the same way as our own. They shoot, they loaf and play cards in their clubs, they butcher pigeons out of traps, they have their race-meetings, they dance much and well; some have yachts of their own. Many of them keep English grooms, and their English—when they speak it—for this reason smacks somewhat of the stable, though they are not usually aware that this is the case. If a Russian autocrat has succeeded in making himself look like an Englishman, and behaves like one, he is happy.

Of winter sports—in which, however, but a small minority of the Russian youth care to take part—there are skating, ice-yatching, snow-shoeing, and ice-hilling. The skating ought, naturally, to be very good in Russia. As a matter of fact the ice is generally dead and lacking in that elasticity and spring which is characteristic of our English ice. It is too thick for elasticity, though the surface is beautifully kept and scientifically treated with a view to skating wherever a space is flooded or an acre or two of the Neva's broad bosom is reclaimed to make a skating-ground. Some of the Russian amateurs skate marvellously, as also do many of the English and other foreign residents. Ice-yachting is confined almost entirely to these latter, the natives not having as yet awakened to the merits of this fine pastime. Ice-hilling, however, at fair-time—that is, during the carnival week, preceding the "long fast" or Lent—is much practised by the people. This is a kind of cross between the switchback and tobogganing, and is an exceedingly popular amusement among the English residents of St. Petersburg.

Snow-shoeing, again, is a fine and healthful recreation; it is the "ski"-running of Norway, and is beloved and much practised by all Englishmen who are fortunate enough to be introduced to its fascinations. It is too difficult and requires too much exertion, however, for young Russia, and that indolent individual, in consequence, rarely dons the snow-shoe.

The Russians are a theatre-loving people, and the acting must be very good to please their critical taste. Many of their theatres are "imperial," that is, the state "pays the piper" if the receipts of the theatre so protected do not balance the expenditure. In paying for good artists, whether operatic or dramatic, the Russians are most lavish, and the Imperial Italian Opera must have been a source of considerable expense to the authorities in the days of its state endowment.

Nearly every Russian is a natural musician, and cannot only sing in tune, but can take a part "by ear." The man with the *balaleika*, or *garmonka*, is always sure of an admiring audience, whether in town or village; and there is not a tiny hamlet in the empire but resolves itself, on holidays, into a pair of choral societies—one for male and one for female voices—which either parade up and down the village street, singing, without, of course, either conductor or accompaniment, or sit in rows upon the benches outside the huts, occupied in a similar manner.

Occasionally, but very rarely, you may see a party of Russian children, or young men and women, playing, in the open air, at one of two games. The first is a variant of "prisoner's base"; the other is a species of ninepins, or skittles, played with a group of uprights at which short, thick clubs are thrown. The Russian youth—those who are energetic enough to practise the game—sometimes attain considerable proficiency with these grim little weapons, and make wonderful shots at a distance of some thirty yards or so.

As for the middle-class Russian sportsman, he forms a class by himself, and is a very original person indeed, unless taught the delights of the chase by an Englishman. In his eyes the be-all and end-all of a true sportsman is to purchase the orthodox equipment of a green-trimmed coat, Tyrolese hat, and long boots, and to pay his subscription to a shooting club. He rarely discharges a gun; the rascally thing kicks, he finds; and the birds *will* fly before he can point his weapon at them as they crouch in the heather at his feet; of course he is not such a fool as to fire after they are up and away. As a rule, however, he goes no farther afield than the card-table of the club-house. Why should he? He has bought all the clothes; and what more does a man need to be a sportsman? I cannot honestly affirm that I ever saw one of these good fellows actually fire off a gun; for whenever I have been informed that such an event is about to take place, I have always done my best to put two or three good miles, or a village or two, between myself and the Muscovitish "sportsman."

THE KIRGHIZ AND THEIR HORSES

FRED BURNABY

The aspect of the country now underwent an entire change. We had left all traces of civilization behind us, and were regularly upon the Steppes. Not the Steppes as they are described to us in the summer months, when hundreds of nomad tribes, like their forefathers of old, migrate from place to place, with their families, flocks, and herds, and relieve the dreary aspect of this vast flat expanse with their picturesque *kibitkas*, or tents, while hundreds of horses, grazing on the rich grass, are a source of considerable wealth to the Kirghiz proprietors.

A large dining-table covered with naught but its white cloth is not a cheery sight. To describe the country for the next one hundred miles from Orsk, I need only extend the table-cover. For here, there, and everywhere was a dazzling, glaring sheet of white, as seen under the influence of a mid-day sun; then gradually softening down as the god of light sunk into the west, it faded into a vast, melancholy-looking, colourless ocean. This was shrouded in some places from the view by filmy clouds of mist and vapour, which rose in the evening air and shaded the wilderness around—a picture of desolation which wearied, by its utter loneliness, and at the same time appalled by its immensity; a circle of which the centre was everywhere, and the circumference nowhere. Such were the Steppes as I drove through them at night-fall or in the early morn; and where, fatigued by want of sleep, my eye searched eagerly, but in vain, for a station.

On arriving at the halting-place, which was about twenty-seven versts from Orsk, Nazar came to me, and said, "I am very sleepy; I have not slept for three nights, and shall fall off if we continue the journey."

When I began to think of it, the poor fellow had a good deal of reason on his side. I could occasionally obtain a few moments' broken slumber, which was out of the question for him. I felt rather ashamed that in my selfishness I had over-driven a willing horse, and the fellow had shown first-class pluck when we had to pass the night out on the roadside; so, saying that he ought to have told me before that he wanted rest, I sent him to lie down, when, stretching his limbs alongside the stove, in an instant he was fast asleep.

The inspector was a good-tempered, fat old fellow, with red cheeks and an asthmatic cough. He had been a veterinary surgeon in a Cossack regiment, and consequently his services were much in request with the people at Orsk. He informed me that land could be bought on these flats for a rouble and a half a *desyatin* (2,700 acres); that a cow cost £3 2s. 6d.; a fat sheep, two years old, 12s. 6d.; and mutton or beef, a penny per pound. A capital horse could be purchased for three sovereigns, a camel for £7 10s., while flour cost 1s. 4d. the pood of forty pounds. These were the prices at Orsk, but at times he said that provisions could be bought at a much lower rate, particularly if purchased from the Tartars themselves. The latter had suffered a great deal of late years from the cattle-pest, and vaccinating the animals had been tried as an experiment, but, according to my informant, with but slight success.

The Kirghiz themselves have but little faith in doctors or vets. It is with great difficulty that the nomads can be persuaded to have their children vaccinated; the result is, that when small-pox breaks out among them it creates fearful havoc in the population. Putting this epidemic out of the question, the roving Tartars are a peculiarly healthy race. The absence of medical men does not seem to have affected their longevity, the disease they most suffer from being ophthalmia, which is brought on by the glare of the snow in the winter, and by the dust and heat in the summer months.

The country now began to change its snowy aspect, and party-coloured grasses of various hues dotted the Steppes around. The Kirghiz had taken advantage of the more benignant weather, and hundreds of horses were here and there to be seen picking up what they could find. In fact, it is extraordinary how any of these animals manage to exist through the winter months, as the nomads hardly ever feed them with corn, trusting to the slight vegetation which exists beneath the snow. Occasionally the poor beasts perish by thousands, and a Tartar who is a rich man one week may find himself a beggar the next. This comes from the frequent snow-storms, when the thermometer sometimes descends to from forty to fifty degrees below zero, Fahrenheit; but more often from some slight thaw taking place for perhaps a few hours. This is sufficient to ruin whole districts, for the ground becomes covered with an impenetrable coating of ice, and the horses simply die of starvation, not being able to kick away the frozen substance as they do the snow from the grass beneath their hoofs. No horses which I have ever seen are so hardy as these little animals, which are indigenous to the Kirghiz Steppes; perhaps for the same reason that the Spartans of old excelled all other nations in physical strength, but with this difference, that nature doles out to the weakly colts the same fate which the Spartan parents apportioned to their sickly offspring.

The Kirghiz never clothe their horses, even in the coldest winter. They do not even take the trouble to water them, the snow eaten by the animals supplying this want. Towards the end of the winter months the ribs of the poor beasts almost come through their sides; but once the snow disappears and the rich vegetation which replaces it in the early spring comes up, the animals gain flesh and strength, and are capable of performing marches which many people in this country would deem impossible, a hundred-mile ride not being at all an uncommon occurrence in Tartary. Kirghiz horses are not generally well shaped, and cannot gallop very fast, but they can traverse enormous distances without water, forage, or halting. When the natives wish to perform any very long journey they generally employ two horses: on one they carry a little water in a skin, and some corn, while they ride the other, changing from time to time, to ease the animals.

It is said that a Kirghiz chief once galloped with a Cossack escort (on two horses) 200 miles in twenty-four hours, the path extending for a considerable distance over a mountainous and rocky district. The animals, however, soon recovered from the effects of the journey, although they were a little lame for the first few days.

An extraordinary march was made by Count Borkh to the Sam, in May, 1870. The object of his expedition was to explore the routes across the Ust Urt, and if possible to capture some Kirghiz *aáls* (villages), which were the headquarters of some marauding bands from the town of Kungrad. The Russian officer determined to cross the northern Tchink, and by a forced march to surprise the tribes which nomadized on the Sam. Up to that time only small Cossack detachments had ever succeeded in penetrating to this locality. To explain the difficulties to be overcome, it must be observed that the Ust Urt plateau is bounded on all sides by a scarped cliff, known by the name of the Tchink. It is very steep, attaining in some places an elevation of from 400 to 600 feet, and the tracks down its rugged sides are blocked up by enormous rocks and loose stones. Count Borkh resolved to march as lightly equipped as possible, and without baggage, as he wished to avoid meeting any parties of the nomad tribes on his road. His men carried three days' rations on their saddles, while the artillery took only as many rounds as the limber-box would contain. The expedition was made up of 150 Orenburg Cossacks, sixty mounted riflemen, and a gun, which was taken more by way of experiment than for any other reason, the authorities being anxious to know if artillery could be transported in that direction.

The detachment reached Ak-Tiube in six days without *contretemps*, after a march of 333 miles, and with the loss of only two lame horses.

WINTER IN MOSCOW

H. SUTHERLAND EDWARDS

Russia in the summer is no more like Russia in the winter than a camp in time of peace is like a camp in the presence of the enemy. Moreover, snow is one of the chief natural productions of the country; and without it Russia is as uninteresting as an orchard without fruit. One always thinks of Russia in connection with its frosts, and of its frosts in connection with such great events as the campaign of 1812, or the winter of 1854 in the Crimea. Accordingly, a foreigner in Russia naturally looks forward to the winter with much interest, mingled perhaps with a certain amount of awe. He waits for it, in fact, as a man waits for a thief, expecting the visitor with a certain kind of apprehension, and not without a due provision of life-preservers in the shape of goloshes, seven-leagued boots, scarves, fur coats, etc.

The house I lived in was in the middle of Moscow; and with the exception of the stoves, the internal arrangement seemed like that of most other dwellings in Europe. The Russian stoves, however, are, in fact, thick hollow party-walls, built of brick, and sometimes separating, or connecting, as many as three or four rooms, and heating them all from one common centre. The outer sides of these lofty intramural furnaces are usually faced with a kind of white porcelain, though in some houses they are papered like the rest of the wall, so that the presence of the stove is only known in summer by two or three apertures like port-holes, which have been made for the purpose of admitting the hot air, and which, when there is no heat within, are closed with round metal covers like the tops of canisters. Sometimes, especially in country houses, the stove, or *peitchka* as it is called, is not only a wall, but a wall which, towards the bottom, projects so as to form a kind of dresser or sofa, and which the lazier of the inmates use not infrequently in the latter capacity. In the huts the *peitchka* is almost invariably of this form; and the peasants not only lie and sleep upon it as a matter of course, but even get inside and use it as a bath. Not that they fill their stoves with water—that would be rather difficult. But the Russian bath is merely a room paved with stone slabs and heated like an oven, in which the bather stands to be rubbed and lathered, and to have buckets of water poured over him, or thrown at him, by naked attendants; and accordingly a stove makes an excellent bath on a small scale. As a general rule, every row of huts has one or more baths attached to it, which the inhabitants support by subscription; but when this is not the case, the peasant, after carefully raking out the ashes, creeps into the hot *peitchka*, and is soon bathed in his own perspiration. He would infallibly be baked alive but for the pailfuls of water with which he soon begins to cool his heated skin. Thanks, however, to this precaution, he issues from the fiery furnace uninjured, and, it is to be hoped, benefited.

THE RED SQUARE, MOSCOW.

When a stove is being heated, the port-holes are kept carefully shut, to prevent the egress of carbonic-acid gas. But after the wood has become thoroughly charred, and every vestige of flame has disappeared, the chimney is closed on a level with the garret floor, the covers are removed from the apertures in the side of the stove, and the hot air is allowed to penetrate freely into the room; which, if enough wood has been put into the *peitchka*, and the lid of the chimney closes hermetically, will, by this one fire, be kept warm for twelve or fourteen hours.

Occasionally it happens that the port-holes are opened while there still flickers a little blue flame above the whitening embers. In this case there is death in the stove. The carbonic-acid gas, which is still proceeding from the burning charcoal, enters the room, and produces asphyxia, or at all events some of its symptoms. If you have not time, or if you are already too weak, to open the door when you find yourself attacked by *ougar* (as the Russians call this gas), you had better throw the first thing you have at hand through the window; and the cold air, rushing rapidly into the room, will save you. A foreigner unaccustomed to the hot apartments of Russia will scarcely perceive the presence of *ougar* until he is already seriously affected by it; and in this manner the son of the Persian ambassador lost his life, some years since, in one of the principal hotels of Moscow. A native, however, if the stove should chance to be "covered" before the wood is thoroughly charred, will detect the presence of the fatal gas almost instantaneously; and having done so, the best remedy he can adopt for the headache and sickness, which even then will inevitably follow, is to rush into the open air, and cool his temples by copious applications of snow. Persons who are almost insensible from the effect of *ougar* have to be carried out and rolled in the snow,—a process which speedily restores them to their natural condition.

One morning there was a fall of snow; and the cream was brought in from the country in jars wrapped carefully round with matting to prevent its freezing. Hundreds of cabbages and thousands of potatoes, similarly protected, were purchased and stowed away. Furlongs of wood (in Russia wood is sold by the foot), were laid up in the courtyard; an inspector of stoves arrived to see that every *peitchka* was in proper working order; and an examiner and fitter-in of windows was summoned to adjust the usual extra sash. At last the windows had been made fast, each pane being at the same time reputtied into its frame. On the window-sill, in the space between the outer and inner panes, was something resembling a long deep line of snow, which was, however, merely a mass of cotton-wool placed there as an additional protection against the external air. Indeed, the winds of the Russian winter have such powers of penetration that, in a room guarded by *triple* windows, besides shutters closed with the greatest exactness, I have seen the curtains slightly agitated when the howling outside was somewhat louder than usual. "The wind," says Gregorovitch in his *Winter's Tale*, "howls like a dog; and like a dog will bite the feet and calves of those who have not duly provided themselves with fur-goloshes and doubly-thick pantaloons." Such a wind must not be suffered to intrude into any house intended to be habitable.

Besides the cotton-wool, which is a special provision against draughts, the space between the two sashes is usually adorned with artificial flowers; indeed, the fondness of the Russians for flowers and green leaves during the winter is remarkable. The corridors are converted into greenhouses, by means of trellis-work covered with creepers. The windows of many of the apartments are encircled by evergreens, and in the drawing-rooms, flower-stands form the principal ornaments. At the same time enormous sums are paid for bouquets from the hot-houses which abound in both the capitals. Doubtless the long winters have some share in the production of this passion for flowers and green plants, just as love of country is increased by exile, and love of liberty by imprisonment.

There are generally at least two heavy snow-storms by way of warning before winter fairly commences its reign. The first fall of snow thaws perhaps a few days afterwards, the second in about a week, the third in five months. If a lady drops her bracelet or brooch in the street during the period of this third fall, she need not trouble herself to put out handbills offering a reward for its discovery, at all events not before the spring; for it will be preserved in its hiding-place, as well as ice can preserve it, until about the middle of April, when, if the amount of the reward be greater than the value of the article lost, it will in all probability be restored to her. The Russians put on their furs at the first signs of winter, and the sledges make their appearance in the streets as soon as the snow is an inch or two thick. Of course at such a time a sledge is far from possessing any advantage over a carriage on wheels; but the Russians welcome their appearance with so much enthusiasm, that the first sledge-drivers are sure of excellent receipts for several days. The *droshkies* disappear one by one with the black mud of autumn; and by the time the gilt cupolas of the churches, and the red and green roofs of the houses, have been made whiter than their own walls, the city swarms with sledges. It is not, however, until near Christmas, when the "frost of St. Nicholas" sets in, that they are seen in all their glory. The earlier frosts of October and November mayor may not be attended to without any very dangerous results ensuing; but when the frigid St. Nicholas makes his appearance,—staying the most rapid currents, forming bridges over the broadest rivers, and converting seas into deserts of ice,—then a blast from his breath, if not properly guarded against, may prove fatal.

It has been said that it is not until the *Nikòlskoi Maros*, or Frost of St. Nicholas, that the sledges fly through the streets in all their glory. By that time the rich "boyars"[1] (as foreigners persist in styling the Russian proprietors of the present day), have arrived from their estates, and the poor peasants, who have long ceased to till the ground, and have not thrashed all the corn, begin to come in from theirs; for, humble and dependent as he may be, each peasant has nevertheless his own patch of land. For the former are the elegant sledges of polished nut-wood, with rugs of soft, thick fur to protect the legs of the occupants; whose drivers, in their green caftans fastened round the waist with red sashes, and in their square thickly-wadded caps of crimson velvet, like sofa-cushions, urge on the prodigiously fast trotting horses, at the same time throwing themselves back in their seats with outstretched arms and tightened reins, as though the animals were madly endeavouring to escape from their control. The latter bring with them certain strongly-made wooden boxes, with a seat at the back for two passengers and a perch in front for a driver. These boxes are put upon rails, and called sledges. The bottom of each box (or sledge), is plentifully strewn with hay, which after a few days becomes converted, by means of snow and dirty goloshes, into something very like manure. The driver is immediately in front of you, with his brass badge hanging on his back like the label on a box of sardines. He wears a sheepskin; but it is notorious that after ten years' wear the sheepskin loses its odour, besides which it is winter, so that your sense of smell has really nothing to fear. The one thing necessary is to keep your legs to yourself, or at all events not to obtrude them beneath the perch of the driver, or you will run the chance of having your foot crushed by that gentleman's heel. Sometimes the horse is fresh from the plough, and requires a most vigorous application of the driver's thong to induce him to quit his accustomed pace; but for the most part the animals are willing enough, and as rapid as their masters are skilful. The driver is generally much attached to his horse, whom he affectionately styles his "dove" or his "pigeon," assuring him that although the ground is covered with snow, there is still grass in the stable for his *galoùpchik*—as the favourite bird is called, etc., etc.

[Footnote 1: It would be equally correct to speak of the English nobility of the present day as "the barons."]

As for the real pigeons and doves, they are to be found everywhere,—on the belfries of the churches, in the courtyards of the houses, in the streets blocking up the pavement, and above all, beneath the projecting edges of the roofs, where you may see them clustering in long deep lines like black cornices.

At home we associate snow with darkness and gloom; but, when once the snow has fallen, the sky of Moscow is as bright and as blue as that of Italy; the atmosphere is clear and pure; the sun shines for several hours in the day with a brightness from which the reflection of the snow becomes perfectly dazzling; and if the frost be intense, there is not a breath of wind. The breath that really does attract your notice is that of the pedestrians, who appear to be blowing forth columns of smoke or steam into the rarefied atmosphere, and who look like so many walking chimneys or human locomotives. And if breath looks like smoke, smoke itself looks almost solid. Rise early, when the fires are being lighted which are to heat the stoves through the entire day, and if the thermometer outside your window marks more than 15°, you will see the grey columns rising heavily into the air, until at a certain height the smoke remains stationary, and hangs in clouds above the houses. Looking from some great elevation, such as the tower of Ivan Veliki in the Kremlin, you see these clouds beneath you, agitated like waves, and forming a kind of nebulous sea, which is, however, soon taken up by the surrounding atmosphere.

It is astonishing how much cold one can support when the sky is bright and the sun shining; certainly ten or fifteen degrees more by Réaumur's thermometer, than when the day is dark and gloomy. And the effect is the same on all. On one of these fine frosty days there is unwonted cheerfulness in the look, unwonted energy in the movements of everyone you meet. If there were the slightest wind with so keen a temperature, you would feel, every time it grazed your face, as if you were being shaved with a blunt razor,—for to be cut with a sharp one is comparatively nothing. But the air is calm; and as the day exhilarates you generally, it makes you walk more briskly than you are in the habit of doing in your *shouba* of cloth, wadding, and fur; and the result is, you are so warm and so surrounded by sunshine, that, but for seeing the cold, you might fancy yourself on the shores of the

Mediterranean instead of on the banks of the Moskva, which is now a long, shiny, serpent-like path of ice. In London, on a damp, foggy, sunless winter's day, when the thermometer is not quite down to freezing-point, the system is so depressed by the atmosphere and the cheerless aspect of the streets, that you feel the cold more acutely than you would do on a sunshiny morning in Moscow with ten degrees of frost. In St. Petersburg, where the winter sun is, "as in northern climes, but dimly bright," and where the city is frequently enveloped in a mist (which is, however, ethereal vapour compared to the opaque fogs of London), the cold is, on the same principle, more severely felt than in Moscow. Nevertheless, in St. Petersburg people go about far more lightly clad than in the more southern towns of the empire,—for St. Petersburg is half a foreign city, and the numerous pedestrians have found it necessary to reject the ponderous *shouba* for a long wadded paletot with a fur-collar. The real Russian *shouba* is undoubtedly very warm; for it enables the Moscow merchant to go upon 'Change, which in the old capital, during the coldest weather, is held in the open air.

In considering the advantages and disadvantages of a Russian winter, one should not forget the question of rain. It is evident, then, that where there is frost there can be no rain; and accordingly, for nearly six months in the year, you can dispense altogether with that most unpleasant encumbrance, the umbrella. For it must be remembered that in Russia the snow does not fall in the soft feathery flakes to which we are accustomed in the more temperate latitudes. It comes down in showers of microscopic darts, which, instead of intercepting the light of the sun, like the arrows of Xerxes' army, glitter and sparkle in the rays as they reflect them in every direction. The minute crystals, or rather crystalline fragments, can be at once shaken from the collars of fur, on the points of which they hang like needles, but above all like Epsom salts; and on the cloth of the men's *shoubas* and the satin of the women's cloaks they have scarcely any hold.

The most pleasant time of the whole winter is during the moonlight nights, when the wind is still and the snow deep on the ground. In the streets the sparkling *trottoir*, which appears literally paved with diamonds, is as hard as the agate floor of the Cathedral of the Annunciation in the Kremlin. In the country, where alone you can enjoy the night in all its beauty, the frozen surface crunches, but scarcely sinks, beneath the sledge, as your *troika* tears along the road as fast as the centre horse can trot and the two outsiders gallop. For it is a peculiarity of the *troika* that the three horses that constitute it are harnessed abreast; and that while the one in the shafts, whose head is upheld by a bow, with a little bell suspended from the top, is trained to trot, and never to leave that pace, however fast he may be driven, the two who are harnessed outside must gallop, even if they gallop but six miles an hour; though it is far more likely that they will be called upon to do twelve. Lastly, the *troika* must present a fan-like front; to produce which the driver tightens the outside reins till the heads of the outriggers stand out at an angle of forty or fifty degrees from that of the horse in the shafts. At the same time the centre horse trots with his head high in the air, while the two who have their existences devoted to galloping have their noses depressed towards the ground, like bulls running at a dog.

There may be enough moonlight to read by when the moon itself is obscured by clouds. But if it shines directly on the white ermine-like snow, which covers the vast plains like an interminable carpet, the atmosphere becomes full of light, and the night in its brightness, its solitude, and its silence, broken only by the bells of some distant team, reminds you of the calmness of an unusually quiet and beautiful day. As you turn away from the main road towards the woods, you pass groups of tall slender birch-trees, with their white silvery bark, and their delicate thread-like fibres hanging in frozen showers from the ends of the branches, and clothing the birch with a kind of icy foliage, while the other trees remain bare and ragged. The birch is eminently a winter tree, and its tresses of fibres, whether petrified and covered with crystal by the frost, or waving freely in the breeze which has stripped them of their snow, are equally ornamental. The ground is strewed with the shadows of the trees, traced with exquisite fineness on the white snow, from which these lunar photographs stand forth with wonderful distinctness. To drive out with an indefinite number of *troikas* to some village in the environs, or to the first station on one of the Government roads, is a common mode of spending a fine winter's night, and one which is equally popular in Moscow and St. Petersburg. These excursions, which always partake more or less of the nature of a picnic, form one of the chief pleasures of the cold season. Of course such expeditions also take place during the day, but, whatever the hour of the departure, if there happen to be a moon that night, the return is sure not to take place before it has made its appearance.

A JOURNEY BY SLEIGH

FRED BURNABY

"Bring out another sleigh," said my friend. "How the wind cuts! does it not?" he continued, as the breeze, whistling against our bodies, made itself felt in spite of all the precautions we had taken. The vehicle now brought was broader and more commodious than the previous one, which, somewhat in the shape of a coffin, seemed especially designed so as to torture the occupants, particularly if, like my companion and self, they should happen to be endowed by nature with that curse during a sleigh journey—however desirable appendages they may be when in a crowd—long legs. Three horses abreast, their coats white with pendent icicles and hoar-frost, were harnessed to the sleigh; the centre animal was in the shafts and had his head fastened to a huge wooden head-collar, bright with various colors. From the summit of the head-collar was suspended a bell, while the two outside horses were harnessed by cord traces to splinter-bars attached to the sides of the sleigh. The object of all this is to make the animal in the middle trot at a brisk pace, while his two companions gallop, their necks arched round in a direction opposite to the horse in the centre, this poor beast's head being tightly reined up to the head-collar.

A well-turned-out *troika* with three really good horses, which get over the ground at the rate of twelve miles an hour, is a pretty sight to witness, particularly if the team has been properly trained, and the outside animals never attempt to break into a trot, while the one in the shafts steps forward with high action; but the constrained position in which the horses are kept must be highly uncomfortable to them, and one not calculated to enable a driver to get as much pace out of his animals as they could give him if harnessed in another manner.

Off we went at a brisk pace, the bell dangling from our horse's head-collar, and jingling merrily at every stride of the team.

The sun rose high in the heavens: it was a bright and glorious morning in spite of the intense cold, and the amount of oxygen we inhaled was enough to elevate the spirits of the most dyspeptic of mankind. Presently, after descending a slight declivity, our Jehu turned sharply to the right; then came a scramble and a succession of jolts and jerks as we slid down a steep bank, and we found ourselves on what appeared to be a broad high-road. Here the sight of many masts and shipping which, bound in by the fetters of a relentless winter, would remain imbedded in the ice till the ensuing spring, showed me that we were on the Volga. It was an animated spectacle, this frozen highway, thronged with peasants who strode beside their sledges, which were bringing cotton and other goods from Orenburg to the railway.

Now a smart *troika* would dash by us, its driver shouting as he passed, when our Jehu, stimulating his steeds by loud cries and frequent applications of the whip, would vainly strive to overtake his brother coachman. Old and young alike seemed like octogenarians, their short thick beards and mustaches being white as hoar-frost from the congealed breath. According to all accounts the river had not been long frozen, and till very recently steamers laden with corn from Southern Russia had plied between Sizeran and Samara. The price of corn is here forty copecks the pood of forty pounds, while the same quantity at Samara could be purchased for eighteen copecks. An iron bridge was being constructed a little farther down the Volga. Here the railroad was to pass, and it was said that in two years' time there would be railway communication, not only between Samara and the capital, but even as far as Orenburg.

Presently the scenery became very picturesque as we raced over the glistening surface, which flashed like a burnished cuirass beneath the rays of the rising sun. Now we approach a spot where seemingly the waters from some violent blast or other had been in a state of foam and commotion, when a stern frost transformed them into a solid mass. Pillars and blocks of the shining and hardened element were seen modelled into a thousand quaint and grotesque patterns. Here a fountain, perfectly formed with Ionic and Doric columns, was reflecting a thousand prismatic hues from the diamond-like stalactites which had attached themselves to its crest. There a huge obelisk, which, if of stone, might have come from ancient Thebes, lay half buried beneath a pile of fleecy snow. Farther on we came to what might have been a Roman temple or vast hall in the palace of a Cæsar, where many half-hidden pillars and monuments erected their tapering summits above the piles of the *débris*. The wind had done in that northern latitude what has been performed by some violent pre-adamite agency in the Berber desert. Take away the ebon blackness of the stony masses which have been there cast forth from the bowels of the earth, and replace them on a smaller scale by the crystal forms I have faintly attempted to describe, and the resemblance would be striking.

Now we came to some fishing-huts, which were constructed on the frozen river, the traffic in the finny tribe which takes place in this part of Russia being very great, the Volga producing the sterlet (a fish unknown in other rivers of Europe), in large quantities. I have often eaten them, but must say I could never appreciate this so-called delicacy. The bones are of a very glutinous nature, and can be easily masticated, while the taste of a sterlet is something between that of a barbel and a perch, the muddy flavour of the former predominating. However, they are an expensive luxury, as, to be perfection for the table, they should be taken out of the water alive and put at once into the cooking-pot. The distance to St. Petersburg from the Volga is considerable, and a good-sized fish will often cost from thirty to forty roubles, and sometimes even a great deal more.

We were now gradually nearing our first halting-place, where it was arranged that we should change horses. This was a farm-house known by the name of Nijnege Pegersky Hootor, twenty-five versts distant from Sizeran. Some men were engaged in winnowing corn in a yard hard by the dwelling; and the system they employed to separate the husks from the grain probably dates from before the flood, for, throwing the corn high up into the air with a shovel, they let the wind blow away the husks, and the grain descended on to a carpet set to catch it in the fall. It was then considered to be sufficiently winnowed, and fit to be sent to the mill. The farm-house was fairly clean, and, for a wonder, there were no live animals inside the dwelling. It is no uncommon thing in farm-houses in Russia to find a calf domesticated in the sitting-room of the family, and this more particularly during the winter months. But here the good housewife permitted no such intruders, and the boards were clean and white, thus showing that a certain amount of scrubbing was the custom.

The habitation, which was of a square shape, and entirely made of wood, contained two good-sized but low rooms, a large stove made of dried clay being so arranged as to warm both the apartments. A heavy wooden door on the outside of the building gave access to a small portico, at the other end of which there was the customary *obraz*, or image, which is to be found in almost every house in Russia. These *obrazye* are made of different patterns, but generally take the form of a picture of saints or of the Trinity. They are executed in silver-gilt or brass relief, and adorned with tawdry fringe or other gewgaws. The repeated bows and crosses made by the peasantry before these idols is very surprising to an Englishman, who may have been told that there is little difference between the Greek religion and his own; but if this is the case, the sooner the second commandment is omitted from our service, the better. It may be said that the Russian peasantry only look upon these images as symbols, and that in reality they are praying to the living God. Let any one who indulges in this delusion travel in Russia and talk to the inhabitants with reference to the *obrazye*, or go to Kief at the time of a pilgrimage to the mummified saints in that sanctuary, and I think he will then say that no country in the world is so imbued with superstitious credences as Russia.

Above the stove, which was about five feet high, a platform of boards had been erected at a distance of about three feet from the ceiling. This was the sleeping resort of the family, and occasionally used for drying clothes during the day. The Russian *moujik* likes this platform more than any other part of the habitation, and his great delight is to lie there and perspire profusely, after which he finds himself the better able to resist the cold of the elements outside. The farm-house in which I now found myself had cost in building two hundred roubles, about twenty-six pounds of our money, and her home was a source of pride to the good housewife, who could read and write, an accomplishment not often possessed by the women of this class in the province of Russia.

By this time our former team had been replaced by three fresh horses, and the driver who was to accompany us had nearly finished making his own preparations for the sleigh journey. Several long bands of cloth, first carefully warmed at the stove, were successively wound round his feet, and then, having put on a pair of thick boots and stuffed some hay into a pair of much larger dimensions, he drew the latter on as well, when, with a thick sheep-skin coat, cap, and *vashlik*, he declared that he was ready to start.

The cold was very intense when we quitted the threshold, and the thermometer had fallen several degrees during the last half-hour; the wind had also increased, and it howled and whistled against the eaves of the farm-house, bearing millions of minute snowy flakes before it in its course. Presently the sound of a little stamping on the bottom of the sleigh announced to me that the cold had penetrated to my companion's feet, and that he was endeavouring to keep up the circulation.

Very soon that so-called "pins-and-needles" sensation, recalling some snow-balling episodes of my boyish days, began once more to make itself felt, and I found myself commencing a sort of double-shuffle against the boards of the vehicle. The snow was falling in thick flakes, and with great difficulty our driver could keep the track, his jaded horses sinking sometimes up to the traces in the rapidly forming drifts, and floundering heavily along the now thoroughly hidden road. The cracks of his whip sounded like pistol-shots against their jaded flanks, and volumes of invectives issued from his lips.

"Oh, sons of animals!"—[whack].

"Oh, spoiled one!"—[whack]. This to a brute which looked as if he never had eaten a good feed of corn in his life. "Oh, woolly ones!" [whack! whack! whack!].

"O Lord God!" This as we were all upset into a snowdrift, the sleigh being three parts overturned, and our Jehu precipitated in the opposite direction.

"How far are we from the next halting-place?" suddenly inquired my companion, with an ejaculation which showed that even his good temper had given way under the cold and our situation.

"Only four versts, one of noble birth," replied the struggling Jehu, who was busily engaged endeavouring to right the half-overturned sleigh. A Russian verst about night-fall, and under such conditions as I have endeavoured to point out to the reader, is an unknown quantity. A Scotch mile and a bit, an Irish league, a Spanish *legua*, or the German *stunde*, are at all times calculated to call forth the wrath of the traveller, but in no way equal to the first-named division of distance. For the verst is barely two-thirds of an English mile, and when, after driving yet for an hour, we were told that there were still two versts more before we could arrive at our halting-place, it began fully to dawn upon my friend that either our driver's knowledge of distance, or otherwise his veracity, was at fault.

At last we reached a long, struggling village, formed of houses constructed much in the same way as that previously described, when our horses stopped before a detached cottage. The proprietor came out to meet us at the threshold. "*Samovar, samovar!*" (urn), said my companion. "Quick, quick! *samovar!*" and hurrying by him, and hastily throwing off our furs, we endeavoured to regain our lost circulation beside the walls of a well-heated stove.

The Russian peasants are not ignorant of the good old maxim that the early bird gets the worm, and the few hours' daylight they enjoy during the winter months makes it doubly necessary for them to observe this precept. We were all up a good hour before sunrise, my companion making the tea, while our driver was harnessing the horses, but this time not three abreast, for the road was bad and narrow; so we determined to have two small sleighs with a pair of horses to each, and put our luggage in one vehicle while we travelled in the other.

Off we went, a motley crew. First, the unwashed peddler who had wished to be my companion's bedfellow the night before; then our luggage sleigh; and, finally, my friend and self, who brought up the rear, with a careful eye upon our effects, as the people in that part of the country were said to have some difficulty in distinguishing between *meum* and *tuum*.

The sun was bright and glorious, and in no part of the world hitherto visited have I ever seen aurora in such magnificence. First, a pale blue streak, gradually extending over the whole of the eastern horizon, arose like a wall barring the unknown beyond; then, suddenly changing colour until the summit was like lapis-lazuli, and its base a sheet of purple waves of grey and crystal, radiating from the darker hues, relieved the eye, appalled by the vastness of the barrier; the purple foundations were in turn upheaved by a sea of fire, which dazzled the eye with its glowing brilliancy, and the wall of colours floating in space broke up into castles, battlements, and towers, which were wafted by the breeze far away from our view. The sea of flame meanwhile had lighted up the whole horizon; the eye quailed beneath the glare. The snowy carpet at our feet reflected like a camera the wonderful panorama overhead. Flakes of light in rapid succession bound earth to sky, until the globe of sparkling light arising from the depths of this ocean of flame dimmed into insignificance the surroundings of the picture.

Presently a sudden check and exclamation of our Jehu told us that the harness had given way, and a conversation, freely interlarded with epithets exchanged between the driver and the peddler, showed that there was decidedly a difference of opinion between them. It appeared that the man of commerce was the only one of the party who knew the road, and having discovered this fact, he determined to make use of his knowledge by refusing to show the way unless the proprietor of the horses who drove the vehicle containing our luggage would abate a little from the price he had demanded for the hire of the horse in the peddler's sleigh. "A bargain is a bargain!" cried our driver, wishing to curry favour with his master, now a few yards behind him. "A bargain is a bargain. Oh, thou son of an animal, drive on!" "It is very cold," muttered my companion. "For the sake of God," he shouted, "go on!" But neither the allusion to the peddler's parentage nor the invocation of the Deity had the slightest effect upon the fellow's mercenary soul.

"I am warm, and well wrapped up," he said; "it is all the same to me if we wait here one hour or ten;" and with the most provoking indifference he commenced to smoke, not even the manner in which the other drivers aspersed the reputation of his mother appearing to have the smallest effect. At last the proprietor, seeing it was useless holding out any longer, agreed to abate somewhat from the hire of the horse, and once more the journey continued over a break-neck country, though at anything but a break-neck pace, until we reached the station—a farm-hause—eighteen versts from our sleeping quarters, and, as we were informed, forty-five from Samara.

RUSSIAN ARCHITECTURE

EUGÈNE EMMANUEL VIOLLET-LE-DUC

The Russian people, composed of diverse elements in which the Sclav predominated at the moment when that vast empire began to be established under great princes and amid incessant struggle, was in too close communication with Byzantium not to have been to a certain extent in submission to Byzantine art; but nevertheless each of these elements was in possession of certain notions of art which we must not neglect.

The Sclavs, like the Varangians, knew scarcely anything but construction by wood, but at a comparatively early period they had already carried the art of carpentry very far, and in many different channels.

The Sclavs (as extant traditions show), proceeded by piles in their wooden buildings: and the Scandinavians resorted to joining and dove-tailing. Thus, the latter early attained great skill in naval construction.

These two methods of construction in wood have persisted till the present day, which fact is easily established on examining the rural dwellings of Russia.

The Sclavs, moreover, as well as the Varangians, possessed certain art expressions which denote an Asiatic origin.

Even in Byzantine art, so far as ornamentation is concerned, there were origins that were evidently common to those that are felt in the Sclav arts; and these original elements are again found in Central Asia.

That ornamentation, composed of interlacings and conventional floral motives, dry and metallic, which was adopted at Byzantium, where it very soon destroyed the last vestiges of Roman art, also appears on the most ancient monuments of the Sclavs, and even on objects that in France are attributed to the Merovingians, that is to say, the Franks who came from the shores of the Baltic.

Thus, Russia was to take her arts, as regards ornamentation, from branches that are far apart from one another in time and distance, but which sprang from a common trunk.

About the Tenth Century, the Russian buildings were of wood; all texts agree on this point, and consequently these constructions could have no part in Byzantine architecture, which does not recall even the traditions of carpentry work.

Towards the Eleventh Century, when the Russians began to build religious edifices of masonry, the structure of which, particularly in the vaulting, is inspired by Byzantine art, they adapted to this structure, together with a sensibly modified Byzantine garb, an ornamentation, derived from Asiatic, Sclavic and Turanian elements in variable, that is to say local, proportions.

CHURCH OF THE REDEMER, MOSCOW.

For at least three centuries, Byzantium was the great school sought by the Latin, Visigothic and Germanic nations of Europe for art teaching, and it was not till the end of the Twelfth Century that the French broke away from these traditions. Their example was followed in Italy, England and Germany more or less successfully. Russia held aloof from these attempts: she was too closely identified with Byzantine art to try any other course; it may be said that she was the guardian of that art, and was to carry on its traditions by mingling with it elements due to the Asiatic Sclavic genius.

All the dominant elements in Russian art, whether they come from the north or south, belong to Asia. Iranians or Persians, Indians, Turanians, or Mongols have furnished tribute, though in unequal quantities, to this art.

It may also be said that if Russia has borrowed much from Byzantium, the art elements among her population have not been without influence upon the formation of Byzantine art. We think even that the influence of Byzantine upon Russian art has been greatly exaggerated, and that Persia may have had at least as much effect upon the course of art in Russia.

However, we must except everything pertaining to images. But even here Asiatic influence makes itself felt, not in the form, but in the preservation of the types. The imagery of the Greek school has never gone out of favour in Russia, and it still holds its place there in the representation of holy personages. In this, Russia shows her attachment to tradition, as all the Asiatic races do, and shows how little her intimate sentiments have suffered modification.

The Russians avoided the influence of the Iconoclasts which was felt so violently in the Western Empire in the Eighth Century, and later still in various parts of Western Europe; among the Vaudois and Albigenses in the Twelfth and Thirteenth Century, the Hussites in the Fifteenth, and the Reformers in the Sixteenth.

But if Russian architecture and ornamentation show marked originality, this does not seem to be the case with the representation of holy personages. These remain Byzantine. It was the school of Mount Athos that supplied Russia with the types, as it did to almost all the Greek Christians of the Orient.

In these representations, we have difficulty in finding a tendency towards realism, which, morever, does not appear till quite late, and does not come to full bloom.

In Russian art, it is possible to find a few Scandinavian traces, or, to be more exact, in the arts of Scandinavia we find some elements borrowed from the same sources whence the Russians took theirs.

Russia has been one of the laboratories in which the arts, brought from all parts of Asia, have been united to adopt an intermediate form between the Eastern and the Western world.

Geographically, she was favourably placed to gather together these influences; and, ethnologically, she was entirely prepared to assimilate these arts and develop them. If she has stopped short in this work, it was only at a very recent period, and when repudiating her origin and traditions, she tried to become Western, in spite of her own genius.

In the first place, the oldest religious edifices of Russia affect slender forms, in elevation, which distinguishes them from the purely Byzantine buildings.

Evidently, the Russians, from the Twelfth Century on, employed in their religious edifices a geometrical plan that was different from that employed by the Byzantine architects, but one very close to that admitted by the architects of Greece during the early years of the Middle Ages.

In Georgia and Armenia, a number of ancient churches, the majority of which are very small, are also of this character. But, while submitting to these dispositions, as soon as they adopted masonry instead of wood for building, the Russians gave quite individual proportions to their religious edifices.

By the Fifteenth Century, Russia had combined all the various elements by the aid of which a national art should be constituted. To recapitulate these origins: We find already among the Scythians some elements of art fairly well developed, foreign to Greek art and derived from Oriental tradition. Byzantium, in constant contact with the people of Southern Russia, made its arts felt there; but in the North, some slight Finnish influences and then some Scandinavian ones, make themselves felt. From Persia likewise, Russia received impulses in art, on account of her commercial relations with that country through Georgia and Armenia. In the Thirteenth Century, the Tartar-Mongol domination was imposed upon Russia, employed her artists and craftsmen, and thus placed her in direct contact with that Mediæval Orient that was so mighty and so brilliant in all its art productions.

At length left to herself, in the Fifteenth Century, Russia constituted her own art from these various sources. But this variety of sources is more apparent than real. It is enough to examine Scythian ornamentation to recognize that it is of a pronounced Indo-Oriental character. Byzantine taste has exerted a preponderating influence upon Russia. But it has been recognized that this Byzantine style is itself composed of very varied elements among which figure most largely the art of Eastern Asia, and that from this Byzantine art Russia likes to appropriate the Asiatic side in particular.

So that we may regard Russian art as composed of elements borrowed from the Orient to the almost complete exclusion of all others.

Moreover, if we follow the streams of art to their sources, we soon come to recognize that the tributaries are not at all numerous.

In the matter of architecture, there are only two principles: structure by wood and concrete structure: grottoes, and construction with clay, and with masonry, which is derived from it. As to construction with cut stones, there results, either from a tradition of building with wood or from concrete construction, grottoes or conglomerate masses, sometimes both, as in Egyptian art, for example.

The innumerable races who issued from the East and finally overwhelmed the Roman Empire had preserved from their cradle their own traditions, and continued to keep up communication with their old homes. Better than any other nation, the Russians preserved these traditions, and they were, so to speak, rejuvenated every time a new wave passed across their territories; for it was always from the northern or southern Orient, from the Ural or the Taurus, that the invaders came. Whether they presented themselves as enemies or colonists they brought with them something of Asia, the great mother of civilizations.

This Russian art, therefore, was never struck with decadence as was the Byzantine art. It did not live solely upon itself, but profited by all that was brought from the Orient. So, when the Eastern Empire fell during the Fifteenth Century, leaving only a pale trace of the last expressions of its arts, Russia, on the contrary, was raising edifices and fabricating objects of great value from an artistic point of view.

The West had only a small share in these productions, but even this was enough to enable Russian art to be distinguished from the arts of the East by a certain freedom of conception and variety in the execution that rendered it an original product full of promise, the developments of which might have been marvellous if the natural course of events had not been hindered by the passion with which high Russian society threw itself on the works of art of Italy, Germany and France.

SCULPTURE AND PAINTING

PHILIPPE BERTHELOT

Western influence was very strongly felt in sculpture and painting in Russia during the Eighteenth and Nineteenth Centuries. Narrowly confined to the representation of conventional types of saints, these arts did not acquire either personality or expression for two centuries. It was not until the Eighteenth Century that they began to raise statues to the memory of Russia's great men: one of the first monuments was consecrated, as was indeed just, to Peter the Great, Russia's great reformer; in his lifetime, Count Bartolomeo Rastrelli the sculptor, father of the architect, executed a *Peter the Great on Horseback*, which was cast in bronze in 1847; but the successors of Peter the Great did not like this group which they did not consider sufficiently animated and would not allow it to be erected on a public square. Catherine II. had Falconet model a *Peter the Great* mounted on a fiery horse climbing up a rock; this bronze group is placed in the centre of the Square of Peter the Great on the Neva, at St. Petersburg. Among the most celebrated works of Russian sculpture, we may cite the bronze monument erected to the memory of Prince Poyarski and the butcher Minine on the Red Square, Moscow (by Martoss, rector of the Academy of Fine Arts, St. Petersburg, in 1888); Lomonossov's monument (by Martoss); those of Generals Barclay de Tolly and Koutousov (1818-1836 after the model by B. Orlovski, placed in front of the Cathedral of Kazan, St. Petersburg); the colossal bust of Alexander I. (by Orlovski); the commemorative monument of Alexander I. (1832, by Montferrand), with a statue of the Angel of Peace, by Orlovski; the statue of Krilov, the fabulist, 1855, by Baron Clodt in the Summer Garden, St. Petersburg; an equestrian statue of the emperor Nicholas I. (by Clodt, 1859, on the St. Mary square); the monument of Novgorod, elevated in memory of the millenary of the Russian occupation (1862), in the form of a gigantic bell containing scenes from Russian history, by Mikiechin; the monument to Catherine II. by Mikiechin, she being represented as surrounded by her generals and statesmen (1874, before the Alexander Theatre); the monument to Pushkin in Moscow (1830, by Objekuchin and Bogomolov); the monument to Bohdan-Chmelnizki, at Kiev (1873, by Mikiechin and other sculptors). The principal Russian sculptors are Popov, Antokolski (statue of Ivan the Terrible, 1871, in St. Petersburg), Tchichov and E. Lanceray. They are characterized by a very pronounced realism that is common to all.

Russian painting has developed in various directions during the last two centuries under the influence of Western Europe; until the first half of the Nineteenth Century the imitation of Italian painting, the classical French school and the execution of strictly academic painting were the three principal paths attempted by the Russian artists. But for half a century, art has found a national expression for itself. At the end of the Eighteenth and beginning of the Nineteenth Century, the principal representatives of religious and historical painting were Losenko (died in 1773), Antropov (died in 1792), Akimov (died in 1814), Ugriumov (died in 1823), Levizki (died in 1822), Ivanov (died in 1823), and Moschov (died in 1839). The landscape and marine painters of greatest repute are Sim. and Sil. Schtchedrin (the first died in 1804, and the second in 1830), Pritchetnikov (died in 1809), F. Alekseiev (died in 1824). Academic painting was cultivated principally by Tropinin (died in 1827), Warnek (died in 1843), Lebediev (died in 1837), Worobiev (died in 1855), K. Rabus (died in 1857), Bruni (died in 1875), Markov (died in 1878), A. Beidemann (died in 1869) and Willewalde. The chief painter of the romantic school is K. Brullov, who formed a school and had numerous scholars. Other romantic painters of repute are Bronnikov and various landscape and marine painters such as Aivasovski, Bogolnibov, L. Lagorio and A. Mechtcherski. Religious and popular painting has A. Ivanov for its representative. The principal realistic painters in genre and historical painting are Fedotov, Makovski, Perov, Polenor, Vereschagin, etc.

STATUE OF PETER THE GREAT AND THE ADMIRALTY
PALACE, ST. PETERSBURG.

Ornamental sculpture seems to be superior to statuary in Russia: it is abundantly practised in the decoration of churches; the innumerable chapels standing at the street corners in honour of some saint possess icons and lamps of bronze and silver; the iconostases of the cathedrals are extremely rich,—gold, silver-gilt, silver, lapis-lazuli, malachite and enamel-work are lavishly employed there. In the churches of Saint Isaac and the Saviour there are many admirable and veritable *chefs d'œuvre* of originality and brilliancy to be found. The industry of bronze and goldsmith's work in religious objects is very flourishing and gives occupation to numerous workmen and artists in Moscow and St. Petersburg. An imperial manufactory produces the mosaics which occupy such a great place in the decoration of the churches.

Industrial arts are very prosperous in Russia and have made great progress during the last century: silken goods are no longer imported from Lyons; and the Russian cabinet-makers produce beautiful furniture, not only in their national style, but in the purest forms of French art of the Louis XV. and Louis XVI. styles. Civil goldsmith's work and jewellery have also been benefited by the national Renaissance: the Emperor Alexander III. restored to honour the national feminine costume for official balls, and ordered works of art to be made after the models of the Muscovite style, and indeed even after the marvels found in the excavations of the Cimmerian Bosphorus. The religious images, particularly those made in Moscow and Kazan, come very near being works of art. Numerous manufactories produce icons painted on wood or copper, ornamented with reliefs of copper, *crysocale*, silver, silver-gilt and gold. The workmen are monks and peasants: each part of the icon—eyes, nose, mouth, hands and feet—is executed by a specialist who always makes the same thing, after the immutable types that the Muscovite convents received from Mount Athos.

RUSSIAN MUSIC

A. E. KEETON

Russian music is the strangest paradox—it owes more to the music of other countries than any other school, yet no music is more thoroughly individual and unmistakable. It clothes itself after the form and fashion of its neighbours, but beneath its garb peeps out a physiognomy indubitably Sclavonic. Its utterances impress us as the most modern—yet the student who would correctly analyze many of its unique characteristics of harmony and modulation is often obliged to take a flying leap backwards over a space of centuries in order to investigate old Church modes, or Persian and Arabian scale systems, both so ancient as to be well-nigh forgotten in Western Europe.

Sixty years ago, there was no Russian school of music, properly speaking; then suddenly it sprang into being. The wonderful rapidity of its growth almost confuses one. Its exponents at once displayed the astonishing receptiveness common to their race. *D'un trait*, as the French would say, they appropriated the knowledge and experience which the Italian and German schools had been slowly amassing for centuries. Technique, form, counterpoint—all these they found ready made to their hand, and borrowed them unstintingly. Had they done this and no more, the onlooker might have dismissed them as clever plagairists, and probably no one would have paid them any further attention. But they had other means at their disposal. Their country contained a treasure-house of native melody and rhythm; a region albeit which few Russians had hitherto thought it worth their while to explore. It is true that, since the middle of the Seventeenth Century, tentative excursions had been made in this direction from time to time, chiefly, though, by outsiders settled in Russia, nor had any of their efforts led to very appreciable results. The man who first turned with serious intent to the pent-up musical resources of his own country was Michael Ivanovitch Glinka. He had sufficient strength of purpose to carry out his designs—he became the founder of the modern Russian school of music and the father of Russian opera.

Glinka belonged to a good if not very wealthy family, who lived upon their estate in the government of Smolensk, where he was born in 1804. From babyhood upwards he delighted his friends and relations by his aptitude not for music alone, but also for languages, literature, zoology, botany—in fact, for each and every intellectual pursuit which came in his way. The brilliance of his college course in St. Petersburg was noteworthy. He quitted it to occupy a civil post under Government, a position, however, which he soon abandoned, in order to devote himself solely to music. Like so many other men of genius, he married a woman quite incapable of comprehending his artistic aims and ambitions; to quote the words of a Russian writer, Madame Glinka, *née* Maria Petrovna, "was only a pretty doll, who loved society and fine clothes, and had no sympathy whatever with her husband's romantic, poetic side." One is glad to state that Glinka never had to struggle with poverty. He died at Berlin in 1857.

He did for Russian music what his contemporary, Pushkin, did for Russian literature, each in his own department representing a national movement. Perhaps it is not too far-fetched a theory to trace this movement to the momentous date of 1812, when it fell to the lot of Russia to administer the first check in Napoleon's triumphant career. Ever since the reign of Peter the Great it had been the fashion to ape foreign habits, to speak foreign tongues, to import foreign music, to mimic foreign literature. But when a foreign invader, who had marched all-conquering through the rest of Europe, appeared in serious earnest at the very gates of Moscow, there was a rebound: slumbering patriotism awoke with a great shout, and, united by a common danger, all classes gathered together for the protection of their Tsar and their Kremlin. To have repulsed a Napoleon was a mighty deed, which could reveal to the Russians of what stuff they were made. It taught them to rely upon each other and be strong in themselves; and as the art of a nation is invariably the outcome of its history, so the rising generation of Russian thinkers looked inwards rather than abroad. Glinka, Pushkin, and their followers sought no foreign aid; they represent a Russian Renaissance. They were content, indeed, to abide by the forms universally adopted elsewhere, but the spirit of their art manifestation was Russian to its core. In literature, Pushkin and Gogol were never weary of delineating their compatriots in every grade of Sclavonic society, whilst Glinka took his musical inspirations from his native folk-songs and dance-rhythms—from the historic chronicles of his country or its legendary lore. In reality, the foreign influences and environment with which he came so continuously into contact served more and more to convince him that Russia in her turn had as great a mission in music as any other nation. For thirty years the idea was gradually gaining strength in his mind. "I want," he said to a friend, "to write an essentially national opera both as regards subject and music; something which no foreigner can possibly accuse of being borrowed, and which shall come home to my compatriots as a part of themselves."

His fame depends solely upon the two operas, *La Vie pour le Tsar* and *Russlan et Ludmille*. That he should have chosen to express himself especially in opera is a significant fact. The unerring instinct of his genius evidently told him that in this form, rather than in purely instrumental music, he would most truly represent that people whose musical aspirations he wished above all else to portray faithfully, and certainly in opera lay his surest way towards enlisting the sympathies of his compatriots. As before remarked, one might have imagined that opera would scarcely ally itself to his personal individuality; it seems probable, therefore, that various salient traits inherent in the Russians as a nation must have led him to the choice. First and foremost, any music which claims to proceed from the very heart of the Russian people must contain a vocal element. So universal a love of singing as exists throughout Russia is to be met with in no other country.

By this one does not mean to infer that Russian cultivated singing, either solo or choral, is in any way superior to what is heard elsewhere. The Russian peasant knows absolutely nothing about voice production, nor, maybe, is he gifted with any unusual vocal material, nevertheless, singing is closely bound up with every rural event of his cheerless existence. During the last half-century many hundreds of the native melodies sung by the Russian country people for generations past have been collected and written down by different musicians—Balakireff, Rimsky-Korsakoff, Prokoudin, and Lisenko amongst others. The variety of these folk-songs is astonishing. They never become monotonous, each song having its distinctive climax, and the air always suits the words. Often the untutored singer has one melody in his *répertoire*, but intuitively he modifies its strains according to the sentiment of his subject.

This general love of music applies as much to the noble as to the peasant. "Where there is a Sclav there is a Song," says a Sclavonic proverb, and no public ceremony or Court function is ever deemed complete in Russia without an outburst of singing to heighten its impressiveness. There is besides a marked dramatic ingredient in the Sclavonic character. The typical Russian loves acting. To discover this, it is only necessary to visit a Russian village and witness the unconscious presentments of lyric drama or of desolate tragedy set forth by the quaint rites of a country wedding or a rustic funeral. Or study a Russian legend. It at once impresses you with its wealth of dramatic situations most concisely defined. In this, the Sclavonic folktale differs radically from its Celtic neighbour. A comparison of the two types suggests that the Russian principally desires a clear statement of facts; a poetic idea which must be extracted from clouds of metaphor conveys but little significance to his mind. An innate love of song, an innate love of acting, a keen perception of dramatic unity, combined with a passionate love of colour and a strong sense of movement—here surely, without any manner of doubt, one has the basis of a well-nigh perfect school of opera. Glinka, the cultivated musician, himself a Russian, thoroughly appreciated these national qualities; indeed they were part and parcel of his birthright. He could assimilate the characteristics of his race and merge them into his own very remarkable originality. The first product of the combined motors was *La Vie pour le Tsar*, given at St. Petersburg in 1836. Fifty years later it had reached its

577th performance, and from all accounts it still retains an undiminished popularity.

THE THEATER, ODESSA.

If we dissect this opera and examine its wonderful mastery of technique and its depth of musical inspiration, it displays beauties which cannot fail to appeal to connoisseurs of every race and school. But regarded as a whole, one is inclined to doubt its ever becoming a standard work outside its native home. Its true scope and meaning can only be justly estimated by a public acquainted with Russia herself, with her people, her history and her innermost modes of thought.

Glinka attached the highest value to the folk-song, of which, as already stated, he found a treasure trove ready to his hand. Nothing, though, was further from his thoughts than to employ this material in *pot-pourri* style. Russians themselves are all agreed that it would be difficult to select one whole folk-song from any single work of Glinka's. It would naturally require a native of Russia with an accurate knowledge of these native tunes to tell us exactly when and where he used them. He seized their mood. In this way he developed every species of Sclavonic folk-song—Great Russian, Little Russian, Circassian, Polish, Finnish—with a passing flavour contributed by Persia, for undoubtedly Oriental music had, at some remote period, influenced its Sclavonic neighbour very strongly. Glinka may be said to have attained his end almost unconscious of his mode of procedure. Determined to compose Russian music, he pursued his idea unremittingly, but it was only towards the close of his life that he began to seriously analyze his effects, asking himself whence he had obtained them and in what essential points they exhibited their nationality. This inquiry involved him in a field of research bewildering in its magnitude, and one which his early death unfortunately prevented him from thoroughly investigating. Nor is the task by any means completed now, some forty years later, although many Russian musicians have thrown considerable light upon its varied aspects. The first step towards a folk-song analysis was the collecting of the melodies in sufficient numbers for comparison. So much being done, it flashed upon Glinka that there was an intimate connection between the Russian folk-song and the most ancient Russian Church music. That is to say, the melody and the freedom of rhythm typical of the folk-song had been evolved by the people, whilst its harmonization, in which lay one of its most striking essentialities, had been bequeathed it by the Church. From all that can be gathered concerning music in Muscovy prior to the introduction of Christianity, it seems justifiable to admit that harmony, or part singing, was already practised amongst the inhabitants, in what manner it is impossible to conjecture. At any rate, when the Church of Byzantium took root there, the Sclav was sufficiently advanced musically to imbibe a new idea. We know that the Byzantine Church modes were purely diatonic, so is the harmonization of the Russian folk-song in its most elementary and uncorrupted form. That the one produced the other is a most natural conclusion. In the oldest of the Russian national melodies Glinka discovered the most clearly defined type of the earliest Christian songs on record.

A wonderful testimony this to the indwelling religious spirit of the Russian people, who change but little and who are singularly tenacious of their customs in spite of all their ready receptiveness. In one sense the folk-song is as rude and hardy as its singer; from another point of view it is a shy, delicate emanation shrinking from all human intercourse outside its own small coterie of familiar voices. In Russia, as in every other country, it has had to be sought in the remote Steppes and far-off districts where foreign influences had never penetrated, and by a curious inverse process its harmonies, of course, transmitted orally, were the means of preserving the Byzantine Church tonality long after this "first cause" had accepted chromatic and enharmonic modulations. In the chief Russian cities and more opened-up parts of the country, the Italian, French, and later on German elements gradually formed themselves into Church as well as secular music, and only within the last sixty years have attempts been made to restore this to its pristine and, perhaps it may be added, somewhat monotonous purity. The minor key in which the Sclavonic folksong was usually couched, together with its extraordinary variety of rhythm and phrase, protected it from this monotony, the minor keys having infinitely richer resources of colour, even when strictly diatonically treated, than the major.

Sclavonic music figures so constantly upon every concert programme in these days that we are probably most of us accustomed to its vagaries of rhythm, or what may be styled irregularity of metre. This is a direct heritage from the folk-song, which Glinka and his successors have borrowed largely.

The leading musical spirits of his day were quick to accredit him a kindred genius. Berlioz welcomed him gladly, and furthered his cause by eloquent writing as well as by obtaining him a hearing in Paris. Liszt was another enthusiastic "Glinkite," and Schumann, unfailingly keen to notice new talent pursuing a new path, speedily drew attention to a Russian who was doing for the music of his country what Chopin and Moniusco had done for Poland. Rubinstein, who was still a boy when Glinka's sun was near setting, grew up with a warm admiration for the founder of his native school, and in 1855 he spent some of his ardour upon a highly laudatory article in the *Wiener Zeitschrift für Musik*, placing Glinka on a par with Beethoven. Glinka thoroughly detesting anything that savoured of flattery, took the young musician soundly to task for his pains; but Rubinstein remained true to his tenets, and later on, when years had matured his judgment, we find him including the name of Glinka with that of Bach, Beethoven, Schubert and Chopin, as the chief germinators of modern music; whilst one of the last acts of his generous public career was a concert given in aid of a national monument to the composer of *La Vie pour le Tsar*. With one or two minor exceptions, successive Russian masters have followed faithfully in Glinka's footsteps. To Borodine, Dargomijsky, Seroff, Balakireff, and Rimsky-Korsakoff a full meed of nationality has been granted. To Rubinstein and Tscháikowski criticism is at present disposed to deny the quality in its most salient features. But their prolific mass of compositions has so far scarcely been sufficiently explored outside their own Russian domain for a final judgment to be hazarded. A nearer inspection of their work, indeed, together with a more accurate study of Russian art as a whole, distinctly leads to the opinion that a revolution of feeling may eventually spring up, especially on the subject of their operas. Also Rubinstein's dramatic works, now mostly dismissed by foreigners as his weakest productions, may in due course be accepted as his finest creations. From the different reasons previously deduced there can be little doubt that in opera Glinka purposely laid the corner-stone of what he earnestly believed to be a true Russian school, and a glance at contemporary musical activity shows that here Russia has every opportunity for distinguishing herself, and that with very little competition.

RUSSIAN LITERATURE

W. R. MORFILL

Of the Russian there are the following chief dialects—Great, Little, and White Russian. The Great Russian is the literary and official language of the Empire. In its structure it is highly synthetic, having three genders and seven cases, and the nouns and adjectives being fully inflected. Its great peculiarity (which it shares in common with all the Sclavonic languages), is the structure of the verbs, which are divided into so-called "aspects," which modify the meaning, just as the Latin terminations *sco, urio,* and *ita,* only the forms are developed into a more perfect system. The letters employed are the Cyrillian, held to have been invented by St. Cyril in the Ninth Century. They are on the whole well adapted to express the many sounds of the Russian alphabet, for which the Latin letters would be wholly inadequate, and must perforce be employed in some such uncouth combinations as those which communicate a grotesque appearance to Polish. It would be out of place here to discuss the Ecclesiastical Sclavonic employed in so many of the early writings composed in Russian. I shall proceed to speak of the literature in Russian properly so-called. The great epochs of this will be—

I. From the earliest times to the reign of Peter the Great.

II. From the reign of Peter the Great to our own time.

The Russians, like the rest of the Sclavonic peoples are very rich in national songs, many (as one may judge from the allusions found in them), going back to a remote antiquity. For a long time, and especially during the period of French influence, these productions were neglected. In the last twenty years, however, they have been assiduously collected by Bezsonov, Kirievski, Ríbnikov, Hilferding and others. The Russian legendary poems are called *Bílini* (literally, tales of old time), and may be most conveniently divided into the following classes:—

1. That of the earlier heroes. 2. The Cycle of Vladimir. 3. The Royal, or Moscow Cycle.

The early heroes are of a half-mythical type, and perform prodigies of valour. To this class belong Volga Vseslavich, Mikoula Selianinovich and Sviatogor. The great glory of the Cycle of Vladimir is Ilya Murometz. The *Bílinas* are filled with his magnificent exploits, either alone, or in the company of Sviatogor.

The national songs are carried on through the troublous times of Boris Godunov, and the false Dimitri, to the days of Peter the Great, when they seem to have acquired new vigour on account of the military achievements of the regenerator of his country. Nor are they extinct in our own time, for we find exploits of Napoleon, especially his disastrous expedition to Russia, made the subject of verse. The interest, however, of these legendary poems fades away as we advance into later days. The number of minstrels is rapidly diminishing; and Riabanin, and his companions among the Great Russians, and Ostap Veresai among the Malo-Russians, will probably be the last of these generations of rhapsodists, who have transmitted their traditional chants from father to son, from tutor to pupil. A great feature in Russian literature is the collection of chronicles, which begin with Nestor, monk of the Pestcherski Cloister at Kiev, who was born about A. D. 1056, and died about 1116.

During the time when Russia groaned under the yoke of the Mongols, the nation remained silent, except here and there, perhaps, in some legendary song, sung among peasants, and destined subsequently to be gathered from oral tradition by a Rîbnikov and a Hilferding. Such literature as was cultivated formed the recreation of the monks in their cells. A new era, however, was to come. Ivan III. established the autocracy and made Moscow the centre of the new government. The Russians naturally looked to Constantinople as the centre of their civilization; and even when the city was taken by the Turks its influence did not cease. Many learned Greeks fled to Russia, and found an hospitable reception in the dominions of the Grand Duke. During the reigns of Ivan the Terrible and his immediate successors, although the material progress of the country was considerably advanced, and a strong Government founded, yet little was done for learning. Simeon Polotzki (1628-80), tutor to the Tsar Feodor, son of Alexis, was an indefatigable writer of religious and educational books, but his productions can now only interest the antiquarian. The verses composed by him on the new palace built by the Tsar Alexis, at Kolomenski are deliciously quaint. Of a more important character is the sketch of the Russian government, and the habits of the people, written by one Koshikin (or Kotoshikin—for the name is found in both forms), a renegade diak or secretary, which, after having lain for a long time in manuscript in the library of Upsala, in Sweden, was edited in 1840, by the Russian historian Soloviev. Kotoshikin terminated a life of strange vicissitudes by perishing at the hands of the public executioner at Stockholm, about 1669.

With the reforms of Peter the Great commences an entirely new period in the history of Russian literature, which was now to be under Western influence. The epoch was inaugurated by Lomonosov, the son of a poor fisherman of Archangel, who forms one of the curious band of peasant authors—of very various merit, it must be confessed—who present such an unexpected phenomenon in Russian literature. Occasionally we have men of real genius, as in the cases of Koltzov, Nikitin, and Shevchenko, the great glory of southern Russia; sometimes, perhaps, a man whose abilities have been overrated as in the instance of Slepoushkin. Lemonosov is more praised than read by his countrymen. His turgid odes, stuffed with classical allusions, in praise of Anne and Elizabeth, are still committed to memory by pupils at educational establishments. His panegyrics are certainly fulsome, but probably no worse than those of Boileau in praise of Louis XIV., who grovelled without the excuse of the imperfectly educated Scythian. The reign of Catherine II. (1762-96), saw the rise of a whole generation of court poets. The great maxim, "*Un Auguste peut aisément faire un Virgile,*" was seen in all its absurdity in semi-barbarous Russia. These wits were supported by the Empress and her immediate *entourage*, to whom their florid productions were ordinarily addressed.

THE LIBRARY, ODESSA.

From Byzantine traditions, from legends of saints, from confused chronicles, and orthodox hymnologies, Russia was to pass by one of the most violent changes ever witnessed in the literature of any country, into epics moulded upon the *Henriade*, and tedious odes in the style of Boileau and Jean Baptiste Rousseau. Oustrialov, the historian, truly characterizes most of the voluminous writers of this epoch, as mediocre verse makers, for claiming merits in the cases of Bogdanovich, Khemnitzer, Von Vizin, Dmitriev, and Derzhavin. Bogdanovich wrote a very pretty lyric piece, styled *Dushenka* based on the story of Cupid and Psyche, and partly imitated from Lafontaine, with a sportive charm about the verse which will preserve it from becoming obsolete. With Khemnitzer begin the fabulists. But I shall reserve my remarks upon this species of literature and its Russian votaries until I come to Krílov, who may be said to be one of the few Sclavonic authors who have gained a reputation beyond the limits of their own country. In Denis Von

Vizin, born at Moscow, but as his name shows, of German extraction, Russia saw a writer of genuine national comedy. Hitherto she had to content herself with poor imitations of Molière. His two plays, the *Brigadier* and the *Minor* (*Nederosl*), have much original talent. No such vigorous representations of character appeared again on the stage till *The Misfortune of being too Clever* (*Gore et Ouma*) of Griboiedov, and the *Revisor* of Gogol. Dmitriev deserves perhaps no more than a passing mention.

The name of Derzhavin is spoken of with reverence among his countrymen: he was the laureate of the epoch of Catherine, and had a fresh ode for every new military glory. There is much fire and vigour in his productions and he could develop the strength and flexibility of his native language which can be made as expressive and concise as Greek. Perhaps, however, we get a little tired of his endless perfections of Felitza, the name under which he celebrates the Empress Catherine, a woman who—whatever her private faults may have been,—did a great deal for Russia.

In Nicholas Karamzin appeared the first Russian historian who can properly claim the title. His poems are almost forgotten: here and there we come upon a solitary lyric in a book of extracts. His *History of the Russian Empire*, however, is a work of extensive research, and must always be quoted with respect by Sclavonic scholars. Unfortunately, it only extends to the election of Michael Romanov. Karamzin was followed by Nicholas Polevoi, son of a Siberian merchant, who hardly left any species of literature untouched. His *History of the Russian People*, however, did not add to his reputation, and is now almost forgotten. In later times both these authors have been eclipsed by such writers as Soloviev and Kostomarov. A new and more critical school of Russian historians has sprung up; but for the early history of the Sclavonic peoples, the great work is still Schafarik's *Sclavonic Antiquities*, first published in the Bohemian language, and more familiar to scholars in the West of Europe in its German version.

With the breaking up of old forms of government caused by the French Revolution, came the dislocation of the old conventional modes of thought. Classicism in literature was dead, having weighed like an incubus upon the fancy and fresh life of many generations. England and Germany were at the head of the new movement, which was at a later period to be joined to France. The influence was to extend to Russia, and may be said to date from the reign of Alexander I. It was headed by Zhukovski, who was rather a fluent translator than an original poet. He has given excellent versions of Schiller, Goethe, Moore, and Byron, and has better enriched the literature of his country in this way than by his original productions. He had, however, some lyric fire of his own; the ode entitled *The Poet in the Camp of the Russian Warriors*, written in the memorable year 1812, did something to stimulate the national feelings, and procure for the poet a good appointment at court.

In Alexander Pushkin, the Russians were destined to find their greatest poet. His first work, *Rouslan and Lioudmilla*, was a tale of half-mythical times, in which the influence of Byron was clearly visible, but the author had never allowed himself to become a mere copyist. The same may be said of *The Prisoner of the Caucasus*, in which Pushkin had an opportunity of describing the romantic scenery of that wild country, which was then entirely new ground. In the *Fountain of Bakchiserai* he chose an episode in the history of the Khans of the Crimea, which he has handled very poetically. The *Gipsies* is a wild oriental tale of passion and vengeance. The poet, who had been spending some time amid the Steppes of Bessarabia, has left us wonderful pictures of the wandering tribes and their savage life. Many Russians consider the *Evgenië Oniegin* of Pushkin to be his best effort. It is a powerfully written love-story, full of sketches of modern life, interspersed with satire and pathos.

A criticism of Pushkin would necessarily be imperfect, which left out of all consideration his drama on the subject of *Boris Godunov*. Here he has used Shakespeare as his model. Up to this time the traditions of the Russian stage—such as they were—were wholly French. The piece is undoubtedly very clever, and conceived with true dramatic power.

Since Pushkin's attempt, the historical drama based upon the English, has been very successfully cultivated. A fine trilogy has been composed by Count A. Tolstoi (whose premature death all Russia deplored), on the three subjects, *The Death of Ivan the Terrible* (1866), *The Tsar Feodor* (1868) and the *Tsar Boris* (1869).

The Russian fabulists, whose name is legion, demand some mention; Khemnitzer, Dmitriev, Ivanov and others, have attempted this style of poetry; but the most celebrated of all is Ivan Krilov (1768-1844). Many of his short sentences have become proverbs among the Russian people, like the couplets of Lafontaine among the French, and Butler's *Hudibras* among ourselves. His pictures of life and manners are most thoroughly national. In Koltzov the true voice of the people, which had before only expressed itself in the national ballads was heard. The life of this sensitive and warm-hearted man of genius was clouded by poverty and suffering.

The poems of Koltzov are written, for the most part, in an unrhymed verse; the sharp, well-defined accent in Russian amply satisfying the ear, as in German. His poetical taste had been nurtured by the popular lays of his country. He has caught their colouring as truly as Burns did that of the Scottish minstrelsy. He is unquestionably the most national poet that Russia has produced; Slepoushkin and Alipanov, two other peasant poets, who made some little noise in their time, cannot for one moment be compared with him; but, on the other hand, he has been excelled by the fiery energy and picturesque power of the Cossack, Taras Shevchenko, of whom I shall speak. Since the death of Pushkin, Lermontov alone has appeared to dispute the poetical crown with him. The short life of this author (1814-41), ended in the same way as Pushkin's—in a duel provoked by himself. Many of his lyrics are exquisite, and have become standard poems in Russia, such as the *Gifts of Terek* and *The Cradle Song of the Cossack Mother.*

In Gogol, who died in 1852, the Russians had to lament the loss of a keen and vigorous satirist. With a happy humour reminding us of Dickens in his best moods, he has sketched all classes of society in the *Dead Souls*, perhaps the cleverest of all Russian novels. No one, also has reproduced the scenery and habits of Little Russia, of which he was a native, more vigorously than Gogol, whether in the pictures of country life in his *Old-Fashioned Household* (if we may translate in so free a manner the title *Starovetskie Pomestchiki*), or in the wilder sketches of the struggles which took place between the Poles and Cossacks in *Taras Boulba*. In the *Portrait* and *Memoirs of a Madman*, Gogol shows a weird power, which may be compared with that of the fantastic American, Edgar Allan Poe. Besides his novels, he wrote a brilliant comedy called the *Revisor*, dealing with the evils of bureaucracy.

Towards the end of the year 1877, died Nicholas Nekrasov, the most remarkable poet produced by Russia since Lermontov. He has left six volumes of poetry, of a peculiarly realistic type, chiefly dwelling upon the misfortunes of the Russian peasantry, and putting before us most forcibly the dull grey tints of their monotonous and purposeless lives.

I have not space to enumerate here even the most prominent Russian novelists. No account, however, of their literature would be anything like complete which omitted the name of Ivan Tourgheniev, whose reputation is European. With the Russians the English novel of the realistic type is the fashionable model. In this branch of literature, French influences have hardly been felt at all. The historical novel—an echo of the great romances of Sir Walter Scott—had its cultivators in such writers as Zagoskin and Lazhechnikov; but at the present time, with the exception of the recent productions of Count Tolstoi, it is a form of literature as dead in Russia as in our own country. The novel of domestic life bids fair to swallow up all the rest, and it is to this that the Russians are devoting their attention.

Tourgheniev first made a name by his *Memoirs of a Sportsman*, a powerfully written work, in which harrowing descriptions are given of the miserable condition of the Russian serfs. Since the publication of this novel, or rather series of sketches, he has written a succession of able works of the same kind, in which all classes of Russian society have been reviewed. No more pathetic tale than the *Gentleman's Retreat* (*Dvorianskoe Gnezdo*) can be shown in the literature of any country. There are touches in it worthy of George Eliot. In

Fathers and Children and *Smoke*, Tourgheniev has grappled with the nihilistic ideas which for a long time have been so current in Russia.

The study of Russian history, so well commenced by Karamzin, has been further developed by Oustrialov and Soloviev.

The Malo-Russian is very rich in *skazki* (national tales) and in songs. Peculiar to them is the *douma*, a kind of narrative poem, in which the metre is generally very irregular; but a sort of rhythm is preserved by the recurrence of accentuated syllables. The *douma* of the Little Russians corresponds to the *bîlina* of the Great Russians.

As might naturally be expected, most Malo-Russian authors of eminence, have preferred using the Great Russian, notably Gogol, who however is very fond of introducing provincial expressions which require a glossary. The foundation of the Malo-Russian cultivated literature was laid by the travisty of the *Æneid*, by Kotliarevski, which enjoys great popularity among his countrymen. A truly national poet appeared in Taras Shevchenko, born a serf in the Government of Kiev, at the village of Kirilovka.

Of the literature of the White Russians, but little need be said, as it is very scanty, amounting to a few collections of songs edited by Shein, Bezsonov and others.

PRESENT CONDITIONS

E. S.

Nicholas I., Tsar of all the Russias (born in 1868), the eldest son of Alexander III. and the Princess Dagmar, daughter of King Christian IX. of Denmark, ascended the throne on the death of his father in 1894. He is descended from Michael Romanof, elected Tsar in 1613, after the extinction of the House of Rurik, and also from the Oldenburg family. Nicholas II. was married in 1894 to Princess Alexandra Alix (Alexandra Feodorovina), daughter of Ludwig IV., Grand Duke of Hesse, and Alice Maud Mary, daughter of Queen Victoria. Their four daughters are: Olga (born 1895); Tatiana (born 1897); Marie (born 1899); and Anastasia (born 1901). The Grand Duke Michael (born 1878), brother of the Emperor, is the Heir Presumptive. The Emperor's vast revenue is derived from Crown domains: the amount is unknown, as no reference is made in the budgets or finance accounts. It consists, however, of more than a million of square miles of cultivated lands and forests, besides gold and other mines in Siberia.

THE TSAR NICHOLAS.

Russia is an absolute hereditary monarchy. The Emperor's will is law, and in him the whole legislative, executive and judicial power is united. The administration of the Empire is entrusted to four great boards or councils: the Council of the State; the Ruling Senate; the Holy Synod; and the Committee of Ministers.

The Council of State, established by Alexander I. in 1801, consists of a president nominated every year by the Emperor and a large number of members appointed by him. This council is divided into four departments: Legislation; Civil and Church Administration; State's Economy and Industry; Sciences and Commerce.

The Ruling Senate, founded by Peter I. in 1711, is really the high court of justice for the Empire. It is divided into six departments, or sections.

The Holy Synod, founded by Peter I. in 1728, has charge of the religious affairs of the Empire. Its members are the Metropolitans of St. Petersburg, Moscow and Kief, the archbishop of Georgia and several bishops who sit in turn. The President is Antonious, the Metropolitan of St. Petersburg. The Emperor has to approve of all the decisions of the Holy Synod.

European Russia consists of Russia Proper (50 Provinces), Poland (10 Provinces), and Finland (Grand Duchy). The population in 1897 was respectively, 93,467,736; 9,401,097; and 2,527,801. Asiatic Russia consists of Caucasia (11 Provinces; population 9,291,000); Siberia (8 Provinces and Regions; population 5,726,719); and Central Asia (10 Provinces and Regions; population 7,740,394). Russian subjects in Khiva and Bokhara number 6,412. Of the total population 128,161,249, 64,616,280 were men and 64,594,883, women. In European Russia the annual increase of population is at the rate of nearly a million and a half. The chief cities of European Russia are St. Petersburg (1,267,023); Moscow (988,614); Warsaw (638,208); Odessa (405,041); Lodz (315,209); Riga (256,197); Kief (247,432); Kharkoff (174,846); Tiflis (160,645); Vilna (159,568); Tashkend (156,414); Saratov (137,109); Kasan (131,508); Ekaterinoslav (121,216); Rostov-on-the-Don (119,889); Astrakhan (113,001); Baku (112,253); Tula (111,048), and Kishineff(108,796). The population of Novgorod, Samara, Minsk and Nikolaieff is between 95,000 and 90,000. Tiflis and Baku in the Caucasus have respective populations of 160,000 and 112,000. The largest towns in the Trans-Caspia are Askhabad (19,500) and Merv (8,750), and those of Turkestan are Tashkend, Namangan Samarkand and Andijan. There are about 50,000 in each of the Siberian towns of Tomsk, Irkutsk and Ekaterinburg.

THE TSARINA.

There has been no census since 1897, but in 1900 the population of St. Petersburg was 1,439,739; Moscow, 1,035,664; and Riga, 282,943. The mortality in the towns is so great that the deaths exceed the births. Emigration is on the increase, and, of late years, the Russians, particularly the Jews, flock to the United States, chiefly through Hamburg, Lübeck and Bremen. In 1900, 49,580 emigrated to the United States; 1,253 to Argentina; and numbers to Canada and Brazil. Emigration to Siberia varies from year to year, but is on the increase. In 1898, 80,000 went and in 1901 from 150,000 to 200,000. There is also much emigration to the Southern Ural and the Steppe provinces.

In European Russia, there is an average of a town or village to every four or seven square miles, and in the Caucasus, one to every nine square miles; but in Asiatic Russia the average varies; for example, in Samarkand there is one to every fourteen square miles, and in the province of Yakutsk, one to every 2,760 square miles.

The principal ports are St. Petersburg, Cronstadt, Narva, Riga, Libau, Pernau and Vindau (on the Baltic); Hango (on the Gulf of Bothnia); Revel, Helsingförs and Wiborg (on the Gulf of Finland); Archangel and Ekaterinsk (Arctic and White Seas); Odessa, Nicolaieff, Sebastopol, Nova-Rossiisk, Berdiansk and Batoum, Taganrog, Marinpol, Rostov and Kertch (on the Black Sea and Sea of Azov); Astrakhan, Derbent and Baku (on the Caspian Sea); Nicolaieffsk, Vladivostok and Petrapaulovsk in Kamtchatka; and Port Arthur and Dalni or Ta-lien-wan (Gulf of Pechili), have been occupied since the Russo-Chinese Treaty of 1898.

The established religion is the Russo-Greek, or Græco-Russian, known officially as the Orthodox Catholic Faith. It maintains the relations of a sister church with the four patriarchates of Constantinople, Antioch, Jerusalem and Alexandria. The Emperor is the head of the church. The Russian Empire is divided into 64 bishoprics, under 3 metropolitans, 14 archbishops and 48 bishops; in 1898, there were 66,146 churches (718 of which were cathedrals), and 785 monasteries. With the exception of the Jewish, all religions are allowed to be professed. There are more than 12,000,000 dissenters scattered throughout the Empire. The numbers are: Orthodox Greek, 87,384,480; Dissenters, 2,173,738; Roman Catholic, 11,420,927; Protestants, 3,743,209; other Christians, 1,221,511; Mohammedans, 13,889,421; Jews, 5,189,401; and other religions, 645,503. In 1903, the Holy Synod received 28,388,049 roubles from the Imperial budget, besides other revenue and gifts.

The Empire is divided into 15 educational districts: St. Petersburg, Moscow, Kasan, Orenburg, Kharkoff, Odessa, Kief, Vilna, Warsaw, Riga, Caucasus, Turkestan, West Siberia, East Siberia and Amur. In some of the primary village schools, there are school-gardens, while bee-keeping and silk-worm culture, as well as trades and handiwork, are taught. In 1900, the Ministers contributed 51,062,842 roubles for schools and universities. The universities are in Moscow (4,344 students in 1902); St. Petersburg (3,708); Kief (2,316); Kharkov (1,340); Dorpat (1,791); Warsaw (1,312); Kasan (823); Odessa (1,116); and Tomsk (549). Helsingfors, Finland, had 1,211 students in 1900-1.

Since 1874 military service has been obligatory for all men from the age of 21. The period of service in European Russia is five years in the active army (reduced by furloughs to four) 13 in the Zapas those who have passed through active service and five years in the Opolchenie, or reserve; in Asiatic Russia, seven years in the active army and six in the Zapas; and in Caucasia, three years in the active army and 15 in the Zapas. The Opolchenie is a reserve force of drilled conscripts.

The Cossacks (Don, Kuban Terek, Astrakhan, Orenburg, Ural, Siberia, Semiryetchensk, Transbaikalia, Amur and Usuri) are divided in three classes; the first in active service, the second on furlough with their arms and horses; the third with arms and without horses. Some of the Cossack cavalry serves with the regular cavalry. Military service is also obligatory in Finland.

The Russian army consists of 31 corps. The lowest estimate of its peace strength is about 1,100,000 with 42,000 officers; the war strength about 75,000 officers, 4,500,000 men and 562,000 horses.

Owing to its widely separated seas, the Russian navy maintains four squadrons: the Baltic, the Black Sea, the Pacific and the Caspian. Cronstadt is the chief base of the Baltic Fleet; Sebastopol of the Black Sea; and

Vladivostok and Port Arthur of the Pacific. The Caspian fleet is comparatively insignificant. In 1903, the navy consisted of 26 battleships, 14 coast defence ships, 24 first-class cruisers, 15 second-class cruisers, 161 gunboats and torpedo craft.

The ocean shipping of the Russian Empire is not relatively large, but its lake and river shipping is very extensive. In 1900, the sea-going marine consisted of 2,293 sailing vessels and 745 steamers.

The total length of railway open for traffic and travel on January 1, 1903, was 35,336 miles (not including 1,753 miles in Finland). Of this 4,965 miles were in Asiatic Russia.

The legal unit of money is the silver rouble of 100 kopecks of the value of 2s. 1.6d., or about fifty cents of American money. The coins called imperial and half-imperial contain 15 and 7-1/2 roubles respectively. There are also credit notes of 100, 25, 10, 5, 3 and 1 rouble.

Russia's chief source of revenue is the liquor traffic. Her chief exports are spirits, tallow, wool, tow, bristles, timber, hides and skins, grain, raw and dressed flax, linseed and hemp. Her principal imports are tea, cotton and other colonial produce, iron, machinery, wool, wine, fruits, vegetables and oil.

Russia is the second largest European grower of wheat. Hemp, flax, potatoes and tobacco are also raised in large quantities. Barley, buckwheat, oats, millet and rye form the staple food of the inhabitants.

Mines of great value exist in the Ural, Obdorsk and Altai mountains, which produce gold, copper, iron, silver, platinum, rock-salt, marble and kaolin or china clay. Rich naphtha springs exist on the Caspian and an immense bed of coal has been discovered between the Donetz and Dnieper rivers.

The Grand Duchy of Finland, which Russia conquered from Sweden and finally annexed in 1808, had a population in 1898 of about 2,595,000 (2,230,000 Finns; 350,000 Swedes; 12,000 Russians; 2,000 Germans; and 1,000 Laps). The chief religion is the Lutheran. The capital is Helsingfors with a population of 111,000, including the Russian garrison. The Tsar of Russia is the Grand Duke; Lieut.-Gen. N. Bobrikov, the governor-general; and V. von Plehwe, Secretary of State. The Diet, convoked triennially, consists of nobles, clergy, burgesses and peasants, but the country is chiefly governed by the Imperial Finnish Senate of twenty-two members. The army consists of nine battalions of Finnish Rifles (5,600 men), and one regiment of dragoons (900 men, with a reserve of 30,000). The chief export is timber and the chief industry iron mines. In 1898, the marine comprised 2,298 vessels of 324,344 tons.

Bokhara and Khiva in Central Asia are vassal states of Russia. Bokhara, bounded on the north by Russian Turkestan, was once the most famous state of Central Asia. Genghis Khan took it from the Arabs in the Thirteenth Century, and it was taken by the Uzbegs, fanatical Sunni Mahommedans of Turkish extraction, in 1505. After the Russian capture of Tashkend in 1865, the Amir Muzeffared-din proclaimed a holy war against the Russians, who invaded his province and captured Samarkand in 1868. By a treaty of 1873, no foreigner may be admitted into Bokhara without a Russian passport. The population is estimated at 2,000,000. The Amir Syed Abdul Ahad succeeded in 1885. The Uzbegs are still the dominant race. The religion is Mahommedan. The chief towns are Bokhara (about 75,000) and Karshi (25,000). The chief products are sheep, goats, camels, horses, rice, cotton, silk, corn, fruit, hemp and tobacco. Gold, salt, alum and sulphur are the chief minerals. There are cotton, woollen and silk manufacturers. Many Indian goods such as shawls, tea, drugs, indigo and muslins are imported. The Amir has 11,000 troops, 4,000 of which are quartered in Bokhara. The Russian Trans-Caspian Railway runs through Bokhara and there is steam navigation on the Oxus. A telegraph connects Bokhara with Tashkend.

The conquest of Khiva, another Uzbeg State also founded on the ruins of Tamerlane's Central Asian Empire, was attempted by Peter the Great in 1717 and again in 1839 by the Tsar Nicholas. On the pretext that the Khivans had aided the rebellious Kirghiz, the Russians invaded Khiva in 1873 and forced the Khan to sign a treaty putting the Khanate under Russian government. The reigning sovereign is Seyid Mahomed Rahim Khan who succeeded his father in 1865. He was born about 1845. The population is estimated at 800,000, including 400,000 nomad Turcomans. The principal towns are Khiva (about 5,000) and New Urgenj (3,000). The religion is Mahommedan. The army consists of about 2,000 men. The chief productions are silk and cotton.

KALKSTRASSE AND THE PROMENADE, RIGA.

In 1898, Russia obtained a lease of twenty-five years from China of Point Arthur and Ta-lien-wan with the adjacent seas and territory to the north. To this the name of Kwang-Tung was given in 1899. Port Arthur, the capital, is a naval station for Russian and Chinese ships. At the end of the port a new town, Dalni, has been founded; it is connected by rail with the Trans-Siberian railway system.

Russia's history in 1903 was marked by general disquietude and turbulence. The disorders among the peasantry in 1902 led to a special committee being appointed to inquire into and ameliorate their condition and also to improve agriculture. On March 11, 1903, the Tsar issued a manifesto promising reform in the government of local towns and tolerance in religion. As little or no improvement was noticed, strike riots resulted in Slatoust (Ufa) and at Nijni-Novgorod, and riots also broke out in the university of St. Petersburg. In May, the Governor of Ufa was assassinated. To these disturbances, the Anti-Semitic outrages were encouraged at Kishineff (Bessarabia) when forty-five Jews were killed, 484 injured, 700 houses demolished, and 600 houses sacked. Strike riots also broke out in South Russia and the Caucasus, particularly in the towns of Kief, Odessa, Baku, Rostov, Nikolaieff. Many smaller towns also suffered loss of life. Military troops were called out to quell the rioters. The policy of Russification was carried on in Finland as well as in the more recent acquisitions. The chief interest, however, lay in the extension of Russia's diplomatic and military policy in the Far East under Admiral Alexeieff (appointed August 13, 1903).

Milton Keynes UK
Ingram Content Group UK Ltd.
UKHW010742080324
438959UK00004B/318